Life and Laughing

Life and Laughing

My Story

MICHAEL McINTYRE

MICHAEL JOSEPH
an imprint of
PENGUIN BOOKS

MICHAEL JOSEPH

Published by the Penguin Group
Penguin Books Ltd, 80 Strand, London WC2R ORL, England
Penguin Group (USA) Inc., 375 Hudson Street, New York, New York 10014, USA
Penguin Group (Canada), 90 Eglinton Avenue East, Suite 700, Toronto, Ontario, Canada M4P 2Y3
(a division of Pearson Penguin Canada Inc.)
Penguin Ireland, 25 St Stephen's Green, Dublin 2, Ireland (a division of Penguin Books Ltd)
Penguin Group (Australia), 250 Camberwell Road, Camberwell, Victoria 3124, Australia
(a division of Pearson Australia Group Pty Ltd)
Penguin Books India Pvt Ltd, 11 Community Centre, Panchsheel Park, New Delhi – 110 017, India
Penguin Group (NZ), 67 Apollo Drive, Rosedale, North Shore 0632, New Zealand
(a division of Pearson New Zealand Ltd)
Penguin Books (South Africa) (Pty) Ltd, 24 Sturdee Avenue, Rosebank,
Johannesburg 2196, South Africa

Penguin Books Ltd, Registered Offices: 80 Strand, London WC2R ORL, England

www.penguin.com

First published 2010

8

Copyright © Michael McIntyre, 2010

All images courtesy of the author except: FremantleMedia (Michael's father with Kenny Everett and
Barry Cryer); © The Sun and 01.06.1984 / nisyndication.com (Newspaper clipping of Michael's
mother with Kenny Everett); Richard Young / Rex Features (Michael with his wife at the GQ
Awards); Dave M. Benett / Getty Images (Michael with Ronnie Corbett, Rob Brydon and Billy
Connolly); Ken McKay / Rex Features (Michael with Prince Charles); Ellis O'Brien (DVD advert at
Piccadilly Circus, Michael on stage at the Comedy Roadshow, Michael on stage at Wembley)

The moral right of the author has been asserted

Set in Garamond MT Std 13.75/16.25 pt
Typeset by Palimpsest Book Production Limited, Falkirk, Stirlingshire
Printed in Great Britain by Clays Ltd, St Ives plc

A CIP catalogue record for this book is available from the British Library

HARBACK ISBN: 978–0–718–15581–0
TRADE PAPERBACK ISBN: 978–0–718–15580–3

www.greenpenguin.co.uk

For Kitty, Lucas and Oscar

I

I am writing this on my new 27-inch iMac. I have ditched my PC and gone Mac. I was PC for years, but Microsoft Word kept criticizing my grammar, and I think it started to affect my self-esteem. It had a lot of issues with a lot of my sentences, and after years of its making me feel stupid I ended the relationship and bought a Mac. It's gorgeous and enormous, and I bought it especially to write my book (the one you're reading now). For the last six months, I've been looking to create the perfect writing environment. Aside from the computer, I have a new desk, a new chair and a new office with newly painted walls in my new house.

When my wife and I were looking at houses, she would be busily opening and closing cupboards and chattering about storage (after a few months of house-hunting, I became convinced my wife's dream home would be the Big Yellow Storage Company), and I would be searching for the room to write my book. The view seemed very important. Previously, views hadn't been that important to me. I prefer TV. Views only really have one channel. But suddenly I was very keen to find a room with a view to inspire me to write a classic auto-biography. Like David Niven's, but about my life and not his.

The house we fell in love with had a room with a beautiful view of the garden and even a balcony for closer viewing of the view of the garden. It was a room with a view. It was perfect. I could create magic in this room. Soon after moving in, I plonked my desk directly in front of the balcony window.

I stood behind the desk drinking in the view of my garden and thought, 'I need a new chair', a throne of creativity. With this view and the right chair, I can't possibly fail.

The big question when office chair purchasing is 'to swivel or not to swivel?' I would love to find out how many of the great literary works of the twentieth century have been written by swivelling writers. Were D. H. Lawrence, J. R. R. Tolkein or Virginia Woolf slightly dizzy when they penned their finest works? I tried out several swivel chairs in Habitat on the Finchley Road for so long that I got told off. I realized a swivel chair would be a mistake. I'd have too much fun. I might as well put a slide, a seesaw or a bouncy castle in my office. So I settled on a chair whose biggest selling feature was that you can sit on it.

With my chair, desk and view sorted, it was time to address the décor. The previous owner had painted the walls of my new office orange. I'll try to be more specific. They were Tangerine. No, they were more a Clementine or maybe a Mandarin. Come to think of it, they were Satsuma. Now, there was no way on God's earth I could write this book with a Satsuma backdrop, so I went to Farrow & Ball on Hampstead's high street. Farrow & Ball is the latest in a long line of successful high street double acts (Marks & Spencer, Dolce & Gabbana, Bang & Olufsen). It's basically paint for posh people. I don't know who Farrow was, or indeed Ball, but I bet they were posh. Maybe I'm wrong. Maybe Ball is Bobby Ball from Cannon and Ball, who tried his luck in the paint industry encouraged by Cannon's success manufacturing cameras.

I perused the colour chart in Farrow & Ball. There are so many colours, it makes you go a bit mad trying to decide. It's also very hard to distinguish between many of them. A quick googling of the Farrow & Ball colour chart reveals ten differ-ent shades of white. All White, Strong White, House White, New White, White Tie . . . you get the idea. I once bought a white sofa from DFS. It was white. If you asked a hundred people what colour it was, I would say that a hundred of them would say it was white. In actual fact, they would all be wrong; it was Montana Ice. I would suggest that even if you asked a hundred Montanans during a particularly cold winter what colour it was, they would say, 'White.'

After a brief discussion with my wife (she's actually colour blind, but I find it hard to reach decisions on my own), I popped for the unmistakable colour of Brinja No. 222. A slightly less pretentious description would be aubergine. Most people call it purple.

My surroundings were now nearly complete: new desk, new chair, lovely view and Brinja No. 222 walls. I placed my Mac on the desk and lovingly peeled off the see-through plastic that protects the screen, took a deep breath and sat down. Unfortunately 27 inches of screen meant that my view was completely obscured. Panic. Why didn't I think of that? The whole window was blocked by this enormous piece of technology. I was forced to move the desk to the opposite wall. I now had a face full of Brinja No. 222 and my back to the view. I would have to turn the chair around at regular intervals to be inspired by my view. I should have bought the swivel chair.

OK, I'm ready. I'm ready to start my book. It's an auto-biography, although I prefer the word 'memoirs'. I think it's from the French for 'memories', and that pretty much sums up what this book is going to be. A book about my French memories. No, it's basically everything I can remember from my life. The bad news is that I don't have a particularly good memory. You know when someone asks you what you did yesterday, and it takes you ages to remember even though it was just one day ago – 'I can't believe this, it was just yesterday', you'll say before finally remembering. Well, I'm like that, except sometimes it never comes to me. I never remember what I did yesterday. Come to think of it, what did I do yesterday?

'Memoirs' just sounds a lot sexier than 'autobiography'. Not all words are better in French. 'Swimming pool' in French is *piscine*, which obviously sounds like 'piss in'. 'Do you piscine the piscine?' was as funny as French lessons at school ever got for me. Only writing BOOB on a calculator using 8008 in Maths seemed funnier. We've borrowed loads of French words to spice up the English language: fiancé, encore, cul-de-sac, apéritif, chauffeur, pied-à-terre, déjà vu. In fact, you could probably speak an entire English sentence with more French in it than English. 'I'm having *apéritifs* and *hors d'oeuvres* at my *pied-à-terre* in a *cul-de-sac*. After some *mange-touts*, I'm sending the kids to the *crèche* and having a *ménage à trois* with my *fiancée* and the *au pair*.' Sounds like a great night.

The good news is I think there's more than enough in my patchy memory for the book. Whatever the French for 'patchy memories' is, that's what this book is. So where better to start than with my earliest memory? I was at a pre-school called Stepping Stones in North London in a class called the Dolphins. I must have been about four years old. I remember it being some kind of music group. We were all in a circle with instruments. I may have had a xylophone, but I can't be sure. What I do remember is that there was the distinct smell of shit in the room. At this age kids are toilet-trained, so whereas only a couple years previously at nursery or play-group the smell of shit was a given, in this environment it was unwelcome.

4

The simple fact was, a four-year-old kid had taken a shit in his or her little pants. It wasn't me. I have never pooed my pants, although as this was my earliest memory, I can't be sure. I remember trying to ignore the smell of shit and just get on with what I was doing, much like being on the top deck of a night bus.

'I smell poo,' said the teacher. Cue hysterical giggling. 'Please tell me if you think it might be you. You're not in trouble.'

Nobody responded. A chubby boy holding a triangle looked slightly guilty to me. A blonde girl with a bongo also looked a bit sheepish.

The teacher enquired again. No response. A third time she asked. You could cut the pungent atmosphere with some safety scissors.

Still nobody came clean about their dirty little secret. Then the teacher announced something that I think is the reason I remember this moment still to this day. She said that if nobody would own up, then everyone must, in turn, pull their pants down to prove it.

Horror. I couldn't believe this. How humiliating. In fact the thought of it nearly made me shit myself. A Chinese kid gasped and dropped his tambourine. One by one, around the circle, we had to stand up and reveal our bottoms to the music group. The tension may have damaged me for life. I remember this unbearable swelling of fear as my turn approached. I frantically scanned the room for the crapping culprit. I ruled out the teacher, although I had my doubts about the elderly woman on the piano. I pinned my hopes on this kid who had a permanently solidified snotty nose. I think everyone can recall the kid in their class at pre-school with a permanently solidified snotty nose. Well, my class had one. He was about four kids to my right, and I prayed it wasn't just the nose area he'd let himself down in.

My prime suspect stood up, seemingly in slow motion, and burst into tears. It WAS him! Thank God. I was saved, but the experience has been permanently etched on my mind. Incidentally, if you were in that circle and were one of the kids who had to pull their pants down, please get in touch. I'd love to know how your life turned out.

It is odd how we remember scenes from our childhood at random. Your first few years are, of course, a total blank. I've got two sons, who are four years and one year old, and they aren't going to remember any of their lives so far. I was going to take them to a museum today. Why bother? I might just send them to their rooms until they're old enough to remember some of this effort I'm putting in.

So everything prior to Poo-gate is a mystery to me. I have to rely on my parents, old photographs and Wikipedia to fill me in. According to Wikipedia, I was born in 1976 on 15 February. However, according to my mother, it was 21 February 1976. I don't know who to believe. One thing they both agree on is that I was born in Merton. I think that's in South London. I'm flabbergasted by this news as I am a North Londoner through and through. My opinion about South London is exactly the same as the opinion of South Londoners towards North London: 'How can you live there? It's weird.' I get a chill when I drive over Hammersmith Bridge. I feel as though I'm entering a different world. I wonder if I need a passport and check that my mobile phone still has a signal. The roads seem to be too wide, they don't have parks, they have 'commons', and everyone looks a bit like Tim Henman's dad.

(I've just realized that I have to be careful about how much personal information I reveal. I think there's already enough to answer most of the security questions at my bank and get access to all my accounts.)

I have details about my birth from my mother, who says she was there for most of it. I weighed 8 pounds and 11 ounces. I'm telling you that because the weight of babies seems very important to people. No other measurement is of interest: height, width, circumference – couldn't give a shit. But the weight is must-have information.

I was a big baby. My mother tells me this, and so does everyone else when they learn of my opening weight. Like it was my fault, I let myself go, I could have done with losing a few ounces, a little less 'womb service' and a little more swimming and maybe those newborn nappies wouldn't have been so tight.

Not only was I a big baby, I was also remarkably oriental in appearance. Nobody really knows why I looked like Mr Miyagi from *The Karate Kid* and, let's be honest, my appearance has been the source of quite a lot of material for me. A midwife asked my mother if my father was Chinese or Japanese. My grandparents thought my parents took home the wrong baby. Questions were asked about my mother's fidelity. My father beat up our local dry cleaner, Mr Wu.

Every year I, like you, celebrate my own birth and the fact that I am still alive on my birthday. This is always a very emotional day for my mother, who annually telephones me throughout the day reliving my birth. She calls without fail at about 3 a.m. telling me that this is when her waters broke, and I get phoned throughout the morning and afternoon with her updating me on how far apart her contractions were. At 5.34 p.m., I get my final phone call announcing my birth, and then she reminds me that I was '8 pounds 11 ounces, a very big baby'.

7

Since I became a comedian, she now adds that the labour ward was also the scene of my very first joke. Apparently, when I was only a few minutes old, the doctor lay me down to give me a quick examination, and I promptly peed all over him. I'm told it got a big laugh from the small audience that included my mother, father, the midwife and the doctor. Knowing me, I probably laughed too.

It was the first laugh I ever got.

2

Why do I look foreign? Let's examine my heritage. My parents are not English people. My father is from Montreal in Canada, and both my mother's parents were from Hungary. I am therefore a 'Canary'. I consider myself British. I have only visited Hungary and Canada once.

My one and only visit to Hungary was with my grandmother and my sister Lucy. I was twenty years old, Lucy was eighteen and my grandma was seventy-nine. My grandmother was an eccentric woman, to say the least. Think Zsa Zsa Gabor or Ivana Trump, and you wouldn't be too far out. She was funny, glamorous and rich. A true character. I will do my best to convey her accent when I quote her.

'Helllow, daaarling', that kind of thing.

This is actually how she wrote English as well as spoke it. Born in Budapest, she claims to have 'rrun avay vith the circuss' as a child before marrying scientist Laszlo Katz. When the Nazis showed up in 1939, they fled their home country and settled in Roehampton, South London (I would have taken my chances with the Nazis). They lived in a Tudor house. You know, white with black beams. Well, according to my mother, my grandma painted the black beams bright blue until the council made her paint them black again three weeks later. She didn't speak a word of English when she arrived and learned it from eavesdropping and watching television, much like *E.T.* or Daryl Hannah in *Splash*.

My grandmother was undoubtedly a bright cookie, and

her vocabulary soon increased enough for her to get by. However, her accent would still hold her back. Trying to buy haddock at her local fishmonger's, she would ask politely, 'Do you hev a heddek?'

Unfortunately, the fishmonger thought she was saying, 'Do you have a headache?'

'No, I'm fine, thank you, love,' he would reply. He thought she was a nutty foreign lady enquiring after his well-being. He was only half right.

The headache/haddock misunderstanding occurred several times until my grandmother burst into tears in her blue Tudor house. She asked her husband through her sobs, 'Vot iz it vith dis cuntry, vy vont dey give me a heddek?'

My grandfather, whose accent was no better, stormed round to the fishmonger's. He called the fishmonger a racist and demanded to know why he didn't give his wife a 'head-ache' when there were several 'headaches' in the window. Luckily, the mistake was realized before they came to blows, which would have resulted in one of them having a genuine 'heddek'.

My grandmother soon became fluent in English, so much so that she became quite the best Scrabble player I've ever encountered. She was even better than the 'Difficult' setting on the Scrabble App for my iPhone and would repeatedly beat her second husband, Jim, a Cambridge-educated Englishman. She was not only a tremendously talented Scrab-bler, but also fiercely competitive and uncharacteristically arrogant when involved in a game, often calling me a 'loozer' or claiming she was going to give me a good 'vipping' or exclaiming, 'Yuv got nothing, English boy!'

I enjoyed countless games of Scrabble with her in my late teens and early twenties. Not only did I enjoy the games, but there were serious financial rewards. You see, the Cambridge-educated Englishman was loaded, having made a fortune as a stockbroker. After his untimely death, my glamour gran was left to fend for herself. So I would visit her, and we would play Scrabble. If I won, she would give me a crisp £50 note, and if I lost, she would give me a crisp £50 note. So you see how this was quite an attractive proposition for a poor student. A lot of my friends were working as waiters and in telesales to make extra money, whereas I was playing Scrabble with my grandma at least five times a week.

You might wonder where these £50 notes were coming from. Well, my glamour gran didn't really trust banks, so when her husband died, she withdrew a lot of money and kept it hidden around her lavish apartment in Putney. I'd open a cupboard in the kitchen looking for a mug and find one at the back packed with fifties. I once found 400 quid in a flannel next to the bath and two squashed fifties when I changed the batteries in her TV remote control.

K5 E1 R1 R1 I1 T1 Z10

'Triple vurd score and "E" is on a duble letteer, so that's sixty-six points. Read it a veep, loozer,' said my grandmother in a particularly competitive mood as she stretched her lead.

Now, although she was a wonderfully gifted wordsmith in her second language, she never learned how to spell many of the words. Often she would get a word that bore no resemblance to the one she was attempting. The best of which was undoubtedly 'Kerritz'. It was a sensational Scrabble word. To use the Z and K on a triple letter score and score sixty-six — exceptional. The only problem was that outside of her mind the word was fictitious. It soon transpired that only the two

11

Rs were correct and that the actual word she was attempting was 'carrots'. I must have laughed for about half an hour.

If I'm honest, I've never really been that into history, neither of the world nor of my ancestors. I hadn't asked many questions about my Hungarian ancestry, and I suppose I must have tuned out if it was ever mentioned prior to my Budapest trip. But the time had come. My grandmother, sister and I were off to half my family's homeland. Astonishingly, nobody had mentioned to me or my sister that we still had family in Hungary; nor did they mention that they were Jewish.

So when we were met at Budapest airport by a man resembling a stocky Jesus Christ, I assumed he was the cab driver. When he kissed me and my sister all over our faces, I assumed he was quite the friendliest cab driver I had ever encountered. When Grandma told us he wasn't the cab driver, I thought for a fleeting moment it was Jesus.

'Heelloo, I im yur Unkal Peeeteer.' His accent was worse than my grandmother's.

It turned out Uncle Peter was the son of my real grandfather's sister, my real grandfather being Laszlo Katz, the Hungarian scientist, and not Jim, the rich English stockbroker who was my grandmother's second husband and the man who enabled us to afford the Hyatt Regency Hotel, Budapest. Are you following this? I'm not and couldn't at the time.

Uncle Peter was Jewish. There was no mistaking that. He had the hair and beard of the Messiah and a trait that is stereotypically shared by Jewish men. He had a nose nearly the size of the plane we'd just got off. I didn't know I had Jewish blood; I always thought that my grandfather was Catholic. In fact, he was. He changed his faith, as Judaism wasn't all that trendy circa 1940. But nobody told me.

Suddenly I'm Jewish. I instantly started to feel more neurotic and speak with the rhythm of Jackie Mason. I turned to my grandmother, 'Oy vey, why did you not tell me already? I thought I was Gentile, but I have Jewish blood pumping through my veins. Did you not have the chutzpah to tell me? Did you think I was such a klutz I couldn't cope with it? You wait till we schlep all the way over here, treating me like a nebbish. This is all too much, I have a headache.'

'Vy have you bought a heddek? Did yu not eat enuf on de plane that you need to smuggel fish? And we just valked through "Nuuthing to declare"!'

Uncle Peter was so pleased to see Lucy and me that it became quite emotional. His mother, Auntie Yoli, and he were the last remaining family in Hungary after the horrors of the war. By Hungarian standards, Peter had done very well for himself. I can't remember exactly what he did, but I know there was a factory involved. He spoke good English and had love in his eyes. But looking at him, I could not help but wonder how I could possibly be related to the man.

In the car park we approached his 4x4. It was by far the most luxurious car on display. 'Shtopp!' hollered Peter, much like the man from the Grolsch adverts. He then took out his keys, pointed a device through the window and waited for a beep. 'It is now safe to enter.' Safe? What was he talking about? 'You must vait for mi to disingage the sacurrity system,' he continued, 'othurwide, verrrryy dangeruss.'

'Isn't it just an alarm?' I asked.

'No, iiit iz gas.'

'Gas? What do you mean?'

'In Hungarry is verrry meny criimes. So if break in my caar, you get gas in fece, verry bed burning in eyes. Blind for meny minnuts,' he said, quite matter of fact.

'You can gas burglars in the face here? What happens if you forget to disengage it and open the car door?'

'I have bin in hosspitaal three times!'

It turned out he had forgotten to turn off his car security system and, on three occasions gassed himself in the face. Each time he was hospitalized. In fact one time, while he was rolling around on the pavement in agony holding his eyes and screaming, somebody had casually taken his keys and nicked his stereo.

It was on hearing this that I was convinced. We are related.

I spent three days learning a lot about Budapest and my family. Unfortunately, the only thing I really remember is Peter gassing himself in the face – oh, and that he had green leather sofas. Hideous. Maybe the self-gassing affected his sight.

I have been to Montreal, my father's birthplace, only once. As has been reported at length in every *Daily Mail* interview I've done, my father died when I was seventeen years old. I recently did interviews with the *Daily Mail* and *Heat* magazine back to back in a hotel in Manchester. The *Mail* grilled me at length about the passing of my dad until I had tears in my eyes. The interview ended, the tape recorder stopped, my tears were wiped, and the *Mail* journalist was replaced by the one from *Heat*, whose first question was 'How do you get your hair so bouncy?', at which point my publicist jumped in: 'Michael doesn't want to answer any personal questions.'

I was in Montreal for the Comedy Festival a few years ago. Montreal is split into French- and English-speakers, and as you can imagine, they don't really get on. My first introduction to French in Montreal was an unfortunate incident in my hotel shower. When the letter 'C' is on a tap, I normally feel pretty confident I'm reaching for the 'Cold' tap. However,

'C' on French taps stands for 'Chaud' which means 'Hot'. I turned up the 'Chaud', thinking it was 'Cold'. When the water got hotter, I simply added more 'Chaud'. I was scalded.

This wasn't the only Anglo-French misunderstanding I encountered in Canada. When businessmen are on the road, often the only highlight is watching pornography in hotel rooms. Sad but true. In fact, checking out of a hotel can feel a bit like confession. 'Forgive me, Novotel Leeds receptionist, for I have sinned; I watched four pornos. I also had two Toblerones, the Maltesers, the sour cream and chive Pringles and five miniature Cognacs from the mini-bar. And I have one of your towels in my bag.'

Checking in to my Montreal hotel, I had a few hours to kill until the gig so, and I apologize to younger readers, I was contemplating the potentially higher calibre of Canadian 'adult' entertainment awaiting me in room 417. The receptionist handed me the key for my room and then enquired whether it was the only key I required.

'Do you want one key?' she asked. However, in her thick French accent this became 'Do you want wanky?' I was startled to say the least. What kind of a hotel was this? I immediately went to my room for a cold shower, but as you know scalded myself.

Being in Montreal, I naturally felt nostalgic for my dad, but, unlike my trip to Hungary, I was alone. I sent an email to my father's brother, Hazen. The last I had heard from him was that he was playing a cross-dresser in a Chinese sitcom (my family have had varying degrees of success in show-business). In the last twenty years, I had had lunch with him once, when he visited London. It was eerie as he shared mannerisms with my father, as well as his accent and intonations.

Hazen had remarried, to a seemingly sweet Chinese lady

who smiled politely through lunch as Hazen reminisced about my dad. He literally didn't stop talking while his spaghetti meatballs went cold in Café Pasta just off Oxford Street. His wife never spoke. 'In all the years we've been married, she's only ever said thirty-seven words to me. Two of them were "I do."' He was funny. He spoke about my father's dry sense of humour and how in the early sixties my dad had come to London as a comedian in search of stardom. And here I was, back in his native Montreal doing the same thing.

In his email, Hazen told me about the neighbourhood where he and my dad grew up in the fifties and places they used to go as kids. In particular, he mentioned my dad's favourite deli. I searched for the neighbourhood and the deli on a map given to me by the concierge. Having located the deli, I was all set to go when I had second thoughts about my sentimental sojourn. I imagined a bustling deli full of lunching Canadians and wondered what I would gain by eating a pastrami sandwich on my own among them. The fact is, my dad wasn't going to be there.

But he lived on in me and he also lived on in his other kids. Aside from my sister Lucy, my dad had two further children after my parents divorced, Billy and Georgina, both of whom I had had very little contact with since my father died. So I found them on Myspace (my computer just underlined Myspace in red and suggested I meant Facebook. Apple iMacs are so cool) and sent messages.

Within hours they both got back to me. Billy, it transpired, was in Vermont for the summer. A mere three hours' drive. A few hours later, there was a knock on my hotel room door and standing there was my father's son, Billy McIntyre. Billy was an all-American kid. He was twenty years old, the lead singer in a band and good-looking. In short, nothing like me. We shared a special few days together that I'm sure would have meant more to our dad than me sitting alone in his favourite deli.

I was in Montreal primarily to work, so Billy came with me to a number of my shows. I introduced him to my fellow comedians as 'my long-lost brother', not realizing that this seemed dubious to say the least. It soon got back to me that the word was I was a homosexual. It looked for all the world as if I had picked up a local rent boy. It never crossed my mind how strange it seemed that I was suddenly hanging around with this young American kid who was also sleeping in my room.

All of the comedians were staying in the same hotel. Billy and I would walk past a gaggle of gagsters who would stop their conversation and stare, muttering to each other about the shameless exhibiting of my new sexual direction. To me, it was an emotional reunion; to everybody else, it was like a gay version of the film *Pretty Woman*.

On my last day of the Festival, I was in the lobby saying goodbye to Billy and slipped him a few hundred quid. It was the big brotherly thing to do, but at this very moment Frank Skinner walked past and gave me a knowing nod. I must admit; it didn't look good.

3

Now, older readers all remember the year of my birth. Not because my entering the world made international news headlines:

CHINESE TAKEAWAY!
BRITISH PARENTS TAKE HOME
ORIENTAL BABY

It's because 1976 was the last baking hot summer. It has become a legendary year, referenced by middle-aged Brits every time there is a heat wave (two hot days in a row), a mini-heat wave (one hot day in a row) or a micro-heat wave (the sun comes out between two clouds). This just winds me up as every spring I, like you, yearn for a long hot summer that never materializes. Well, it turns out I was actually alive for the best summer of them all. London was scorching and everyone was brown (although I was yellow due to jaundice). It was my first experience of weather and it was fantastic. I thought I lived in California, my mother didn't need to buy me clothes for eight months, my first word was 'Nivea'.

In truth, the heat wave of 1976 was probably greatly exaggerated. In future years when we talk about the winter we've just endured, we'll probably add a few inches of snow and deduct a few degrees from the temperature and the wind chill factor. When our grandchildren are longing for snow, we will wax lyrical about the snow of 2010 (of course, when

I am a grandparent, I will then look almost exactly like Mr Miyagi so I will 'Wax lyrical ON, Wax lyrical OFF' about the snow of 2010*):

'The blizzard lasted six long weeks. Sixteen feet of snow fell solidly. They were using a blank white sheet of paper for the weather forecast. Cars, houses, entire villages, disappeared. The whole country was housebound apart from Torvill and Dean, and Omar Sharif, who had experienced similar conditions during his portrayal of Dr Zhivago.'

I think Sharif would also have coped well in the heat wave of 1976, thanks to his sterling work on *Lawrence of Arabia*. Anyway, this isn't Omar Sharif's autobiography, it's mine, so let's get back to it. I'm born, it's hot, and I move into a tiny flat with my parents in Kensington Church Street, London. My birth certificate states that at the time my father was a 'Record producer'. I know bits about his career in comedy, but little about his days in the music industry other than that he had one big hit, the novelty record 'Grandad' by Clive Dunn, which was number 1 for three weeks in 1971.

My mother, who has produced no novelty records about family members, was beautiful. I'm basing this on old photographs. In every one, she looks stunning, but let's be honest, she would have weeded out any less than flattering photos over the years and destroyed them. This is what women do; they constantly edit their photo albums so that history may remember them looking their best. Old people basically get the best photo from their youth and use it as a sort of publicity shot – 'Look at me, I could have been a model, I had an 18-inch waist, I got asked for ID at the pictures when I was thirty-two.' That's the great thing about being old – you can

* This joke requires the viewing of *The Karate Kid*, the original film starring Ralph Macchio.

say what you like to your grandkids. Not only because they weren't there, but also because they're not really listening.

Personally, I am particularly un-photogenic. Cruelly, it is suggested that people who are not photogenic are ugly. I had some stand-up material along those lines about passport photos and how people hide them claiming, 'It's a terrible photo, I'm really ugly in it, I don't look anything like this.'

If this was true, they wouldn't get past immigration, but the fact is they do. The immigration guy never says, 'You don't look anything like this photo. This photo is of an ugly person. You, on the other hand, have a sculpted beauty that brings to mind a young Brando. I will not let you into this country, you gorgeous liar.' No, they look at your ugly photo and then look at your ugly face and let you go to baggage reclaim.

I've been lucky enough to be photographed by some seasoned snappers, but it is very difficult to get a good shot of me. I would say that I am happy with about 1 in 10 photos of me. I would say that my wife is happy with maybe 4 in 10 photos of her. Therefore the odds of getting a good photo of us together are 0.4 in 10 (I wasn't just reading the word 'BOOB' on my calculator in Maths). To put it another way: very unlikely. The odds on a family photo where my wife, our two boys and I look good all at the same time: impossible. The result is that there are very few photos of my wife and me together that haven't been deleted or destroyed by one of us.

To get a photo of my wife and me together, somebody else has to take it. On our honeymoon in the Maldives, we kept taking photos of each other; me in bed alone, her swimming alone, me in a hammock alone, her in a jacuzzi alone. The woman in Boots, Brent Cross, developing our holiday snaps must have thought we'd each gone on an 18–30 singles holiday and not pulled. Who was I supposed to ask to take our photo? I've never really taken to asking waiters when you have to explain that your camera works in exactly the same way as every other camera on earth – 'it's the button on the right' – and it still takes them so long to work it out that you develop a slightly annoyed smirk, ruining the photo.

Having no photos of us together on our honeymoon simply wouldn't do. So on the last day when I had one photo remaining on our disposable camera, I asked a sweet gentleman called Nizoo who was delivering room service if he could take a photo. 'Of course,' he agreed, before standing up as straight as he could and smiling inanely at us. He was under the misapprehension that we wanted to photograph him. I didn't have the heart to tell him that it was us I wanted him to photograph. The upshot is that the only couple who appear in my honeymoon photos are Nizoo and myself.

I imagine the woman in Boots, Brent Cross, sitting in the darkroom thinking, 'Ah, sweet, he met someone right at the end.'

My mother may also have looked good in 1976 because she was nineteen years old. Yes, I am the result of a teenage pregnancy. My father, on the other hand, was thirty-seven. He was a cradle snatcher, which was good for me as I was now sleeping in the vacated cradle. Thirty-seven! That's four years older than I am now, and I'm writing my autobiography. He had a whole life before me. Born, as you know, in Montreal, he was named Thomas Cameron McIntyre, but changed his name to Ray Cameron to make this book slightly more confusing. Ray Cameron was his stage name. My mum called him Cameron, showbiz associates called him Ray, his mother called him Tommy and I called him Dad.

He decided that he'd have a better shot at fame and fortune with a new name. Loads of celebs have changed their name.

In most cases I think artists would have found the same success with their original names: Elton John (Reginald Dwight), Cliff Richard (Harry Webb), Kenny Everett (Maurice Cole), Michael Caine (Maurice Micklewhite), Tina Turner (Anna Bullock), Omar Sharif (Michael Shalhoub – I'm obsessed with him today), Meatloaf (Steak Sandwich – I made this one up). In some cases, however, you can see why a change was necessary. Would you have been comfortable listening to 'Wonderful Tonight' by Eric Clapp? Laughing at *Fawlty Towers* with John Cheese? Or watching *Newsnight* with Jeremy Fuxmen (I made this one up, too)?

According to his brother Hazen, when we chatted in Café Pasta, the young Thomas McIntyre originally wanted to be a singer, but suffered a serious throat infection (I don't remember the details) in his teens. He lost his voice for months, communicating by writing things down. Apparently he already had a wonderfully dry sense of humour, but his time spent voiceless meant he couldn't waste any words when communicating through notes. This sharpened his comedy mind, and he often presented notes that had surrounding Canadian people in stitches. When he could speak again, his singing voice was lost, but his comedy voice was found. He started to perform stand-up locally with success before crossing the pond to try his luck in the bright lights of London. This might be a romanticized version of events, but I like it, so I'm going with it.

In the early Swinging Sixties, my father, who was in his early swinging twenties, was performing live comedy in swinging London. The sixties stand-up scene was very different to what it is today. There were no comedy clubs. This was the age of cabaret and variety. My dad was the MC, introducing dancing girls and novelty acts while telling jokes in between. I feel extremely lucky to have some of his actual scripts. Only one of them, dated 11 November 1962, mentions a venue, the nightclub Whiskey a Go Go. I researched it thoroughly (typed it into Google) and it seems to have been the original name of the Wag Club in Wardour Street and is described as a 'late-night dive bar'. The office for Open Mike Productions, who make *Live at the Apollo* and *Michael McIntyre's Comedy Roadshow*, is just a few doors down Wardour Street. In the last few years, I have spent countless days working there.

In fact, I've probably spent more time than I should have at the Wardour Street office. This is mainly due to Itsu, the sushi restaurant at number 103. I'm a big fan of raw fish. Although Itsu itself is synonymous with poisoning Russian spies with Polonium-210, the sushi that doesn't contain radiation is divine, particularly the scallops. Itsu has one of those carousels, where you sit down and the food just passes by you: salmon, tuna, squid, miso soup, edamame beans. I once saw a Samsonite holdall around the time Terminal 5 opened at Heathrow. You pick what you want from colour-coded plates that relate to their price, and I literally cannot stop eating. My rule is that once the plates are piled up so high that I cannot see the carousel, I should probably get the bill.

I'm glad there isn't an Itsu closer to home. You know the expression 'There are plenty more fish in the sea'? Well, I don't think that's the case any more. What I don't understand about the Russian spy murderers is, how did they know he was going to pick the Polonium-poisoned piece from the carousel? Maybe they just wanted to kill somebody at random. Like Russian roulette, they poisoned one piece of sushi and watched it go round and round the carousel waiting for one unlucky luncher to select it. It could have been some advertising exec but ended up being a Russian spy. I don't know.

What I do know is that it's a bloody cheek having 12.5 per cent service included in the bill. I picked the dishes off the carousel and brought them to my table. The waiter only takes them away. I figure this is worth a maximum of 6 per cent.

It's incredible to think that as I sit in Itsu arguing over the service charge in front of a tower of empty plates resembling the Burj Khalifa building in Dubai, fifty years earlier my dad was performing just a few yards away, clutching these very notes I have in my hand today.

It's fascinating for me to see my dad's notes. A comedian's notes tend to make little sense. They will consist of subject headings and key words. My dad's notes say things like 'Westminster Abbey', 'School teacher', 'The house bit' and 'Your horse has diabetes . . .' Comedians carry around these scribbles of key words that they hope contain the DNA of a good gag. Looking at some of the notes from my last tour, it's the same kind of thing: 'Wrinkle cream', 'Morning', 'Last day sunbathing'. I once thought it would be fun to swap notes with other comics on the bill and try to make jokes about each other's subjects onstage. This suggestion wasn't met with much enthusiasm in Jongleurs, Leeds, circa 2005.

In among the notes there is a script, and it's hilarious. So here's my dad in a Soho nightclub in 1962:

I'd like to tell you a bit about myself . . . I'm one of the better lower priced performers . . . I'm from Canada. I realize that it may be a little difficult because you've never heard of me here but don't let it worry you 'cause I have the same problem in Canada . . .

But it's real nice to be here . . . I brought my wife over with me . . . You know how it is . . . You always pack a few things you don't need . . .

24

We had a very interesting flight over here, we came on a non-scheduled airline . . . You know what that is? . . . That's the type of airline who aren't sure when the crash is going to be . . . You see, they use old planes . . . In fact this one was so old that the 'No Smoking' sign came on in Latin . . .

But don't get me wrong it wasn't all bad . . . There were only a few things that I didn't like . . . For instance when I fly I like to have . . . Two wings . . .

It's such a treat to have so many attractive ladies in the audience . . . Especially for me . . . Because I come from a very small town . . . And I don't want to say the girls in my home town were ugly, but we had a beauty contest there once . . . And nobody won . . .

They finally picked one girl and called her the winner, actually she wasn't that bad . . . She had a beautiful bone structure in her face . . . Those eyes . . . Those lips . . . That tooth . . . She had this one tooth right in the front and it was three inches long . . . The first time I saw her I thought it was a cigarette and tried to light it . . . To see her eating spaghetti was really something . . . She used to put her tooth right in it and spin the plate . . . But I married her anyway . . .

I got married because I wanted to have a family and it wasn't long before we had the pitter-patter of tiny feet around the house . . . My mother-in-law's a midget . . . I told her to treat the house as if it were her own . . . And she did. She sold it . . .

I hope you found that as funny as I did. I particularly like the 'I thought it was a cigarette and tried to light it' bit. This is proper old-school stuff, wives and mother-in-laws being the butt of the joke. I don't know if he wrote all of it, some of it or none of it. I know that comedians back in those days used to share jokes around a lot, but nevertheless it's still funny. I have gags, I couldn't really survive without punchlines, but a lot of my material is observational or mimicry. It's a different approach to making people laugh – it makes me laugh, which is why I say it. But you can understand how 'old-school' comedians can be baffled by 'alternative' comedy, because there are so few proper 'gags'. 'Where are the jokes?' they'll say, normally in a northern accent. For me, it's quite simple: if people are laughing, it's comedy . . . or tickling.

Browsing my dad's notes, I'm not sure he was the most confident performer. There are two pages entitled 'No Laughs', back-up in case the jokes weren't working. Here are some of them:

Well, I wasn't born here, but I'm certainly dying here.

That gag is twenty years ahead of its time. It's just your bad luck that you had to hear it tonight.

Well, from now on, it's a comeback.

I don't mind you going to sleep, but you could at least say goodnight.

Ouch. I certainly never had a plan for dying onstage. I've always found that once you've lost an audience, there's nothing you can do to win them back.

Comedians talk about stand-up in very hostile terms. If you have a good gig, you 'killed', and if you have a bad gig, you 'died'. It's kill or be killed. Witnessing a death onstage is excruciating. Experiencing it is indescribable. The worst death I ever saw was during my brief stint at Edinburgh University, years before I took to the stage myself. I never knew the comic's name and haven't seen him since. This career path was certainly evident that night, as he performed to near silence. It was a

26

packed audience of about 400, including a gallery. The comedian was fighting for his life, sweating, dry mouth, throwing every joke he could think of at it. No response. People were turning away, chatting among themselves.

Now, I don't know if it was thrown or dropped, but somehow a lit cigarette originating from the gallery landed on the comedian's head. As it burned away atop his full head of hair, the audience started noticing the cigarette and giggling. Unaware of the lit cigarette, the comedian's eyes lit up, too. 'I've cracked them!' he was thinking. He then started to loosen up, moisture flooded back into his throat, the sweat on his brow began to clear, and he confidently launched into more material. Flames started to plume from his head. The giggles now escalated into fully blown laughter. He thought he was Richard Pryor, but looked more like Michael Jackson making a Pepsi commercial.

'You're on fire, mate!' someone shouted from the crowd.

He took this as a compliment.

'Do you like impressions?' he said, feeling like a star.

The audience were now weak from laughter, tears rolling down their student faces as he broke into his 'Michael Crawford', not realizing he was already doing a pretty good 'Guy Fawkes'. It looked for all the world as though this 'dying' comedian might die for real. People were laughing so hard at the situation, they were unable to tell him he was ablaze, and he was so thrilled at the response to his 'ooh Betty' to notice. Eventually, just after he'd commented on the non-existent smoke machine, he ran from the stage screaming. It was a horror story and not for a moment was I thinking, 'That's what I want to do for a living.'

However bulletproof you think your 'set' is, a comic can die onstage at any time. From what I've been told, my dad didn't need to use his 'No Laughs' jokes very often. He opened for the Rolling Stones and lived for a while with Irish comedian Dave Allen, who told my mum years later that my dad was extremely talented. But, unlike myself, I don't think his vocation was to perform, and his move behind the camera began when he devised the comedy panel show *Jokers Wild* for Yorkshire Television. Hosted by Barry Cryer, the format was simple: Barry would give two teams of three comedians a subject to make a joke about. During the joke, a member of the other team could buzz in and finish it for points. It's like *Mock the Week* but with flares, corduroy and more manners. The show was a hit and ran for eight series, regularly featuring Les Dawson, John Cleese (Cheese), Arthur Askey, Michael Aspel and my dad himself.

As indicated by my birth certificate, my dad was primarily involved in the music industry. It was during *Jokers Wild* that he met Clive Dunn and recorded 'Grandad'. He and his partner Alan Hawkshaw (who signs his emails 'Hawk') were writing and recording songs. I met Alan when I was about thirteen. He's a hilarious character. My dad, my sister and I went to his enormous house in Radlett, Hertfordshire. Music had been good to the Hawk, one piece of music in particular. He wrote a thirty-second tune that made him a fortune. Can you guess it?

Here's a clue . . . It's exactly thirty seconds long.

Here's another . . . Du-du . . . Du-du . . . De-de-de-de . . . Boom!

Yes, that's right, *Countdown*.

(I actually met Carol Vorderman once in a lift. I got in and she was standing at the numbers and asked me, 'What floor?' If I couldn't make a joke in these circumstances, I'm in the wrong business. 'One from the top and four from anywhere else, please, Carol.')

Those thirty seconds netted the Hawk a fortune. His house had its own recording studio, swimming pool, snooker room. He gets paid every time it's played, that's every weekday at about 4.56 p.m. He actually gets paid by the second, so the longer it takes for people to guess the conundrum, the more money he makes. You can imagine him in the eighties, turning on the telly at 4.55 p.m., hoping the contestants can't decipher the conundrum so that he can afford a better holiday.

Countdown aficionados (judging by the number of adverts they have for Tena Lady in the break, *Countdown* is mainly watched by women who pee in their pants) will know that if the contestant buzzes in to guess the conundrum, the clock stops. If they correctly identify the jumbled-up nine-letter word, the game is over. However, if they get it wrong, the clock restarts, which means more money for Alan. You can only imagine the excitement in the Hawk household, whooping and cheering when they guess incorrectly, wild applause, back-slapping and champagne corks popping when the tune reaches its 'De-de-de-de . . . Boom' climax.

My sister and I loved Alan as soon as we met him. He was a charming and personable man. Within moments of our arriving, he sat at his grand piano and dramatically played various TV themes he had written that we might recognize, including the original *Grange Hill*. It's wonderful to see someone so proud of their work, and I have to say his rendition of *Countdown* was one of the most moving thirty seconds of my life. We drove for a pub lunch in his new Japanese sports car, in which he played all his own music, announcing, 'I only ever listen to my own music in the car.'

As the pub was about ten minutes away, I remember thinking, 'I'm glad he has an extensive canon of work – otherwise we'd have to listen to *Countdown* twenty times back to back.'

So Alan and my dad were writing music and producing records in the sixties and seventies. In 1975, my father found a song and was looking for a singer. This is basically record producing in its purest form. He held auditions in his small office off Trafalgar Square, and in walked my mum, a bleached-blonde beauty young enough to be his daughter. 'If you can sing half as good as you look, we're going to be rich,' observed my dad.

She couldn't. Her audition was appalling. If she was on *The X-Factor*, Louis would have said through his giggles, 'I'm sorry, you look great, but I don't think singing is for you'; Danni would have said, silently seething over how gorgeous Cheryl looks, 'It was a bit out of tune'; Cheryl would have diplomatically said, 'I think you're luverly, but I think you're a bit out of your depth singing, sorry, luv'; and Simon would have said, 'I give up', and then walked off set, immediately cancelling *The X-Factor*, *American Idol* and *Britain's Got Talent*, retiring from showbusiness to become a recluse with nobody knowing his whereabouts, apart from Sinitta.

My father's reaction was less drastic. One thing led to another and before you knew it, I was peeing on the doctor in a hospital in Merton in 1976, which probably came as a relief to the doctor as much as me due to the Sahara-like temperatures.

4

When my mum fell pregnant (an odd expression: 'Wow, you're pregnant, what happened?' 'I fell . . . on top of that man') with my sister Lucy, we moved in search of more space. We found it in a ground floor flat in leafy Hampstead. I know what you're thinking – Kensington? Hampstead? La-di-da. I know. There's no denying I had a pretty decent start. This is primarily due to my grandma ('Helloo, daaarling') marrying Jim, the wealthy Scrabble-losing stockbroker.

I can only imagine my father's face when he found out this beautiful nineteen-year-old had rich parents too. And you can only imagine my grandma and Jim's faces when they found out their daughter was marrying a thirty-seven-year-old Canadian comedian who went by several different names and whose greatest success was producing Clive Dunn's 'Grandad'. The relationship between my dad and grandparents was uneasy, to say the least. My mother recalls how on their first meeting my dad addressed the thorny issue of their wealth, saying, 'I'm a bit worried about your money.'

To which my grandmother replied, 'Don't vorry about it, you're not gettiing it.'

Relations certainly weren't improved when my dad sold their holiday home in Malta, which Grandma and Jim had put in my mother's name for tax reasons. I tried to talk him out of it, but my vocabulary was limited to 'Ma', 'Da' and 'Shums' (my word for 'shoes'). I threw up on his shoulder, but it had little impact. The Maltese house was sold, and the Hampstead flat bought with the proceeds.

My mother was expecting her second child. I wasn't. I thought she'd let herself go. I didn't know she was about to give birth to a rival. I was the centre of attention at home. I was used to having everything my own way. I was the main man. Then one day my mum suddenly lost a tremendous amount of weight and there was this baby stealing my lime-light. 'Isn't she beautiful?', 'Can I hold her?', 'Look at those little hands', 'Adorable', gushed friends and relatives.

'Michael, do you want to say hello to your new little sister?' my dad asked.

'Keep that little bitch away from me,' I tried to say, although all that came out was, 'Ma, Da, Shums.'

It was a shock to have competition at home, but I had to see the positives of having a sibling and a growing family. Unfortunately, I couldn't and decided to try to kill my sister instead. According to my mother, up until Lucy was about six months old, I made several attempts on her life. Much like a Mafia hit, I would win her and my parents' trust before striking. I would gently stroke her cheek, before trying to suffocate her with her own frilly booties. I would sweetly comb her hair, and then bash her in the temple with the brush. I poisoned her rusks with red berries I found in the garden and tried to drown her so many times that we had to take separate baths.

I'm pleased to say I finally accepted my sister and together we got on with the business of growing up in the eighties. But, in truth, there was another child in the house. Our mum. To give you an idea of the age gap, my mum once sprained her ankle and my father rushed her to Casualty, where the doctor said, 'If you would like to just pop your leg up on

Daddy's knee.' This pissed my dad off so much he sent my mum straight to bed without a story.

In America, she would only have just been allowed to drink alcohol, but here she was raising two kids and learning on the job. It's a job she did wonderfully well, with only the occasional hitch. For example, normally an adult would tell the kids to buckle up in the car, but nobody wore a seatbelt in my mum's mustard-coloured Ford Capri. My sister and I would just bounce around in the back, occasionally clinging on to the front seats for survival. And remember, there were no speed bumps in those days. By the end of a journey, I would often end up in the front and my sister on the ledge in front of the back window with Bronski Beat playing at full volume.

Family cars containing young kids will always be untidy. However, this is usually confined to the back. Not my mum's Capri. The Capri was filthy in both the children's area and my mum's area. Strewn all over the front of the car would be crisp packets, bits of old chewing gum, magazines (yes, she would read at the traffic lights), Coke cans, old lipsticks and cassettes with unwound tape hanging out of them.

Occasionally my mother would clean the car, by throwing things out of the window, in traffic. Once she threw so much litter out of the car at rush hour on the Finchley Road that my sister and I sat open-mouthed in amazement in the back. Literally, she chucked about four magazines into the street while Kajagoogoo blared out of her Blaupunkt stereo. Moments later somebody got out of their car, picked up my mum's discarded debris, and threw it back into our car. Unperturbed, my mum promptly threw it out again. This continued all the way between St John's Wood and Hampstead.

Once, when we went shopping on Hampstead High Street,

my mother loaded the boot with groceries, put me in the back seat and drove off. A few miles later, she started to get a nagging feeling she'd forgotten something. PG Tips? Shake n' Vac? Culture Club's 'Do You Really Want to Hurt Me?' on 7-inch vinyl from Our Price? No, my sister Lucy, who was still in her pram on the pavement fifteen minutes later when we returned. 'Why didn't you say anything?' my mother screamed, blaming me.

'Hey, I've been trying to kill that bitch for months,' I said, although this came out as 'Ma, Da, Shums.'

After I moved to Tanta in Egypt with my Lebanese Catholic parents Joseph and Abia . . . (Oh no, I've slipped back into Omar Sharif's autobiography. What's wrong with me?)

In my teens, I fell ill (nothing serious, don't worry) and checked in at the doctor's surgery reception in Hendon. The receptionist handed me my medical notes and said, 'Please give these to the doctor, and you're not allowed to look at them.'

'Of course not,' I lied.

Moments later, out of sight, I had a flick through my little malady memoirs. I got quite nostalgic about my 'pain in the abdominal area' of March 1987, my 'blurred vision' of May 1985 and my 'soreness in left ear' of November 1983. What surprised me, however, were the first few entries. 'Michael not talking. Parents worried.' 'Michael still not talking, just grunting. Parents increasingly concerned.' 'Michael only saying a few words. Worrying rate of development. Should be monitored. Only says "Ma", "Da" and "Shums".' I was shocked to find out that my early medical history was remarkably similar to Forrest Gump's. Apparently my sister spoke before me despite being two years younger. Her first words were 'Is Michael retarded?'

My younger son, Oscar, is nearly two and only has one word, 'hoover', which he calls 'hooba'. Out of all the things in the world, why 'hoover'? My oldest, Lucas, who is four and a half – his first word was 'car'. I have no idea why, but I suppose you've got to start somewhere. Maybe they'll go into business together one day and run 'McIntyre Brothers', a car valeting service.

So my memories really start to kick in at our Hampstead flat, which I remember to be quite dimly lit. Maybe at my parents' height this was 'mood lighting', but from where my sister and I were crawling, it was just dark. The flat was in a big old Edwardian building that also contained three other flats.

The room I remember most is the living room. This is odd, because it's the only room that my sister and I were strictly forbidden to enter. I became obsessed with the living room, presumably because it was out of bounds. The living room was darker than the rest of the house, with dark green sofas and lots of plants. Because I was only two foot tall, to me it was like an indoor night jungle with soft furnishings. 'Don't go in there, that's Mummy and Daddy's special room.' Special room? What goes on in that mini-Jurassic Park of theirs?

My wife and I do the same today with our kids. We don't let them in the living room because it's our special room that we want to keep nice. I'm sure many people reading this can relate to keeping the front room child-free. But if I'm honest, my wife and I never go in there, and nor did my parents ever go in theirs. Let's face it, the country is filled with homes, each with an immaculate room that nobody goes in. We buy and rent accommodation and don't use all of it. The only time we've used our living room, and the only time I remember using the living room in my childhood Hampstead flat, was on Christmas Day. It's a room reserved for one day of the year. This is OK if you live in a mansion, but this was a cramped flat. It made no sense to me as I toddled around that we'd cordoned off part of it for just one day of the year.

One dinnertime, while enjoying a beef broth vegetable medley compote, I addressed my parents: 'This living room situation is a joke. Why don't you sub-let it? I was chatting to a girl at playgroup, and she says her parents do the same thing. Maybe we could solve the homeless problem if we, as a nation, open up our unused front rooms? We'd have to kick them out on Christmas Day, but the rest of the year would be good for them. And that's another thing. If it's just a "Christmas room", why don't you leave the Christmas tree and decorations up all year? And why have you got so many plants in such a dark room, have you never heard of photo-synthesis? What kind of people are you?'

Unfortunately, my rant sounded more like an episode of *Pingu*, and my dad just muttered, 'We should go back to the doctor, his speech isn't improving at all.'

My parents' actual room was not out of bounds. Every morning my sister and I would climb into our parents' bed. I would always go on our dad's side and Lucy would always go on our mum's side. I don't know why it was always this way round. All I know is that, with all due respect to my father, I got the bum draw, almost literally. We must have been very young at this time; in fact this might rival Poo-gate as my earliest memory. I love cuddling my two boys but seldom wonder what the experience might be like for them. They are little, soft and wonderful. I am not.

Well, I vividly recall these early-morning cuddles with my dad. Not only was he a big naked hairy man, but his mouth was about the size of my little head. I will never forget his hot cigarettey breath blasting into my tiny face. At regular intervals, my hair would be blown horizontal as I would try to avoid it, like Keanu Reeves avoiding bullets in the *Matrix* trilogy.

Morning breath (something I have discussed at length in stand-up) is bad enough – cigarettes certainly don't improve things. Occasionally my father would be sipping coffee in bed. The combination of morning breath, cigarette breath and coffee breath became almost lethal. I think he was one garlic clove away from actually killing me. I would peek over to the other side, where Lucy and my mother were enjoying day-beginning cuddles and then return to my father's life-threatening monster breath blowing a gale into my face. Come to think of it, maybe this is what was affecting my vocal cords. Maybe my morning dad cuddles also shaped the way I look. Nowadays I always look a bit windswept and squinting, which is exactly how I would have looked in the eye of his breath-storm.

My dad was a heavy smoker. Outside of his wives and children, the two great loves of his life were Marlboro and Camel. He began smoking as a twelve-year-old in Montreal when, believe it or not, smoking was encouraged for health reasons. Then, your 'five a day' referred to cigarettes. It was as if he smoked every minute of the day. Remember in those days there were no restrictions on smoking. So he'd be smoking in restaurants, on aeroplanes, in cinemas, on the bus, on the Tube. He was smoking when he said his marriage vows, he smoked while sleeping and when he swam underwater. My dad never managed to quit.

I myself started smoking as a teenager and smoked about a pack of Marlboro Lights a day until my mid-twenties.

Giving up was one of the biggest achievements of my life. I read Allen Carr's book *How to Stop Smoking* and would recommend it to anybody trying to kick the filthy habit. In fact, I have recommended it many times, including to a very sweet, chain-smoking former tour manager of mine who then accidentally read Alan Carr's *Look Who It Is!*, the 2008 autobiography by everyone's favourite camp comedian. He then bizarrely reported, 'I read that Alan Carr book you told me about. I thought it was hilarious and yes, I have been smoking less, thank you.'

Apart from my parents' room and the living room, the rest of our Hampstead flat is a bit of a blur. Strangely, comedy was already in the building as living in the flat above was the comedy writer John Junkin, who appeared with the Beatles in the film *A Hard Day's Night*. I don't ever remember him upright. He was always sitting, in fact almost lying, in his chair, and he seemed to have most of his life around his neck. His glasses were on a cord hanging around his neck, as were his lighter and a bottle opener. I think he might have also had a compass and maybe a medal for the longest time sat in one chair. Even as a toddler who could only grunt I thought, 'That's odd.' The other bizarre thing in the Junkin household was the astonishing amount of Lucozade. This family was addicted to Lucozade. The whole flat had a sort of orange glow, like David Dickinson's bathroom.

John was married to Jenny. Jenny and my mother became the best of friends almost immediately, chatting to each other, from their respective flats, through makeshift telephones made of plastic cups and string. My mother's name was Kati, pronounced 'Cottee' (I can't believe I haven't mentioned this before), but Jenny called her 'Coke', a nickname that stuck for some time. Looking back, it seems the

Junkins were really into fizzy drinks, what with the Lucozade everywhere and calling my mum 'Coke'. When Jenny fell on John, she too became pregnant and had a child called Annabelle, which was disappointing as my sister and I had a side bet she would be called 7-Up or Dr Pepper.

Soon after we moved into our dimly lit Hampstead flat underneath the Junkins' Lucozade-glowing abode, my dad's career in comedy began in earnest. Barry Cryer was hired to write for a zany and wildly talented radio DJ, Kenny Everett. Kenny was moving to television with *The Kenny Everett Video Show* on Thames TV. Barry, who had worked with my dad on *Jokers Wild*, brought him in to help with a segment of the show. The three of them hit it off immediately, and to such an extent that my dad was hired for the whole series. The chemistry between Kenny, Barry and my dad was perfect, and they laughed their way through series after series of a show that was getting up to 20 million viewers.

In those days there were only three channels, BBC1, BBC2 and ITV. It must be impossible for teenagers, reading this book on their iPad, to fathom such a thing. It wasn't really so bad. The only real difference is that in 1980 someone would ask, 'What's on TV tonight?' and ten seconds later the reply would be 'Nothing', whereas in 2010 when someone asks, 'What's on TV tonight?' it takes half an hour before somebody says, 'Nothing.'

TV was so much simpler then. Today I can hardly keep up with technology. I've just got HD; now I'm told it's all about 3D. 3D technology is truly amazing, and soon we will get to experience it in our own homes. The problem I have is that, sure it's amazing if you're watching *Avatar*. I've seen *Avatar*. It's unbelievable – you feel like you can reach out and touch the Na'vi characters and are surrounded by the landscape of

Pandora, and you can practically smell it. But do we really want to be sitting at home watching TV and feeling like we can reach out and touch Jeremy Kyle? I don't want to feel surrounded by the Loose Women, and I certainly don't want to feel I can practically smell Alan Titchmarsh.

For parents, TV is a salvation. It's well-earned time off. 'Sit down and watch this, kids, while I briefly return to a life I left behind.' My four-year-old, Lucas, even has his own mini-DVD player, so while Oscar's watching *Teletubbies*, he'll be watching *Finding Nemo* on his portable. (When school was cancelled for a week during the snow, I think he watched every U and PG film ever made. He had to start on the 12s and 15s. When the snow finally melted, he was halfway through *Carlito's Way*.)

When I was a kid, my sister and I watched our fair share of telly. 'Don't sit too close or your eyes will go square,' our mum would say before getting back to her colouring in. (The 'eyes going square' risk fascinated me, as did the 'if you sneeze with your eyes open, your eyes will pop out' claim. I spent countless hours trying to get my sister to sneeze while sitting too close to the TV, hoping her square eyes would pop out.)

We watched all the classics that will hit readers of a certain age with nostalgia. My favourites were *Sesame Street*, *The Perils of Penelope Pitstop*, *Battle of the Planets* and *Buck Rogers*. I could tolerate *Rainbow* but was not a fan of *Playschool* or *Blue Peter*; I found the presenters really patronizing. I know they were talking to children, but I just thought they were acting weird. The much-loved Floella Benjamin, for example, I couldn't stand her. She was just way too over the top for me (and her first name sounded like a vaccine). I preferred the company of Big Bird, the Cookie Monster, Mr Snuffleupagus, and Bert and Ernie.

It was years later when it struck me that Bert and Ernie must be gay. 'Good night, Bert', 'Good night, Ernie' – they were sleeping in the same bed. I know this may come as a Michael Barrymore/George Michael/Rock Hudson-scale shock to some, but the evidence is there. They were flatmates. Flatmates would normally have their own room or at least have their own bed – if not, then it's got to be a 'head to toe' sleeping arrangement. Flatmates in the same bed sleeping head-to-head? Gay.

We only had a television in our parents' room, and Lucy and I would sit on the floor in front of their bed. Occasionally, we would watch TV as a family. The main event was always *The Kenny Everett Show* because it was 'Daddy's show'. *The Kenny Everett Show* was famed for the rule-breaking sound of the crew laughing at the sketches rather than canned laughs or the laughs of a live studio audience. My dad had the biggest booming laugh. He would constantly be laughing uproariously. So the laughter on *The Kenny Everett Show* was mainly my dad, which would have a twofold effect when we watched the show at home. He would be laughing on the TV and laughing behind me in his bed. I could barely hear the jokes.

Another evening I recall when we watched TV as a family was the launch of Channel Four in 1982. At last we would be getting a fourth channel. We gathered in my parents' bedroom for what was a spectacular anti-climax. *Countdown*. I think the whole nation felt let down and immediately went back to the BBC and ITV, apart from Alan Hawkshaw, who went shopping.

People look back fondly at a time with so few channels because the nation was all watching pretty much the same thing. We therefore had more in common with each other, leading to what the Americans call 'water-cooler moments'. This is when people discuss the previous night's television at the water-cooler. This expression has crept into our nation's lexicon (I know, 'lexicon', quite a fancy word for me). I think 'water-cooler moments' are purely an American thing, and the expression has no place over here. British people don't speak to each other anywhere, let alone at water-coolers. The only thing a British person has said to another British person at the water-cooler is 'There's no more water' or 'We need more cups' or 'Sorry'.

I do think, though, that the multi-channels of today are great for kids. There are countless kids' channels that are on twenty-four hours a day. If you have kids (or just enjoy unchallenging TV), it doesn't matter what time it is, you can turn on the telly and watch *Ben 10* or *Bob the Builder*. Whereas in the early eighties, my sister and I could only watch television intended for us at certain times, which led to us watching a lot of TV that wasn't intended for us. I remember watching a lot of snooker on BBC2. My mother was forever trying to find Ray Reardon and Cliff Thorburn figures in toy shops. The film *The Towering Inferno* was on seemingly every day during the 1980s. It was on more than the weather forecast. It would be the news, *The Towering Inferno*, then the weather. Every time I turned the TV on, Robert Wagner was hanging out of a burning building. It was repeated so many times, I think I once watched it back to back.

It was during my childhood TV viewing that I found out I was heterosexual. I can actually pinpoint the moment. It was in 1983, so I was seven years old and watching Billy Joel's 'Uptown Girl' video featuring the model Christie Brinkley. She was gorgeous. I felt peculiar. I revisited those feelings a few times pre-puberty, and approximately every seven seconds post-puberty. Lynda Carter's *Wonder Woman* was a favourite, as was golden-bikini-clad Princess Leia, obviously, and there was a scene in *Flash Gordon* (the camp one with music by Queen – 'Flash, Aaaaa!') where Princess Aura is being whipped that I rewound so many time the video tape broke – as did the video player and the television. (I've just looked the clip up on YouTube. Tremendous.)

I got carried away a bit there with eighties television – back to the story. So there I was with my vocabulary of three words watching *The Towering Inferno*, toddling around our little Hampstead flat, keeping out of the living room, with my baby sister who I had made feel a bit like Sarah Connor from *The Terminator*. I was being raised by my mum, who looked more suited to Wham!'s 'Club Tropicana' video, and by my chain-smoking, booming-laughing, *Kenny Everett Show*-writing dad.

My family. All together. But not for long.

That's a very dramatic end to quite a light chapter. It's designed to make you read on.

5

A child's job is relatively simple. At breakfast-time your goal is to eat the sweetest option available, Frosties, Ricicles, Sugar Puffs, or ideally just a bowl of sugar with a sprinkle of sugar. If you're leaving the house, you want to leave it until the last possible minute when your mother reaches a certain decibel of helplessness. Then you must lose one shoe – 'For Chrissake, where's your other shoe?' – and avoid wearing a coat regardless of the temperature: 'I don't wunna wear a coat.' When in the road, your goal is to avoid handholding and to explore the city on your own. Splashing in the bath is fun, but everything else in the bathroom is unnecessary. You never want to brush your teeth, and if you're a boy having your hair washed, you will scream like a girl, and if you're a girl, you will just scream.

At mealtimes, you will find one food that you like (chicken nuggets, pasta) and stick to it. Despite your parents' claim that vegetables are good for you, you and other kids know the truth. They are deadly and to be avoided at all costs; the only things good for you are sweets, chocolate and ice cream. 'Bedtime' is a concept created by adults, but in actual fact does not exist. There is no time of bed. Sleep is not needed. Do everything you can to delay getting into bed. When finally in bed being read a story, always aim for one more story than has been agreed. Shouting 'One more!' usually does the trick.

As a parent your job is to threaten your children, often with death, so they do what you want. 'If you don't wear a coat, you will die of pneumonia', 'If you don't hold my hand, a car will hit you and kill you', 'If you don't brush your teeth, they will rot and fall out, then you can't eat and you will die', 'If you don't wash your hair, you will get worms living in it that will eat into your head and kill you', 'If you don't eat your vegetables, your bones will crumble and you will die', 'If you don't go to bed now, I will strangle you to death.'

The problem is that kids don't really believe their parents' threats. Personally, I didn't listen to my mum because she wasn't wearing a coat, ate Frosties and screamed when my father washed her hair. I think they should have broadcast a fake *Newsround* every day with John Craven saying things like, 'Today, previously healthy Jamie Dunn, aged five and a half, from Milton Keynes, died instantly from pneumonia after leaving the house without his coat. Jamie's mother said, "I warned him, but he just didn't listen." Today's weather will be warm, but nothing like 1976. Stay tuned for *The Towering Inferno*.'

My sister and I would not only be battling our mum for more sweets and toys, but also be in competition with each other for various childhood perks.

'I want to go first.'

'No, I want to go first.'

'Let your sister have a bite.'

'No, it's mine.'

'I want the window seat.'

'No, I want the window seat.'

'I want to sit in the front.'

'No, I want to sit in the front.'

Which is why it came as a surprise when we got bunk beds, and I said, 'I want the top bunk' and my sister answered, 'OK.'

'No, I want the top bunk,' I replied automatically.

'I don't want it,' reiterated my sister.

45

I couldn't believe this. The top bunk is where it's at. Elevated sleeping is the Holy Grail of child slumber. I can see our room, indeed the world, from a new perspective from up there, like the students in *Dead Poets Society* standing on their desks. 'Are you sure, Lucy?'

'Yes, Michael, I don't want to sleep on the top bunk.' *Carpe diem*, I'm taking it. That night our dad read us a story, kissed us goodnight and dimmed the light, leaving us just enough illumination not to be scared.

'Lucy?' I said from my upper berth.

'What? Don't interrupt me, I'm drifting off to sleep,' came the reply from beneath. Like all little girls, she was articulate and advanced beyond her years.

'Why didn't you want the top bunk?'

'Because the ceiling is going to fall down in this room, and it's safer down here,' she answered factually.

'No it isn't,' I said.

'Do you see that crack in the ceiling? That will worsen and the ceiling will fall,' she insisted.

'Don't be stupid,' I said, before losing consciousness.

Every night, without fail, my sister would go to bed muttering about how the ceiling was going to cave in. I thought she was mad. And then, one day, the ceiling fell in. I remember my dad coming home from work with a smile on his face, which soon disappeared when he saw my mum and me standing in the front porch in tears with bits of ceiling in our hair. We weren't hurt, although I received a glancing blow from one of the Junkins' Lucozade bottles. (Luckily, it was a 125 ml, and in the days before the '25% Extra Free'.)

Lucy was at the kitchen table combing the hair of a My Little Pony, rocking backwards and forwards, saying, 'I told you', looking like a character from a Japanese horror movie.

For a while after her disaster prophecy, I was quite fearful of Lucy, especially when she became best friends with Annabelle Junkin from upstairs. Annabelle had fiery red hair and fair skin. Lucy and Annabelle standing together at the end of a corridor looked like a scene from Stanley Kubrick's *The Shining*. I would spend days hiding behind plants in the out-of-bounds living room. Was my baby sister some kind of modern-day Nostradamus? Soon we settled back into a relationship typical of siblings with a two-year age gap. We fought with each other and loved each other. We slept in the same room, had baths with each other, ate with each other and went to pre-school together.

My pre-school, Stepping Stones, the scene of the Poo-gate incident that scarred me for life, was a stone's throw from our Hampstead flat. Mum would drop us off in her Capri every morning, although sometimes she let me drive. Lucy would go to her class and I to mine. I certainly didn't enjoy it there, but what I hated more than anything else in my life, then or since, was school lunch.

Still to this day I cannot eat peas because of the memory of the Stepping Stones peas. They made me feel sick to my stomach. Just the smell of peas now and I am catapulted back in my mind to those horror school lunches when I was five years old. Sitting at long tables, with the white noise of children chatting and cutlery clattering, I would stare at my 'lunch', intermittently retching. The teachers would prowl up and down the tables like Dementors from *Harry Potter*, making sure you ate all your food. There was categorically no way I was going to put those peas in my mouth. So I would take a handful of them and, when the teacher wasn't looking, throw them on the floor under the table. I got away with it. Every day, if I didn't like something, I would subtly

47

throw it on the floor. Some days I would just tip up the whole plate.

I don't really understand why I was being made to eat all my food when it was so disgusting. This was a private school; my grandmother ('Heelooo, daarling') was paying good money for this. The teacher should come over to my table and say, 'Is everything all right with the food, sir?'

I would reply, 'No, the peas are making me vomit.' Then he would apologize profusely, immediately remove my plate and take some money off the school fees as a goodwill gesture.

But we had to finish our revolting food or be forced to. So I took drastic measures, and, to be honest, I thought I was a genius to be getting away with it. However, it transpired that the teachers were fully aware of my devious dumping. In fact, unbeknownst to me, they were watching me in the wings and giggling as I tried to get rid of my peas, like Steve McQueen discarding earth in *The Great Escape*. Everyone had been watching and laughing, even the kids. It was soul-destroying. The teachers had a word with my mum, and soon peas were off the menu, and have been ever since.

While I was throwing peas on the floor, my mum was throwing magazines out of her car window and Lucy was predicting domestic disasters, my dad's career continued to blossom. *The Kenny Everett Show* moved to BBC1 on Thursday nights after *Top of the Pops*. The nation was in love with 'cuddly Ken' and our life was becoming quite glamorous. Kenny was just about the most famous man in the country. Many readers will remember, but for younger readers who don't, Kenny Everett was a sensation. It's difficult to think of the equivalent today. His show was being watched by more people than watch *The X-Factor*. He was hysterically funny and loveable. Kenny and my dad clicked creatively, but Kenny and my mum clicked in every other way. My mum, 'Coke', became quite the fag hag. They became the best of friends. In fact, I remember my mum together with Kenny more than I remember my mum together with my dad.

The weekly shop is probably the least glamorous part of life. Not for my mum. The nation's favourite funnyman, Kenny Everett, would join her in Waitrose, Temple Fortune. Kenny in his beige bomber jacket with fluffy collar and my blonde mum in her dungarees, would pick up a bottle of champagne each from 'Aisle 12, Alcohol and Beverages', then return to 'Aisle 1, Fruit and Vegetables', pop open their bottles of bubby and giggle their way round the supermarket. Kenny was such a megastar he could do as he pleased. The Waitrose staff loved it. Crowds of onlookers would gather outside as word spread on the normally sleepy suburban high street. Kenny would be cracking jokes about detergents and biscuits between signing autographs and swigging Bollinger, while my mum would be laughing hysterically, sometimes from inside the trolley.

After the shopping was done – 'Come on, Coke, I'm ravenous' – it would be off to La Sorpresa in Hampstead for lunch, where the Italian waiters welcomed them with open arms.

'Mr Kenny, Miss Coca-Cola, hello, come have seat, favourite table.'

In they would stumble. Kenny was in the closet at this time, so everyone thought they were a couple. My mum would often be referred to as 'mystery blonde' in the tabloids. There was so much goodwill towards Kenny (he once knocked over a cyclist in his BMW who proceeded to ask for an autograph) that lunch was usually on the house. Either they would frame the cheque or just refuse payment. Once

Kenny didn't have a pen and wrote the cheque using tooth-paste they'd just bought from Waitrose. 'You're so funny, Mr Kenny.'

He wouldn't just eat for free, but also take whatever he fancied from the restaurant. 'Do you like this vase, Coke?'

'I love it,' giggled my mother. 'I quite like that ashtray, too.' They would leave the restaurant with most of the tableware (and once a lamp) with the full blessing of the Italian owner, who would be laughing and applauding his celebrity guest as Kenny and my mum walked out with nearly enough furnishings to open their own Italian restaurant.

After lunch they would pick up Lucy and me from school. You can only imagine the looks on the other conservative parents' faces when my mum walked through the school gates in fits of laughter on Kenny Everett's arm. As the schoolchildren came out, Kenny would guess their future professions: 'Accountant', 'Wrestler', 'Osteopath', 'Dictator'. The kids themselves went nuts with excitement. When the future accountant, wrestler, osteopath and dictator saw Kenny, it was bedlam. The day after the first time Kenny collected me from school, my popularity rocketed.

'Is Kenny Everett your dad?', 'Is Kenny Everett your dad?' I must have been asked a hundred times by everyone from my friends to the teachers, dinner ladies and, coolest of all, the big boys. This was a crunch moment for me. I'd gone from pea-dropping freak to potentially the most popular boy in school, and it seemed to hinge on my response. 'Is Kenny Everett your dad?'

I paused, thinking of my real dad, who I loved and was my hero. 'Yes, Kenny Everett is my dad,' I said. I was the most popular kid in school.

My popularity lasted a term and a half until the fathers'

race at sports day. I don't think there has been as much excitement surrounding a hundred-metre dash since Jesse Owens claimed Gold in the 1936 Berlin Olympics. I was terrified about my lie being revealed. My dad looks nothing like Kenny Everett. On the morning of sports day, I tried to convince my father not to attend, but he was breathing hot coffee, cigarettey morning breath into my face at the time, which I think muffled my request. The crowd was enormous, every pupil and parent focusing on the starting line. Other events occurring elsewhere on the sports field were completely ignored as child competitors looked confused as to why their parents hadn't shown up to cheer them on.

'Where is he? Where is he?' murmured sections of the crowd. Some parents had dressed up as their favourite *Kenny Everett Show* characters; I saw three Sid Snots and a Cupid Stunt. I couldn't bear to watch. When my dad was introduced there was a gasp from the crowd. Not before or since has an athletics crowd been so disappointed (Ben Johnson's 1988 cheating doesn't come close). The Cupid Stunt ripped off his wig and stormed off to his car, still in his fake tits.

'Kenny Everett's not your dad', 'Kenny Everett's not your dad', 'You're a liar', 'Liar', said everyone from my friends and the teachers, to the dinner ladies and, worst of all, the big boys. I was the least popular kid in school.

Oh, and I should also mention my dad came last in the race, and in the wheelbarrow race I fell and landed head-first on a fake egg, from the earlier egg-and-spoon race, which gouged my eye. All in all, a terrible day.

This wasn't the only time I lied as a child. There is one lie that I have carried with me until this very moment, in this very book. In the summer holidays after my disastrous sports day, we went on holiday to Florida. We stayed at the Hilton

Fontainebleau, an enormous hotel seen on the opening credits of *Miami Vice* with Don Johnson. Lucy and I loved it there. There was a waterfall and waterslide into the pool. My father got into a row with the manager at breakfast because a pot of coffee cost differing amounts depending on how many people were drinking it, even though it was the same sized pot. So if ten people had a sip each, it cost ten times the amount of one person drinking the whole pot. It makes me angry just thinking about it. Anyway, that's not why I'm telling you this.

During our stay a major motion picture was being filmed at the hotel, resulting in part of the pool being closed for a few days. The film was the cult classic *Scarface* starring Al Pacino. The poster has adorned the walls of just about every teenage boy's bedroom of the past twenty-five years. There's a scene where the camera pans across the beach, and I claimed that I was in the shot for a split second. Everybody believed me. I have been gaining credibility over my *Scarface* appearance ever since. People don't question it – they just say, 'Wow, cool, you were in *Scarface*, that's awesome.' I wasn't. I lied.

Kenny and my mum weren't just spending days together; they were partying into the night, too. My dad was literally from a different generation to my mum, so after a hard day's writing or filming, he just wanted a good meal, a hot bath and a thousand Marlboros. The problem was his wife was in her early twenties and wanted to party. It's a bit like getting a Labrador; they're really cute and blonde but a lot of work. 'Coke' had devoted much of her youth to motherhood. You just don't see a lot of pregnant or breastfeeding women in nightclubs. But now the kids had been weaned and she wanted to go out with her new girlfriend, Kenny Everett. My dad was happy, it meant my mum could burn some of her youthful energy in the company of homosexuals who were no threat to him.

So my mum would dance the night away at nightclubs such as Heaven and Stringfellows. In fact, for years there was a photo of them together adorning a wall inside Stringfellows. My dad would catch up on their exploits in the tabloids the next morning. Kenny would make up a different name for my mum every time they were papped coming out of a club; my favourite was 'Melody Bubbles'. Heaven is, and was, London's largest and most renowned gay club. Melody Bubbles would be the only girl in there, dancing the night away with just about every gay man from the 1980s, including Freddie Mercury, Boy George and *Sesame Street*'s Bert and Ernie.

Today, there is a comedy club that uses Heaven nightclub between 8 p.m. and 11 p.m., before it is open to gentlemen of a certain persuasion. I've performed there many times; it's actually a great space for comedy. On leaving the venue, I've seen the gay men queuing for entry to the club. Security seems to be quite an issue. They have an airport-style metal-detecting security arch outside. I don't know if they are worried about weapons or drugs or if it is some kind of 'gaydar' machine that beeps if you're not gay.

Next to the detector was a gentleman frisker who looked like Jean-Claude Van Damme in a muscle vest and tight white jeans. It seemed obvious that the queue would much rather be frisked than not. There was huge disappointment when there was no beep. I saw one man make his own beeping sound and then jump into the arms of the frisker. People were holding whatever metal they could get their hands on to guarantee the detector sounded. One guy wasn't leaving anything to chance and had dressed as a knight.

The presence of Kenny and his television show dominated my early years. I visited the TV studio several times and watching the show was the highlight of the week. There would be various props, bits of wardrobe, posters and VHSs from the show knocking around our Hampstead flat. In among them were these postcards with an image of big red smiling sexy lips on them. I don't remember what the reference was, perhaps something to do with Hot Gossip, the Arlene Phillips-choreographed dancers who appeared on the show. I was very familiar with these cards being used for scribbles around our home, shopping lists, phone messages, that kind of thing.

After days of having a wobbly tooth, the landmark occasion of my first tooth falling out was approaching. Your teeth falling out is grim, it's literally like a bad dream, but the carrot was, of course, the Tooth Fairy. When my tooth finally freed itself from my mouth, I was to leave it under my pillow, whereupon a fairy would, in effect, buy it from me. The going rate in 1982 was a pound. Strangely, I think it still is a pound. The Tooth Fairy has obviously never heard of inflation. In fact if milk tooth prices rose in line with, say, house prices, by 2007 the price would have reached £14 (although now it would have dropped to about £12.50). What I never understood about the Tooth Fairy is, what exactly is she doing with these teeth she's collecting? She must have millions of children's milk teeth. Sick. And where does she get the money from? I bet MI5 have a file on her.

Anyway, my tooth finally fell out and I placed it under my pillow. In the morning I was thrilled to find a crisp £1 note under my pillow and something else unexpected. The Tooth Fairy had also left a calling card. It was a card with a photo of a set of glistening perfect white teeth. I immediately recognized this card to be one of the many identical cards from *The Kenny Everett Show* that were scattered all over our flat. I was confused. Why would the Tooth Fairy have one? Could … my mum … be … the … Tooth Fairy? I ran into my mum's bedroom. 'Mum, are you the Tooth Fairy?' I enquired.

'Why would you say that, darling?' she replied convincingly.

'Because there was one of these cards under my pillow and even though it had an image of teeth, which one would associate with the Tooth Fairy, I know these are cards from Daddy's show.'

It was at this point my mother cracked under surprisingly little pressure and gave up all her parenting secrets in one of the most shocking and devastating moments of my life. 'You've got me, you worked it out,' she confessed. 'I am the Tooth Fairy and the Easter Bunny and Father Christmas, don't tell your sister.' Bang, bang, bang. Three in one go.

I can't imagine that in the history of parenting a mother has ever delivered such damaging revelations in such quick succession. I may have been on to the Tooth Fairy, but not for a second had I doubted the authenticity of the Easter Bunny and certainly not Father Christmas. I was mute for three whole days. My parents and all parents for that matter are liars. Well, I wasn't going to be part of their deceit, so I told my sister. Lucy said she already knew and was humouring our parents. Then she said, 'Planes will strike towers in New York City.' I didn't realize at the time she was predicting the horrors of 9/11; I just thought, 'She's been watching *The Towering Inferno* again.'

Kenny's merchandise may have shattered my childhood innocence, but Kenny the TV comic was going from strength to strength. He was tremendously talented and, as my mother fondly remembers, deeply funny all the time. But harnessing his talent for a half-hour television series still took some doing, and by all accounts it was my father who was mainly responsible. Barry Cryer remembers: 'Ray was pretty much directing the show.'

Kenny's co-star, Cleo Rocos, recalls, 'Ray was the heartbeat of the show. Kenny wouldn't be Kenny without him. He was the pioneer and driving force.' Dad had become a major player in the comedy industry, unofficially writing, directing and producing one of the biggest shows on television, but officially he was just a co-writer. It was time to make a career move.

So my dad took a giant showbusiness leap. He made a film. The film was called *Star Wars*. If only. The film was called *Bloodbath at the House of Death*. He wrote, directed, produced, edited, appeared in and raised the finance for it, quite a step-up from television co-writer. If it came off, we'd be rich. The film starred Kenny Everett at the height of his powers, the legendary Vincent Price ('Darkness falls across the land . . .'), Kenny's TV sidekick Cleo Rocos and Billy Connolly's wife, Pamela Stephenson.

Last week I met Billy Connolly, a hero of mine, at an awards ceremony. I was very nervous about introducing myself. I thought he may remember my father, as he appeared himself on *The Kenny Everett Show* and his missus starred in my dad's movie, but not for a moment did I think he'd recognize me. I loitered near him while he was talking to the comedian Rob Brydon, and then he caught my eye. 'Youu, it's you!' he hollered as only Billy Connolly can.

'Hello, Billy Connolly,' I said, more posh than usual (I always get posher when I'm nervous).

'I was on the train last year,' said The Big Yin, 'and I saaw *Time Out* magazine. The headline was "King of Comedy", big letters. And it was YOU. It was fuckin' youu! King of Comedy? I've never fuckin' heard of you. Who is this guy? I thought. I'm the King of Comedy. I spat out ma sandwich. I'm sittin' there with bits of sandwich on my newspaper and in ma beard.' Billy Connolly knew who I was because he didn't know who I was. I was thrilled nevertheless.

We then had a photo taken, which consisted of, from left to right, Ronnie Corbett, Rob Brydon, myself and Billy Connolly. Referring to our heights, the photographer said, 'Look, you're getting bigger and bigger.'

To which I replied, 'In talent.' That's another thing that happens when I'm nervous. I get a bit cheeky and arrogant.

'Who said that? Who said that?' cried Corbett.

'The King of Comedy strikes again,' sarcastically noted Connolly. We had a brief and nice chat, but I could sense he thought I was posh, cheeky and arrogant. He vaguely remembered my dad, but when I brought up *Bloodbath at the House of Death*, he simply said, 'Pamela's been in a lot of shit movies.' I think that pretty much sums up how my dad's film was received. For all the hope and hype, he may have bitten off more than he could chew.

The film was a horror spoof. The strap line was 'The film it took a lot of guts to make'. I think that towards the end of filming the budget may have been a bit tight. The final scene of the film is an *E.T.* spoof: a spaceship departing and E.T. running through the woods. The spaceship leaves without him, and E.T. says, 'Oh shit, not again!'

My reasoning for suggesting there may have been financial issues with the production is that the voice-over artist my dad hired to play E.T. was a six-year-old. Me. I had only recently been speaking in sentences that didn't involve the words 'Ma', 'Da' and 'Shums', and here I was doing voiceovers. And swearing. I was a pretty cool six-year-old.

When people met me and asked, 'Are you at school, little man?' I would reply, 'Yeah, but I'm mainly involved in the film industry. I do impressions, mainly extraterrestrial at the moment but I'm looking to diversify.'

Prior to the film's release, everything seemed to be on the up. My parents' Capris were replaced by BMWs, and when the Junkins moved out of London, we bought their flat and also convinced the owner of the remaining flat in the building to sell. We suddenly owned this massive Hampstead house. Well, we actually owned three flats in a massive Hampstead house. We had three kitchens and a million bedrooms, and my sister and I had unimaginable amounts of fun running around it. Kids love to play house – well, until the renovations started, we each had our own apartment. Suddenly I was a voice-over artist with my own place in Hampstead. I was a great catch when I was six. I didn't know at the time that it would take me over twenty-five years to be doing so well again.

My parents, however, were not getting on. I know they argued a great deal, but I only really remember one row in particular. It seemed so trivial. Lucy and I could hear the yelling from our respective flats and even as little people couldn't understand why they would be arguing over such a thing. Grapefruit. My dad was livid over the fact that there was no grapefruit for breakfast. I suppose when two people reach a point when they can't stand each other, they argue over everything. Although remembering the Florida Hilton coffee quarrel, maybe Dad was just very argumentative at breakfast-time. It got pretty heated – I think a La Sorpresa vase may have been smashed at some point. Looking back, the way Mum was shopping in Waitrose, Temple Fortune, it's a wonder there was any food in the house at all, let alone grapefruit.

Parents try to protect their children, so I wasn't fully aware of their problems. As a child, your parents are the two people you love most in the world. To hear them fighting is horribly confusing and upsetting. As I sat on the stairs listening to them arguing, I didn't know that in just two school sports days' time, I would have two dads in the fathers' race (and still no Kenny Everett).

6

I am not superstitious in any way, I don't believe in anything supernatural or paranormal. Fortune-tellers, mediums, psychics are all, in my opinion, nonsense. I've watched those 'talking to the dead' shows, and they just don't make any sense to me. The medium calls out common letters, 'I'm getting a G.'

Then several people in the audience start responding: 'It's Gary', 'It's Gordon', 'It's Grandma.'

If the medium could talk to the dead, why are the dead only giving him the first letter of their name? This is an amazing opportunity for the dead. They must have a lot to talk about, and some pretty major information like: what happens when you die? Is there a God? What's the meaning of life? No, apparently they would rather play some kind of afterlife version of 'Guess Who?' Also, the letters the medium gets are always very common, to give himself the best chance of a response. You'll never see one of these shows when the psychic says, 'I'm getting an "X"', to a silent audience.

Until a French widow stands up and says, 'That must be Xavier!'

When my mother lived alone in Kensington Church Street, very soon after meeting my father at his auditions, she wandered into a psychic bookshop a few doors down from her. She'd walked past it almost every day, but today found herself browsing the occult. There were Tarot card readers in the back, and, with time to kill, she was enticed into a reading. She was young, impressionable and open-minded. Rather than a mystical woman in flowing robes leaning over a small candlelit table, her reader was a relatively normal-looking man. She turned the cards over, and the card reader was immediately shocked by what he saw. My mother was a little concerned by his reaction. 'Is everything OK?' she enquired.

'Can you just wait there a second?' Without waiting for a response, he left her sitting there alone. She started to panic, and by the time he returned had not only convinced herself she was dying, but had doodled a 'Will' on a receipt from her handbag.

The Tarot card reader had brought mystics who worked in the shop to view the cards. All four of them had similarly excitable reactions. 'What is it?' my mother asked.

Her original reader spoke: 'You are pregnant.'

'I'm not,' insisted my mum. In actual fact, she was, but didn't know it yet. Most people find out they're pregnant from a missed period, a home pregnancy test or a big tummy. It's rare to learn this from a Tarot card reader in the back of a psychic bookshop.

'You will have a son,' continued one of the other readers who had been summoned. 'He will be world-famous, everybody will know his name, he will do wonderful things. He is special.'

The rest of her reading contained equally far-fetched information about her future. 'You will have many children. You will live in an old house for five years, and then you and your husband will be separated by the seas and by death. That will be £6.50, please.'

My mother left the bookshop in a trance and went immediately to Boots the chemist just around the corner. It briefly crossed her mind that maybe the Tarot readers have a deal with

Boots whereby they predict certain things that send people immediately to the chemist – 'You are pregnant', 'You have a cold sore coming', 'Your hair will go grey' – to boost sales of Clear Blue, Zovirax and Just For Men. My mum purchased the pregnancy test and rushed home. It was positive.

She was overcome with the romance of what had just occurred and clutched her stomach. She felt like the Virgin Mary. 'I am carrying a special son,' she thought to herself. If she gave birth to a baby girl, the whole thing would have been off. But I was born a boy (although slightly camp).

As more and more of the Tarot card reader's predictions came true, my mother became convinced I was some special chosen child. It impacted a bit on my relationship with her when I was a child. Once at dinner I jokingly replaced my glass of water with a glass of Blue Nun, and she crossed herself, fell to the floor and started kissing my feet. At parent–teacher evenings when she was told that I wasn't fulfilling my potential and that I was lazy, she wouldn't really care, remembering Jesus was a carpenter until his thirties. As long as I was achieving in Woodwork, she wasn't bothered about English and Maths. The Tarot card revelations certainly affected me. I was about five or six years old and was learning about the world around me. She had only recently delivered the Tooth Fairy/Easter Bunny/Father Christmas triple blow, when she told me I would grow up to be famous.

It gave me confidence when I was young. I felt that I had a magical secret and that I was special. My mother recently told me that she often thought of the mystical bookshop, which spookily closed down soon after her visit, and wondered as I grew up what path to fame I would take. When I became a successful comedian, I said to her, 'I'm famous now, Mum, just like you said I would be. Are you proud?'

To which she said: 'I was hoping you'd make some kind of medical breakthrough, a cure for a disease or something.'

It's a shame the Tarot card reader couldn't have been a bit more specific: 'You are carrying a child, a son. He will become an observational comedian. I see great importance in the words "Man" and "Drawer".'

Whereas my mother is a believer, I am a sceptic. Every once in a while these psychics are going to get lucky. It's statistics. Maybe the person who visited the bookshop immediately after my mother was also predicted fame and fortune and then got hit by a bus on Kensington High Street moments later. If I'm honest, I'd rather it wasn't true anyway – I'm not a fan of destiny. What's the point of living your life if it's all mapped out ahead of you? And if these Tarot card readers were so accurate, why couldn't they foresee their bookshop closing down? Anyway, if the Tarot reader's prophecies were to come true, there was to be strife before my glittering future. If we were to 'live in an old house for five years', our time was nearly up, and the 'separated by seas and death' prediction was a bit of a worry.

It certainly didn't seem like we were about to move from Hampstead. We were in the process of developing our three flats into one big house. I remember living with builders for some time. Our lives were dominated by workmen shouting, sledgehammers smashing, skips loading, wheelbarrows wheeling and dust billowing. My sister, whose own oracle-like qualities seemed to be confined to the destruction of buildings, babbled constantly about walls and ceilings tumbling. The builders were fun and friendly, probably due to my mum. My mum was the type of lady at whom builders whistle. Builders' whistles often fall on deaf ears, but now when they whistled, my mum would bring them tea. I remember one of them, Steve, inviting me to punch him in the stomach. This was wildly exciting for me. Steve was like a real live He-Man. 'What? As hard as I can?' I questioned, overestimating my own seven-year-old strength.

'Sure,' Steve confidently replied. So I swung with all my might and connected flush with Steve's rock-like stomach. He didn't even flinch. I couldn't believe it. I hit him again, this time with a run-up, but he barely noticed. It was like living with the Incredible Hulk. My friends would come to my house just to punch him in the stomach.

One of my friends, Barnaby, accidentally punched the wrong builder in the stomach – 'Oi! Fuck off, you little shit.' Barnaby burst into tears and didn't come round again.

The house itself soon started to take shape and began to be decorated. Because it was the mid-eighties, my mother settled upon a theme for her lovely new home. Hideous. An expression I heard a lot when growing up and, thankfully never again, was 'rag-rolling'. 'Rag-rolling' is when you take a painted wall and ruin it. I can only imagine it was invented by mistake. Someone in the eighties must have leant on a wall without realizing it was newly painted and in the process not only invented 'rag-rolling', but also the equally tasteless paint splattered shirt which was all the rage at the time. What was wrong with people in the 1980s? I think the singer Sade was the only person who looked good.

My mother was looking less like Bananarama and more like Krystle Carrington every day. Her shoulder pads were so large she was once late picking me up from school because one of them wedged in the door of her new BMW 3-Series. The builders had to widen the doorways so she could get around her own home. She used every fad going to create what in the eighties was a dream home, but in hindsight was the stuff of nightmares. Looking back, I'd rather have lived in my father's fictional 'House of Death'. Loud bright colours were the order of the day. The out-of-bounds dark living room now had sky-blue rag-rolled walls and custard yellow carpets. Even though I was now allowed in, I banned myself from entering. The kitchen walls were Barbara Cartland pink with white stripes. Upstairs was worse. My mum employed more painting techniques of the era. There was a lot of 'stencilling' in the bedrooms and 'marbling' in the bathrooms. Marbling was painting made to look like marble. The results were criminal. A couple of the bedrooms were stencilled with swirls that were so disorientating it was difficult to keep your balance.

The fittings and fixtures were even more offensive. We had white cowboy doors between the pink kitchen and peach dining room. It was like a scene from the alternative ending of *Brokeback Mountain*, the version where they live happily ever after. The pièce de résistance of our new Hampstead house of horrors was undoubtedly the master bathroom. The bath had golden taps beside a spout in the shape of a swan's neck and head. The water would shoot out of the swan's mouth, like it was vomiting. The black loo was so over-stylized that it was actually unusable. The loo seat was angled in such a way that it pushed one's bottom cheeks together, thus blocking nature's course. It was difficult enough to poo with a vomiting gold swan staring at you, but the design fault made it physically impossible. It became a 'show loo', just for decoration. The whole house was a bit like that.

I don't remember my father being around while the work was being done. He must have been making or editing his film. I know that he was also travelling to America a lot as he was putting together the sketch show *Assaulted Nuts*, which was co-produced by the US cable network HBO.

What I do remember is sitting in our newly converted loft playing with excess rolls of carpet and coming across my mother's Filofax (an eighties must-have) and seeing a note to her from Steve, the builder with an iron chest. 'I love you,' it read. Why would Steve the builder love my mum? I was shocked. At this moment, my mother walked in. 'Have you seen my Filofax, darling?' She saw me sitting on the fluffy new carpet, the blood drained from my young face. 'Are you all right, Michael?'

'No,' I said, barely audible. 'The room is spinning.'

'I know, Michael, that's the stencilling. That's the effect I'm going for. You'll get used to it, it's very trendy.'

I showed her the Filofax. 'What's that mean?' I asked fearfully. Unfortunately, it had flicked to another page, 21 June.

'The summer solstice,' she explained. 'That's the first day of summer, I think.'

'No,' I said, riffling through the Filofax to find the incriminating page. 'That. What does that mean?'

I thought confronting my mother with evidence of her adultery would be dramatic, but it was nothing of the sort. 'I love Steve, we love each other. I thought you knew that.'

I genuinely couldn't believe how blasé she was being. 'No, I didn't.'

'We've been together for a while. Why do you think he's always here?'

'To decorate,' I said truthfully.

My mum chose to downplay the gravity of the situation. Either that or she was so in love with the builder that she was blissfully unaware that she was married with two kids. I thought for a moment that maybe these avant-garde painting techniques were responsible for my mother's seduction. She did seem to be in a trance-like state. Maybe she was just

Steve's latest victim, and he was some kind of decorating Derren Brown using a combination of rag-rolling, stencilling and marbling in a series of gaudy colours to hypnotize house-wives.

My memories of our final days in Hampstead are not only hazy, but also confused by the fact that a lot was kept from Lucy and me to 'protect' us. This was a messy divorce with kids involved, and I was one of the kids. My dad came back from America to a strange and hostile environment. I can't imagine what it must have been like for my father. A man's first instinct when he learns his wife is cheating on him is to attack the other man. 'Who is it? Where is he?' Unfortunately in this instance, it was Steve, the iron-chested builder. My dad could have punched Steve repeatedly in the stomach, and Steve wouldn't have even noticed – he would have just carried on rag-rolling while listening to his Sony Walkman. Your partner cheating on you is bad enough. If she cheats on you with a bigger man, it's the worst-case scenario. What are you supposed to do when you catch them together? 'Hey, that's my wife. Get off her or I'll hit you, and then you'll hit me and I'll be hospitalized.'

What if your partner cheats on you with a hero of yours? At the time of writing John Terry has just lost his England captaincy for alleged adultery. But what if he was sleeping with the wife of a Chelsea season ticket holder who proudly wears a John Terry replica shirt, and it's days before the European Cup Final? What would be the husband's reaction then? Initially he would be shocked and angered by the infidelity of his wife before noticing his idol in his bed. 'How could you do it this to me, you fu— There's only one John Terry, one John Teeeeery, there's only one John Terry. Look who it is, love, it's JT!'

'I know, I'm having sex with him.'

'You all right, JT? Can I get you some water or something? He's got the final on Wednesday night, so you should go on top, love. He's got to save his energy. Careful, darling, mind his metatarsal, that's six weeks out, that is.'

The marriage was over. They weren't happy. My dad was working hard, my mum was playing hard, and when they were together they were arguing hard. They were from different generations and the gap was never going to close. A friend of my mum said to her at the time of the separation, 'Children grow up and leave home, and that's all you're doing.'

My grandmother was thrilled to learn that the marriage was over and swigged from a glass of fine champagne. 'Daarling, you are doing the right thing, he vas no gud for you. Start egen, I vill help you vith money.' Then my mum told her about Steve. She choked, vintage champagne spluttered from her mouth and through her nose 'Vot? The builder? I'm feeling faint, Jim, Jim, get my pills . . .'

I haven't really gone into much detail about Grandma's rich husband Jim. For all his business prowess and swollen bank account, he was very much a secondary figure in my grandmother's home. He acted and looked like a butler, very English, very proper, very upright. He occasionally smirked or scowled, hinting towards true feelings that he never voiced. He fetched my grandma's pills. 'You're telling me you are in luv with the rag-rohleeer?' she continued. 'Vell, you vont get a bean out of me. He is after the money, and he's not getting any.' My grandmother believed everybody was after her money.

In hindsight, I think my parents' marriage breakdown was inevitable. I've met them both, and they genuinely had nothing in common. I'm surprised it lasted as long as it did. Although my mum was spending a lot of time with Kenny and his friends, it was only a matter of time before she met a heterosexual man. People who are single are often encouraged to 'get out there, don't just wait for Mr Right to come knocking on your door'. Well, in my mother's case, Mr Right smashed the door down, installed a new one, then painted and rag-rolled it. They were in love and determined to start a life together, a life with Lucy and me. My home was broken. The Hampstead house was put on the market.

Let's just put the divorce to one side for a moment. Park the divorce. I want to talk about house prices. It was 1983 and we owned a substantial house in Hampstead. I also want you to put the décor of the house to one side. Park the décor. Park it next to the divorce.

Because of a wonderful website, with which I became obsessed when I was house hunting called houseprices.co. uk, you can now find out the price of homes sold anywhere in the UK. We sold our Hampstead house in 1983 for £330,000, a substantial amount of money at the time, even today. At the peak of the market in 2007, the same house was sold for £4.2 million. Here's a question: why the fuck didn't the Tarot card reader mention that? The house increased in value by £160,000 a year. Would this knowledge have saved my parents' marriage? (I've just un-parked the divorce.) I don't think so. But maybe it would have prevented them from selling their goldmine with hideous interior. (I've just un-parked the décor.) For that kind of money, Steve could have built a dividing wall and they could have split the house. Lucy and I would still live with both our parents, and in twenty-five years we would all walk away millionaires.

It wasn't to be. The house was sold, bizarrely, to the Osbournes. Any relation? Yes, it was them, the actual Osbournes. Sharon and Ozzy and little baby Jack. Kelly Osbourne had just been born at the time. This is from Sharon's autobiography: 'Ozzy arrived for the birth and I took him to see somewhere I found in Hampstead. It was Victorian, semi-detached with a garden, not enormous but somewhere to put the pram . . . It needed a lot doing to it, but the price was good and it had great potential.'

This is an historic moment: the overlapping of two celebrity autobiographies. It's interesting, the different perspectives. For Sharon, the house was 'not enormous'; for me, it was 'enormous'. Sharon felt it 'needed a lot doing to it'; for me, it was 'hideous'. It also said in her book that it was the first place that felt like a family home. The house certainly had the potential to be one; unfortunately, we were the wrong family. I doubt that when my father bought all the different flats and sat down with his architect, he said, 'I want to create the perfect family home, for the Prince of Darkness.'

I had obviously never heard of Ozzy Osbourne. It may not come as a shock to you to learn that I never went through a 'heavy metal' phase. For all I knew, Black Sabbath was just another date in my mum's Filofax. Before the MTV television series that endeared Ozzy and his family to the world, he was primarily known for eating the head of a bat. When my mother told me to tidy my room 'because a man who bites the heads off bats is coming round to look at it', I thought it was a threat. I've never cleaned my room so well in my life. Inspired by my mother's Capri cleaning, I usually just threw rubbish out of the window, but this time I had the place immaculate. 'All right, I'll do it! Please don't let the man bite my head off.'

The proceeds of the house sale were divided equally between my parents so each could start a new life. My father rented a house belonging to friends in Hertfordshire, and my mum, Steve, Lucy and I bought a house in Golders Green. So that was it, a new chapter in my life was beginning. Annoyingly, this is my autobiography and I haven't actually reached the end of the chapter – bad planning on my part. I feel I need to introduce Steve to you properly, as he now looks all set to become my stepfather. No, maybe I should end the chapter here.

I think I will.

A new chapter in my life had begun. I didn't know it at the time, but it was Chapter 7. There was a new man in my mother's life, and because I was only seven years old and Lucy five, there was a new man in ours as well. We were the baggage that my mother came with.

Steve was pretty much the same age as my mum and looked almost identical to Patrick Swayze. Much to his embarrassment, his mother entered him into a Patrick Swayze look-alike contest by sending in a photo. He came second. I genuinely don't know how he didn't win; either it was rigged or the real Patrick Swayze entered. Steve was often mistaken for the Hollywood star in the most unlikely locations. 'Oh my God, are you Patrick Swayze?'

'No, do you really think Patrick Swayze would be buying paint in Wickes on the North Circular? Oh, look over there! It's Tom Selleck looking at drills.'

Steve was young, more *Point Break* than *Donnie Darko*. He was an aspiring painter in the artistic sense but was painting in the painter/decorator sense to make ends meet. He grew up in Brixton with its predominantly West Indian community. He spoke in Jive as a party trick. His father was an electrician and his mother a dental nurse. On his first day of school he wore shorts, not knowing that the 'all boys should wear shorts' rule was ignored by every other boy at the school. This trouser-length faux pas led to him being ridiculed and locked all day in the cupboard that housed the fuse boxes and electrical meters. When Steve finally made it home, his father asked, 'How was your first day at school?'

'Much like your day at work, Dad, except I didn't have a torch,' he replied. The following day, now wearing trousers, he approached the largest of the bullies who had locked him up and punched him in the mouth, knocking several teeth out.

The father of his now front-toothless victim squared up to Steve's father at the end of school. 'Hey, your kid has knocked my kid's teeth out.'

'What do you want me to do about it? I'm an electrician,' was Steve's father's now legendary response. 'You want my wife for that. She'll book you in for an appointment with the dentist.'

For all the punching in the stomach and 'history of violence' on his first day at school, Steve was and is the gentlest man I have ever met. He likes stamp-collecting and bird-watching and is extraordinarily passive and sweet-natured. Lucy and I liked him immediately. You might have expected the opposite reaction. Here was a man breaking up my family. But I didn't see it that way. My parents were so unsuited to each other. It was now warfare. The last thing I wanted was for them to be together. How can two people who hate each other make a happy home?

Our Golders Green house was built in the 1930s. It required some work, but Steve was determined to do it all himself, not just to save money but also because his new girlfriend had a history of sleeping with contracted builders. It was detached with four bedrooms, a small kitchen, small living room, dining room and one bathroom. It was perfect for a young Jewish family. The main drawback was that none of us were Jewish. My mother's father was Jewish (remember

Laszlo, the Hungarian scientist whose sister's son was Uncle Peter, the guy who gassed himself in the face?), but one Jewish relative is not enough to make you particularly welcome in the neighbourhood.

Although the house was a good size for the money, He-Man builder Steve could easily do any work necessary, and though it was only about two miles from our old Hampstead house, it was like moving abroad. I felt a bit like Harrison Ford in *Witness*. Golders Green is properly Orthodox Jewish. Everyone has skullcaps, long hair with side-curls, all black clothing and Volvos. Volvos are very popular with Jewish people; they refuse to buy German cars (with good reason) so BMWs, Mercedes, Audis, Volkswagens and Porsches are all out of the question. There are of course many other good-quality cars that aren't German, but everybody in Golders Green seems to go for the Swedish Volvo. The Volvo, of course, is famed for being the safest and strongest vehicle on the road, so if they saw a Nazi, they could run him over with minimal risk to themselves.

I don't think we did ourselves many favours when we first arrived in my mother's new BMW 3-Series with Kraftwerk playing on the stereo. Adjacent to our new home was some outside space, a park that my mother christened 'Dog Shit Park'. She told the neighbours she'd christened it 'Dog Shit Park', but they just slammed the door: 'We don't believe in Christ.' The council wasn't as stringent with dog fouling in those days. In the mid-eighties most of the dogs didn't even have collars, as all the punks were wearing them.

Golders Green's high street was an excellent shopping parade, if you're kosher. There are shops and bakeries that not only seem to have been there since the beginning of time, but have the same people in them. Grodzinski's was a coffee shop that had the same collection of old Jewish ladies, in the same seats, sipping the same coffee, every time I walked past. The high street seems to be in some kind of a time warp. Chains of shops would go out of business elsewhere but remain open in Golders Green. I think today there are still a C&A, Wimpy, Cecil Gee, Woolworths and Our Price.

The best thing about Golders Green, and the reason I still go back, is the I. Warman-Freed chemist. Most chemists keep regular business hours. Boots, for example, is usually open from 8.30 a.m. to 6 p.m. So you have to fall ill, or require any form of medication or remedy, between these hours. If you have a cold sore and want to adhere to the advert that tells you to buy Zovirax 'at the first sign of tingling', you can't outside certain times. In fact between 6 p.m. and 8.30 a.m., every ailment known to man must be treated with Nurofen from the petrol station or a visit to Casualty. It's a wonder this situation is tolerated. Well, there is one group of people who would never tolerate such a state of affairs. Jews. Which is why smack-bang in the middle of Golders Green Road is I. Warman-Freed, the all-night chemist. I don't know who I. Warman-Freed was, but he certainly understood the neuroses of Jewish people. You know when the *Harry Potter* books are released and people of all ages queue around the block? Well, the I. Warman-Freed pharmacy counter is like that twenty-four hours a day.

During the week, I lived in Golders Green in what felt like an FBI witness relocation 'safe house'. On the weekends Lucy and I would stay with our dad in his temporary accommodation. Strangely, it's from this point on that my memories of my father are much stronger. He was obviously very busy with work prior to the divorce, but now in his 'weekend dad' capacity, he made the most of our time together. Being apart from his kids was heartbreaking for him and he desperately wanted to make us feel we had a new home with him as well as in Israel – sorry, Golders Green. Seemingly within minutes of his separation from my mother, there was a new lady in his life.

While my mother was being romanced in plaster of Paris by Steve in scenes not dissimilar to the film *Ghost*, my father had met a twenty-seven-year-old Floridian sweetheart during his frequent visits to America. I'm not aware of the details; all I remember is that Lucy and I went to visit him in his rented cottage, and there she was, Holly Hughes.

The best way accurately to describe Holly is that she was 'American'. She had rosy cheeks and wore leggings with baggy T-shirts. She was bubbly and confident and in love with my dad. It was extraordinary, after some home renovations and a business trip, I suddenly had two mums and two dads. Holly had been working in the music business and from what I remember had been very successful.

She brought American culture into my life for the first time. I say 'culture'; I mean 'food'. Holly introduced us children to a standard of eating that would have had Jamie Oliver pressing charges. 'Jiffy Pop' was a highlight; this was basically a saucepan-shaped package that you heated on the hob until it created a big aluminium (a word she couldn't pronounce) balloon filled with popcorn. 'Sloppy Joes' were a lowlight; these were hamburger buns covered in a sort of super-sweet Bolognese sauce. I don't know who 'Sloppy Joe' was, but he was almost certainly clinically obese, and so would Lucy and I have been if our dad had won custody. In general, Lucy and I loved Holly's weekend cooking, and her hot chocolate is the best I've ever tasted.

This split lifestyle that Lucy and I were leading had some

major perks. My dad was definitely trying to make up for his enforced absence by spoiling us. He bought us top-of-the-range BMXs to explore the Hertfordshire countryside. My metallic blue Raleigh Burner was the love of my life thus far. Lucy and I were kitted out with all the latest cycling accessories: helmets, gloves, knee and elbow pads, flashing lights and sirens. We looked like something from outer space. I actually think some of the local farmers reported alien sightings.

My dad was certainly flush with cash at this point, and apart from our lavish divorce-inspired gifts he purchased himself a gorgeous silver BMW 635 CSI. I don't know what the 'CSI' stood for, but it was top of the range and had something to do with making it go faster – either that or the previous owner was murdered in it. The major excitement about his new car was that it had a phone in it. Nowadays, everyone has a phone on them all the time. But in 1984 it was tremendously state of the art. People saw car phones as the future of technology (the Carphone Warehouse did, but they now sell as many car phones as Blockbuster Video sells videos).

My dad's car phone was the envy of all my friends, and all his friends for that matter. It was long and sleek and sat proudly next to the handbrake. Unfortunately, it was also about the same size as the handbrake, which led to dangerous mishaps. When the phone rang, he would pick up the handbrake by mistake, sending the car into a spin. Or he would stop on a hill, reach for the handbrake, but pick up the phone by mistake and roll into the car behind. The phone itself barely had a signal, and when he got one the conversation would only last long enough for him to say he was in the car. 'Hi, I'm in the car, I'm on the car pho– Hello?' It was basically a device for informing people he was driving.

My sister and I loved his BMW 6-Series. On a Friday afternoon, Daddy would pick us up from school in his magnificent sports saloon. We would hurtle up the M1 motorway at law-breaking speeds. Lucy and I would pick cars ahead of us to overtake while I would be shouting out our speed, '116, 117 . . . 120 miles an hour!' It's only looking back that I realize just how dangerous this was, not to mention highly illegal. I know it sounds strange, but our dad was using the car to bond with us. He was desperate. He had lost his kids for five days of the week, and he had to make up ground, at 120 miles per hour. He had to cram a lot into his two days and wanted to make us happy. So if that involved expensive presents and treating the motorway like a Grand Prix track, so be it.

The BMW 6-Series happened to be my mum's dream car. She had a 3-Series, but every time we drove past a 6-Series, she would state her intent: 'I love that car, I want one.' She likes cars, my mum. In general, she's a pretty good driver, despite the lack of seat belt and occasional magazine-reading. Where her driving falls down, however, is at the set of traffic lights on the Finchley Road at the junction with West End Lane. Her misunderstanding of the filter light system resulted in three collisions in the very same place.

The insurance company kept saying to her, 'You've already told us about this accident.'

To which she would shamefully reply, 'I'm sorry, I've done it again.' Unfortunately, this junction was on the school run. Lucy and I would have to brace for impact twice a day.

Even though things were tight financially and Steve was searching for a more substantial job, when my mother received some money from her late father's estate, she decided to blow it on a BMW 6-Series. The problem was that she only had £7,000 to spend. My dad's 6-Series had cost closer to £25,000. Thanks to *Autotrader* or *Loot* or something of that ilk, we found one for £6,995. It was a light blue 633i with plenty of miles on the clock and fewer extras than my BMX Raleigh Burner, but it was a 6-Series (although it may have been two 3-Series welded together). It was perfect. We spent the £5 change on petrol and went on one of those 'new car drives' where you aren't actually going anywhere, just cruising around. Unfortunately, because we lived in London, we got stuck in roadworks for an hour and a half and reached a top speed of 7 mph. Typical.

The sensible decision was taken not to tell my grandmother about the 6-Series. Her reaction would not have been: 'Good vor you, luvely car, fuel injection, wery classy, you deserve, mast get burglar gassing device, very populer in Hungaaary.' It would more likely have been: 'You blow money on ztupid car, you vasters, I will cut you out of my vill.' She tended to use her money as a weapon, and threatened to cut us out of her 'vill' about every thirty to forty minutes. 'Michael, come end give yur grenny a hug, or I vill cut you out of my vill.' 'These kerritz are burned, Kati, I vill cut you out of my vill.'

We were the poor relations, and Grandma revelled in it. When she visited, she would bring us food from her fridge that had passed its use-by date as a gift. Whenever she found loose change on our floor or behind the sofa, she would accuse my mother of wasting money and would preach her mantra: 'Look avter ze pennies and ze pounds vill take care of themselves', forgetting that marrying a millionaire also helps. So the decision was taken to keep the new car a secret. When we visited her, we would drive our old 3-Series and when she visited us we would hide our new 6-Series up the road. It simply wasn't worth the trouble. Grandma would much rather her daughter was eating out-of-date dinner surrounded by jars of 1ps and 2ps, than cruising around in a new set of wheels.

The first time my mum dropped Lucy and me off at our dad's rented cottage in her light blue 633i BMW, parking it alongside his silver 635 CSI, all hell broke loose. He accused her of purposefully undermining him by buying the same car as him, the car Lucy and I loved so much. It was horrific. The 'grapefruit' row was nothing compared to the 'BMW 6-Series' row. Steve and Holly were both present and embarrassed. They peeled off to one side and chatted awkwardly. 'I gather you brought a lot of Jiffy Pop over from the States, the kids really love it,' Steve said, searching for conversation.

'Are you Patrick Swayze?' replied Holly.

Meanwhile, my parents were screaming at each other in the drive between their respective shiny new BMWs, like an episode of *Top Gear* gone wrong. He was accusing her of buying the car to spite him, and she was adamantly denying it. At the end of the argument, my mum and Steve were ordered off my dad's rented accommodation. 'Come on, Steve, we're leaving,' cried my mother.

To add insult to injury, Steve then got into my dad's BMW by mistake. 'I can't fucking believe this,' commented my dad to Holly.

'Is that Patrick Swayze?' she replied.

Steve and my mum then leapt into the correct car and sped off at an impressive 0–60 in 6.8 seconds. The result of this ugly scene was that my mum was banned from my dad's house. In future, Lucy and I were to be dropped off at a neutral location, the Swan Pub near Hemel Hempstead, to be bundled from one BMW 6-Series to another.

Jewish architect David Rosenberg was another proud new

car owner in Golders Green. He had infuriated his neighbours by buying a Mercedes 500SL, a German car. He was a chancer who began selling ice creams in the City before convincing a Japanese customer to let him redesign his offices. He made money wherever the opportunity presented itself. He once shut his own fingers in the door of Barclays Bank and sued them for a small fortune.

He was cunning and crafty, the kind of guy who does well on *The Apprentice* with Lord Alan Sugar, doesn't win, and then gets booed on *The Apprentice – You're Fired* with Adrian Chiles. He was also a terrible driver and had so many accidents he was considering shutting his fingers in another bank door to pay the astronomical insurance premium on his new sporty motor. Steve, my mum, Lucy and I met David in a head-on collision on Redington Road, in Hampstead. Our short and disruptive romance with our seven-grand sports saloon ended just weeks after it had begun.

Lucy and I were in the back, Mum was in the passenger seat, and Steve was driving. Redington Road is a residential road, home to the rich and famous. We had friends living there, the married actors John Alderton and Pauline Collins. John and Pauline's youngest son, Richard, was at school with Lucy and me, and they had hit it off with our mum at the school gates. By sheer coincidence, David Rosenberg's Mercedes and our BMW crashed directly outside the home of the *Forever Green* stars. They both heard the impact and rushed outside. The scene they found was not pleasant. Both cars were written-off, or 'totalled', as Holly would have said. I had managed to cling on to the seat in front of me, Lucy injured her leg and my mother's head smashed through the windscreen.

Because David Rosenberg had been involved in so many car accidents, his only concern was liability. He jumped out of his broken car, camera in hand, photographing the crash site. He was collecting evidence. Hilariously, these photos were self-incriminating because his car was clearly on the wrong side of the road. So while the stars of *Please, Sir* and *Shirley Valentine* were recovering us from the wreckage, David Rosenberg was busy proving beyond all reasonable doubt that the accident was his fault.

Distraught and slightly concussed, my mother telephoned my grandmother and told her about the accident. Thank God, everyone had escaped with only minor injuries. The car, however, was unsalvageable. She totally forgot that Grandma was unaware we owned the car involved. It still hadn't dawned on her when Grandma and Jim came round the following day with a bag full of goodies past their use-by date, to console us. They were twenty minutes late so I peeked out of the window to find them in our driveway, circling the 3-Series inspecting the non-existent damage. I ran downstairs. 'Grandma and Grandpa are outside.'

'Why don't you let them in?' Steve said.

'They're inspecting the 3-Series. Why did you leave it in the drive?'

'Shiiiiiit,' my mum screamed. At that moment the doorbell went. 'What am I going to say?' They had put themselves in the awkward position of having to explain how their un-salvageable car had been miraculously restored to its former state in less than twenty-four hours. They briefly considered climbing over the garden fence and making a run for it, but Lucy's bruised leg wasn't up to it. The doorbell sounded again. My mother finally opened the door.

'Helloo, daaarling, ze car it is fine. Vot is going on?' My mother began lying through her teeth. She explained how the crash wasn't as bad as she first thought.

Steve chipped in with the classic line, 'The damage was mainly internal.'

Grandma and Jim didn't believe a word of it and pretty soon the truth came out. 'You vucking liars, I'm cutting you out of my vill,' she yelled as she sped off.

Grandma wasn't speaking to us, the car only had third-party insurance so was lost, and Steve was struggling to find a job to support his new family. The BMW 633i had caused nothing but trouble. But then, out of the light blue, the 6-Series saga had a happy ending. David Rosenberg had perused his photos of the crash and realized he was the guilty party and his insurers would punish him for this. He regretted taking the photos, but treasured the one of him and John Alderton, one of his favourite actors. David popped over to our house to discuss the situation.

He was charming and very keen to strike a deal with my mum and Steve. Making polite conversation, they found themselves discussing David's new business venture. He had recently founded a new architectural company and purchased a snazzy new computer design system and was looking for somebody to operate it. 'What a coincidence,' lied the job-hunting Steve, 'I can do that.' A visit to WHSmith and a few days and nights cramming later, Steve landed himself a job at David's company. He worked there for the next ten years.

8

Some time during my domestic turmoil, I started 'big boy' school. I went to a lovely school called Arnold House in St John's Wood, London. I wore a bright red blazer with dark trim. It looked like a ladybird costume. Unlike Steve's first day, when he was beaten and locked in a cupboard for wearing shorts, everybody in the Arnold House Junior School obeyed the rules and wore tiny little shorts, like the ones worn by footballers in the seventies. At break-time there were more goose pimples in the playground than on a battery farm in the Arctic. Matters were made even worse for me as my mum put my shorts in the wrong wash, not only shrinking them but also giving them a slightly golden sheen after they shared the machine with one of her *Dynasty*-inspired trouser suits. I was going to school in hot pants looking a bit like Kylie Minogue in the 'Spinning Around' video.

Arnold House is a private all-boys school and cost my father a fortune. It was oddly formal. I remember referring to all my friends by their second names. My best friend, Sam Geddes, was known as Geddes, and I was McIntyre. The school register in the morning sounded like a list of advertising agencies. Teachers had no names at all and were called 'sir' or 'miss'. When the teacher walked into the classroom, all the boys would stand up until 'sir' told them to 'Be seated.' What's that all about? It's the wrong way around. I'm paying a fortune for this school; shouldn't the teacher call me 'sir' and stand up when I walk in?

The school was also a bit religious. Every morning we gathered in the gym for assembly and recited the Lord's Prayer. The headmaster, Mr Clegg, would lead and the teachers and whole school would mumble along: 'Our Father, who art in heaven, hallowed be thy name . . . Give us this day our daily bread . . . And forgive us our trespasses, as we forgive them that trespass against us . . . For thine is the kingdom, the power, and the glory, for ever and ever . . .'

At the end, we'd all very loudly say, 'Amen.' Every day I said this, for six years. I didn't have a clue what it meant and nobody explained it. I remember thinking, 'What daily bread? I had cereal this morning', 'Does this mean I'm allowed to trespass?', 'Why should I forgive people who trespass against me?' There was a grassed area in front of the junior school that had a 'No Trespassing' sign. I used to walk across it safe in the knowledge that God would forgive me.

Academically I was unpredictable. One year I was literally bottom of the class in every subject. I got 4 per cent in French, 7 per cent in History and got lost on the way to the Geography exam. My Maths was so bad that I didn't actually know what per cent meant. My poor grades may have been due to my problems at home, or simply because I already knew I was going to be wildly successful thanks to the Tarot cards. My mum didn't seem to mind at all.

My end-of-year report was a collection of slips of paper written by the teacher of each subject. It was so awful that I threw most of it in the bin and only gave her PE (Physical Education) and RE (Religious Education). She didn't notice and was thrilled that I had 'a keen interest in Sport' and was 'Very attentive during Bible readings'. It didn't seem to concern her that I was only learning two subjects or that I was all set to be the next David Icke.

My dad, on the other hand, did notice. 'Where's the rest of your report?' He was livid and lectured me for hours on the importance of school, not to mention the astronomical school fees he was paying to keep me there. Something he said to me registered and I became determined to succeed at school. I became a 'swot' overnight. I found out what per cent meant and then gave it one hundred.

I remember the teachers thinking I was stupid, in particular Mrs Orton, the French teacher. She had good reason after my 4 per cent in the exam. Mrs Orton was one of those teachers who was never totally in control of the class. It didn't help that her English was limited and when she wanted us to 'be quiet', she would shout 'Shoot' and then smack the blackboard with the blackboard rubber. I presume she was trying to say 'Shut up', but for some reason it came out of her mouth as 'Shoot!' Every time she said 'Shoot!', the class would giggle, which would only make her repeat 'Shoot!', and again smash the blackboard. For most of the forty-five-minute lesson, she would be shouting, 'Shoot!' and banging the blackboard with its rubber.

Before and after lessons, my friends and I would impersonate Mrs Orton to each other with much hysteria. It was during one of these muckabouts that one of us noticed there was a gap behind the blackboard. The blackboard was positioned against the corner leaving a little space behind it. After a little encouragement, we convinced the smallest kid in the class, Watson, to try and squeeze in. We must have lost track of time because just as he jammed himself between the wall and the blackboard, Mrs Orton entered to begin her French lesson.

Watson ducked down and the rest of us scrambled to our seats. Mrs Orton addressed the class, oblivious to the hiding

Watson. We tried to contain ourselves but the situation was too much to bear. Pockets of sniggering broke out. Then Mrs Orton, true to form, smacked her rubber on the blackboard and shouted 'Shoot!' This was probably the first time in my life I properly got the giggles. The whole class fell into total hysterics as she continued to shout 'Shoot!' louder and louder and hit the board harder and harder with Watson wedged behind it. As far as I remember he was in there for the whole lesson.

Even though Mrs Orton never knew why we were laughing, she was always looking at me and singling me out as the culprit of whatever shenanigans were occurring. She saw me as a waster, a loser and an idiot. My 4 per cent just proved her suspicions. But now I was on a mission. I concentrated, I learned. I studied in the school library at break-time, I read my textbooks in the car on the school run, I got my mum and my sister to test me constantly, I played Survivor's 'Eye of the Tiger' as I did my homework.

When the exams came I had never been more prepared for anything in my short life. Still to this day, I remember most of my results. Maths 78 per cent, Geography 87 per cent, History 82 per cent, Science 83 per cent, French 92 per cent. I came top of the class in every subject. My mum was thrilled (but she was thrilled when I only studied PE and RE), my dad was proud, but the person I was most looking forward to seeing was Mrs Orton. From 4 per cent to 92 per cent, quite an improvement. I sat waiting in the classroom for the French lesson to begin, enjoying my newfound status. I was top of the class. I was a champion.

The teacher walked in, but it wasn't Mrs Orton. We were told that she had left the school and this new guy, Mr Sissons, was taking over. It transpired that Mr Sissons marked the exams. Mrs Orton was gone, and she was unaware of my dramatic turn-around. I was truly gutted. Where had she gone? Nobody knew. There was a rumour somebody had finally shot her. About ten years later, I was playing tennis in a park when I heard an unmistakable sound from the next court: 'Shoot!' I looked over and there she was, planting a forehand volley into the net.

I ran over to her, forgetting I was now nineteen years old and a decade had passed. 'Mrs Orton,' I screeched, 'I got 92 per cent.' Naturally, she had no recollection of me whatso-ever. I apologized and we continued our respective games.

Academically, that was my one good year. I never again worked so hard or scaled those heights. I suppose I just wanted to prove to myself and to my dad I could reach the top, and having done that I slipped back down to the middle. I never again excelled in any subject. I was a bit like Blackburn Rovers when they won the league in 1992. One subject I certainly never excelled in was Music. I am simply not musical in any way. I can barely press 'play' on the stereo. My dad, of course, had a musical background and was very keen for me to take up an instrument. More specifically, he wanted me to learn the piano. He owned a piano for me to practise on so he was especially keen for this to be my instrument of choice.

My best friend at the time was Gary Johnson. Gary was tremendously cool. He was a fair-haired American, liked basketball and had his own 'ghetto blaster'. When my mum asked him what he wanted to be when he grew up, he said, 'Black.' Gary said guitars were cool, so my mind was made up. The guitar was the only instrument for me. I argued with my dad for hours. The 'guitar' row was our biggest to date, and it was only when I threatened divorce that he eventually backed down. He begrudgingly bought me a guitar and booked me in for lessons at my school. Gary said my guitar wasn't cool – he'd meant electric guitars. So I didn't attend a single lesson. The guitar sat in my Golders Green bedroom in its case, untouched. My dad didn't live with us so he would never know. I was now only seeing him every other weekend. He and Holly were as in love as Steve and my mother, and bought a big country house. She had been living in LA and he in London, but they now decided to pursue an English country life together.

Holly dreamed of an idyllic rural life and my dad set about making this dream a reality. The house they bought, Drayton Wood, had 35 acres of land, a swimming pool, a tennis court, stables and two paddocks. They purchased a Range Rover, of course. Kitted themselves out in new wellies and Barbours, and filled their property with two dogs (a Great Dane called Moose and a sheepdog named Benjie), two cats (Marmalade and Turbo), three horses (Nobby, Dancer and Lightning), two cows (Bluebell and Thistle) and six geese (I don't remember their names), no partridges and several pear trees.

It was a wonderful place for Lucy and me to visit, and they seemed to adjust well, apart from the occasional mishap. The geese, for example, weren't quite as successful as my father had hoped. 'Geese are great watchdogs, the best,' said my dad.

'What about dogs? Aren't they the best watchdogs?' I challenged.

'No,' my dad insisted, refusing to follow my logic. 'Geese are much better watchdogs than dogs.' So rather than rely on the dogs or indeed install an alarm, he got six geese. On their first night at Drayton Wood, we went to sleep safe in the knowledge the geese would alert us to any unwanted guests by honking. In the morning, we awoke to find six dead geese. My father had forgotten about the food chain. A fox had eaten his new alarm system. It turned out our watchdogs needed watchdogs.

Visiting my dad in the countryside was a real adventure. I had horse-riding lessons, rode my BMX, went swimming, played fetch with the dogs and tennis with my dad. It was the perfect weekend getaway. Holly created her dream country kitchen with copper pots hanging from the ceiling and more herbs and spices than I knew existed. She would prepare a variety of dishes with varying success for our juvenile palates. Regardless of how much we enjoyed it, Lucy and I always reported back to our mum that it was 'disgusting'. Complimenting our new mum's cooking to our real mum would not have been a wise move.

At one lunch, my dad and Holly had several people over. I don't recall the occasion. There must have been about ten of us sitting at the large dining room table. My father at the head, telling stories accompanied by his own booming laugh. I was a child surrounded by adults, so the only time I was involved in conversation I was asked typical questions like, 'What school do you go to?', 'Do you enjoy it there?' and 'What's your favourite subject?'

'Hey, Michael,' asked my dad, 'how are your guitar lessons coming along?'

'You must be a real Jimi Hendrix by now,' Holly added.

I had been bunking off my guitar lessons for a year at this point. It had actually been so long that I had forgotten I was supposed to be going.

My heartbeat quickened, my voice trembled slightly as I mumbled, 'Fffine.'

My dad addressed the whole table: 'Michael begged me to get him a guitar. I wanted him to learn the piano, but he was so adamant.'

90

My mum, Kati Katz, a teenage
pregnancy waiting to happen.

An early publicity shot of new Canadian
comedian Ray Cameron, my dad.

'Hellooo Daaarlings!' My glamour Gran.

Me, during my brief stint as an East End Crime Lord.

My mother wondering whether she'd accidentally picked up a Super Mario Brother from the hospital.

My dad and me eating breakfast in bed – the scene of his morning-breath cuddles.

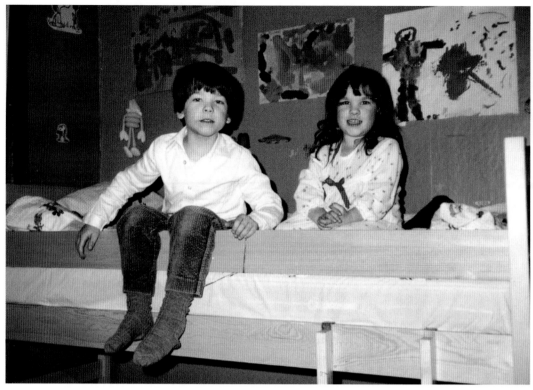

On the top bunk with my sister Lucy, where she correctly predicted the ceiling would fall down.

Lucy and me in the bath in Hampstead. Check out the wallpaper and the tassles on the side of the bath, not to mention the razors within easy reach of children.

In my garden in Hampstead, trying to get away from Lucy and our
neighbour Annabelle in a scene not dissimilar to *The Shining*.

When my parents weren't loving, teaching and raising me,
they liked to dress me up as chart toppers from the 70s.

Kenny Everett, in Sid Snot guise, with Barry Cryer and my dad in their heyday, caught in a rare moment not laughing at each other's jokes.

Dad and the legendary actor Vincent Price on the set of *Bloodbath at the House of Death*. Known for his quirky unconventional directing style, my father insisted that his crew should be holding a polystyrene cup at all times.

'Wine, women . . .' I think it was more like 'Champagne, men . . .' Kenny and my mum, going by the name Marianne, just back from Waitrose.

WINE, women – and now song. Kenny Everett's got the lot! He and friend Marianne are pictured celebrating his new job with London's Capital Radio after the BBC had fired him for the second time. © The Sun and 01.06.1984 / nisyndication.com

Here I am in my trademark suit with my mum and Kenny on her birthday.

My family. All together.

'Adam Ant doesn't play the guitar,' interrupted Holly. Everybody laughed at the 'adamant' and 'Adam Ant' mix-up. I thought maybe I was saved and the conversation would turn to New Romantic pop. I was wrong.

'What songs can you play?' asked my dad with a mouthful of Holly's finest 'Sloppy Joe'. I was terrified and tried to change the subject.

'Have you told everybody about the geese? And how you murdered them,' I suggested.

'Oh yes, I will. But first I want to know what songs you can play on that guitar I bought you.'

How was I going to get out of this? I had to remain calm, but my heart was nearly beating out of my chest. I flicked my eyes to Lucy, who knew I hadn't even taken the guitar out of its case. She looked almost as terrified as me.

'Er-er-eeerm,' I stuttered.

'Come on,' reiterated my dad. 'You've been learning the guitar for a year, what's your favourite tune?' All eyes were fixed on me; I felt like throwing up. I couldn't think of a single piece of music ever written.

'The . . .' I began.

'The what?' pushed my dad.

'The National Anthem,' I said finally.

The whole table looked confused. A bit of 'Sloppy Joe' dribbled out of the side of Lucy's mouth. 'The National Anthem?' said my dad, surprised.

'That's very patriotic,' somebody else interjected.

'Yes,' I said, realizing I had some work to do to be convincing, 'I love it, I just love playing it, I love our country, I love the Queen, I'm really good at it. Aren't I, Lucy?'

'Yes,' Lucy assured everyone. 'He's brilliant at it, he plays it all day.'

'OH MY GAD!' interrupted Holly in her thick US accent. 'Cameron, I can't believe I forgot. I've got an old guitar upstairs in one of the boxes, I'm going to go and get it.'

'What a great idea,' agreed my father. 'After lunch Michael can play the National Anthem.'

The blood drained from my body. I was in hell. I wanted the ground (all 35 acres of it) to open up and swallow me. Holly disappeared to look for the guitar. My mind was racing. What was I going to do? Should I feign illness or injury? I was in the midst of a nightmare. My dad began telling his geese manslaughter story. It seemed like only seconds before Holly returned, tuning her old guitar as she walked towards me. My father cut short his anecdote. 'You found it, great!' Holly placed the guitar in my trembling hands. The whole table turned to me.

'Stand up, Michael,' my father directed.

I stood up, awkwardly holding the alien instrument. This was the moment, the moment I had to admit my lie. The moment to reveal the shameful truth, that I was not so much Jimi Hendrix as the Milli Vanilli of school guitar lessons. I decided to go for it. I don't even know if I decided. I found myself strumming the guitar and singing, 'God save our gracious Queen, long live our noble Queen . . .' I sang it as loud as I could, to mask the fact that I was just randomly strumming. It sounded horrific; my audience looked puzzled.

'EVERYBODY!' I encouraged. 'God save the Queen, de, de, de, de, Send her victorious . . .' Everybody sang along, just about managing to hide my out-of-tune, random guitar-playing. I belted out the last line with lung-bursting pride, like Stuart Pearce at a World Cup: 'LONG TO REIGN OVER US, GOD SAVE THE . . . QUEEEEEN . . . YEAH!' The most embarrassing moment of my life was over. I took a bow and received uncomfortable applause. It turned out I had fooled nobody, and later that night when the guests had departed, my father took me aside. 'Michael, I think we need to talk.'

I wasn't punished for skipping my guitar lessons. My humiliation at lunch was considered punishment enough. Also, my excellent exam results weighed in my favour. I claimed I had been too bogged down with work to learn an instrument.

My dad was pleased with my now glowing school reports. I don't know why but I was particularly good at Latin. I was a 'Latin lover', but not in the sense that pleases women. I was also quite sporty. This might be difficult for you to believe. I opened the batting for the cricket team and was top scorer for the hockey team.

If you think hockey is a bit of a girlie sport, wait until you hear this: my posh private school taught boxing. An ex-boxer, I forget his name, whose face featured the obligatory flat nose, taught us the Queensberry Rules once a week. Fine, you might think. Boxing is good for exercise and co-ordination. Well, at the end of the year a boxing ring was set up in the gym, and there was a tournament when all the parents came to cheer their posh offspring beating the shit out of each other. Come to think of it, with me speaking Latin and boxing in front of a passionate mob, I was like a young Maximus Decimus Meridius in *Gladiator*.

A champion was crowned for every school year. I actually won in the first year, defeating Sam Geddes by a technical knock-out. Sam and I are friends to this day, and I haven't stopped reminding him of my victory for the past twenty-five years. I'm sure he'll be thrilled to learn it's mentioned in my book. I'm sorry, Sam, but the fact is my speed, silky skills and breathtaking power were too much for you. I gave you a boxing lesson. I destroyed you.

In the second year, I wasn't so successful. Maybe after a year as the champ I wasn't as focused. I'd put on a few pounds. I got complacent. 'I could have been a contender.' But I think the real reason I lost was that I fought Ralph Perry in the final. Let me explain what Ralph Perry looked like. Imagine Mike Tyson as a white ten-year-old. I was no match for him. Perry, who later served time for GBH and assaulting a beauty queen, gave me a beating and I lost my crown. I burst into tears when the result was announced and refused to shake Ralph Perry's hand and told him to 'fuck off' in Latin. My dad gave me a long lecture about sportsmanship and told me to use my jab more. But there was to be no rematch. The school woke up to the fact that making kids fight each other was perhaps a bit barbaric and boxing was stopped altogether.

So that just left sports day as the only occasion for my parents to witness my physical prowess. My two sets of parents decided to try to get along 'for the sake of the children'. So my mum, Steve, my dad and Holly chose my sports day as the starting point for their new positive relationship. The venue was Cannons Park, a large sports field set up for athletics. It started well; my four parents were smartly dressed, the sun was shining and the rumour that Patrick Swayze was my dad was going some way to make up for the Kenny Everett debacle of two years earlier. The problem was that this wasn't a dynamic which was going to work. There was far too much resentment, pain and anger between my mum and dad and their new sidekicks. It was excruciating to witness them pretending to get on and fake laughing at each other's jokes.

My event was the long jump and I won. I jumped 3.03 metres, but due to a mix-up the distance was recorded as 3.30 metres. I still would have won, but those extra 27 centimetres meant that I smashed the school record. In fact, I still

94

hold the Arnold House School record for the Under-9 long jump due to this error. Twenty-five years that record has stood. The teachers and headmaster fully expected me to become a professional long jumper. But the time has come to reveal the truth. While I'm in such a confessional mood, I would like to add that I was also on anabolic steroids.

I was so pleased with my record-breaking jump that I rushed into the arms of my dad and then I rushed into the arms of my mum and then I rushed into the arms of my other dad and then I rushed into the arms of my other mum. Then came the surreal fathers' race. It was agreed that both my dads would compete. This was fine by the school, who had encountered this situation before. In fact there were so many additional parents due to broken marriages, they had to run heats.

My dad took his place on the starting line alongside Steve and the other fathers. There was no starting gun, which was a relief because I'm sure at some stage one of my parents would have snatched it and opened fire on the other. Instead Mrs Orton was responsible for starting the race, 'On your marks, get set, shoot!' My dad got off to a bad start, an even worse middle and painfully slow end and finished in last place. Steve won the whole race. My dads had finished in first and last place.

As I celebrated Steve's win, I didn't think about my real dad's feelings. I was too young. Maybe he saw the funny side. It can't have been easy.

But little did I know that in just two more school sports days' time, I would have FOUR dads in the fathers' race (this isn't true).

9

Girls make up half of the population. Girls are what most boys want. There comes a time when a boy's entire life revolves around the pursuit of girls. There are girls reading this book: 'Hi.' I went to an all-boys school. This was a terrible idea. I learned nothing about girls; they were like alien creatures to me. I had such a late start getting to know the fairer sex that it definitely put me at a disadvantage.

I'm not just saying all schools should be mixed; I'd like to go beyond that. I think as soon as you're born you should be shown a girl to begin your education. Then at school you should have to study each other's gender as a subject. 'What's your timetable today, McIntyre?'

'Maths, Geography and then double Girls.'

Also, in addition to French and English, you should be taught 'French Girls' and 'English Girls'. In fact you may as well include 'Latin Girls'; any information about any girl from history can be beneficial in unravelling the extraordinary complexities of females.

Girls, however, probably wouldn't even need one entire lesson in 'Boys', the teacher rounding the lesson off with '. . . so if they're grumpy, they're probably hungry. OK, girls, we seem to have finished twenty minutes early. So you're free to fiddle with your split ends until break-time.'

I began my phenomenally unsuccessful pursuit of the opposite sex when I was about twelve years old. Sitting outside the school gates on a wall, in her crimson uniform, clutching her violin, was twelve-year-old Lucy Protheroe. She was Christie Brinkley, Princess Leia, Wonderwoman and Princess Aura rolled into one. Lucy's younger brother was at my school and every few days she would collect him and walk to their home just around the corner. From the moment I saw her, it was like a thunderbolt had hit me. The problem was that for her (to continue the analogy), there was no change in the weather conditions; maybe a slight breeze, but nothing more.

I was becoming more independent and had started to take the number 13 or 82 bus from Golders Green to school. These were the old-style London buses, the ones with a conductor and that you just jumped on and off. Nowadays if you miss the bus, the doors close, you curse and you wait for the next one. In those days, you never felt like you'd missed the bus as you could hop on at any time when it stopped in traffic. I would see a bus in the distance in traffic and go tearing after it. It would tease me by always being close enough for me to think I could catch up. I once chased a bus for my entire journey to school.

School finished at 4.30 p.m. and from 3.30 onwards my heart was aflutter at the prospect of Lucy perched on the wall outside. Every day I walked through the school gates and looked to my right to see if she was there. If she wasn't, I would be deflated for a few moments but soon be daydreaming again about seeing her the following day while sitting on the bus home (or running behind it). If she was there, I would try, and fail, to be cool.

The first problem was the fifty-yard distance between us. I would see her and smile and she would see me and smile. So far, so good. Then I had to walk to her with her staring at me. I knew how to walk, I had been walking for about ten years at that point and had been practising walking throughout my day at school. But I felt so self-conscious under her gaze that my walking skills abandoned me. My normal straightforward walking style was temporarily replaced by a swagger that even Liam Gallagher would have laughed at. I also struggled with direction, often colliding with other people, painfully smacking my hand against a lamp post or brushing along the hedge that ran from the school gate to the wall she was perched upon.

By the time I reached her (covered in leaves and with a sore hand), my mouth would be so dry from nerves that occasionally no words came out at all, just a sound similar to the one a dog makes when you accidentally step on its foot.

We would have an awkward conversation while she would flick her hair from one side to the other. This hair flicking was really quite something. She had fair hair in a bob and would move all of it to one side of her face and then a few moments later flick it back to the other side. I don't know if this was a habit or if she couldn't decide which side looked better; all I know is that it made me look like a tennis specta-tor, regularly shifting my head to the left and right to follow it. It only added to the hypnotic effect she was having on me.

Between her bobbing hair, she was beautiful. I was fresh-faced, narrow-eyed and chubby. I may not have looked like Matt Goss from Bros but I was determined to maximize whatever attributes I did have. My best feature was, and is, my perfect teeth. The problem is that I don't know if teeth are that high up the list of what girls find attractive. But it's all I had, so I felt I needed to show them off. I would thrust them out of my mouth, like a Bee Gee at the dentist. So I basically looked like a Chinese Bee Gee watching the tennis dressed as a ladybird wearing Kylie Minogue's hot pants. I hoped she fancied me.

She didn't.

We had one 'date'. I flew her to Paris on a private jet and we watched the show at the Moulin Rouge and spent the night at the Ritz. Not quite. We went to the Odeon cinema in Swiss Cottage. Our romance was as successful as the film we saw, *Slipstream* starring Mark Hamill. Exactly. She said there wasn't the right chemistry between us. I was devastated, heartbroken, and blamed my chemistry teacher.

Lucy was just the first in a long list of infatuations with girls that never came to fruition. In fact until I met my wife, Kitty, when I was twenty-two years old, my love life may have been the least successful in history. Teenage girls simply weren't interested in me. Nowadays, I have plenty of teenage girls screaming my name at my gigs, waiting outside and trembling when they meet me. Where were they when I needed them? If only I had released my first DVD when I was thirteen.

When Lucy rejected me, I was heartbroken. 'There're plenty more fish in the sea' tends to be the consoling wisdom of your friends. But it was useless.

'I don't want a fish,' I would squeal with my head in my hands.

'It's just an analogy,' my friends would explain.

'Well, it's a shit analogy, fish stocks in Britain have reduced by 10 per cent due to overfishing, the EU have tried to step in and introduce quotas, but it's no use, I'll never meet another girl.'

That summer I went to Corfu with my best friend Sam, who had forgiven me for beating him in the boxing (it wasn't just a beating, it was a devastating display of my superiority). Sam is properly posh, he's the real deal. He has lords and ladies on one side of the family and royalty on the other. He's in line to the throne, although it would have to involve a lot of unforeseen deaths or a bomb at a Royal wedding he was running late for. I spoke just as 'proper' as him. As you know, my dad was Canadian and my mum from Hungarian stock. I don't have Sam's pedigree, but in his presence I too sounded like an aristocrat.

I've always picked up other people's accents very easily. The problem is that rather than use them as an impression I tended to keep them. Without a doubt I get this from my mum, who embarrassingly takes the accent of whoever she is talking to and starts speaking like that herself. This led to countless cringeworthy scenarios during my youth. If she was in an Italian restaurant and the waiter said, 'Whatta can I getta you?' she would reply, 'I woulda like a Spaghetty Bolognesey anda Garlico Breado, thank you, yes, please.' What made it worse was that she wasn't that good at accents and would sound more like Manuel from *Fawlty Towers*. (I'd like to add that Andrew Sachs, who played Manuel, is a very fine actor, and I'd like to wish him and his family well.)

The worst was when she addressed Pila. Pila was a very sweet little Filipino lady who cleaned our big Hampstead house during the few months we were rich. Pila could barely speak English, so in return, my mum would barely speak English back to her. 'Mis . . . Kati . . . would . . . like . . . me . . . do . . . now?' Pila would hesitantly enquire.

'Pi . . . la,' my mum would respond equally slowly, 'must . . . you . . . now . . . very please . . . do . . . How do you say? . . . Ironing?'

The habit nearly became dangerous in a newsagent when my mum was buying some magazines from a six-foot dreadlocked West Indian man. 'Whatsup, Blood,' rapped my mother, 'I is lookin' to buy dis here readin' material, Jah Rastafari.' Luckily Steve and the newsagent were old friends from Brixton, and he managed to diffuse the situation.

So Sam and I went to Corfu sounding like Princes William and Harry. We went with his parents, Hugh and Harriet, his brother Luke and his friend from Eton (wait for it . . .) Quentin Farquar. Hugh always wore corduroy trousers that were one size too small for him, even on the beach. Harriet was lovely jubbly, Luke was like Sam, but older, and Quentin was a perfectly named posh wanker.

I'll never forget Quentin turning to me on the flight and embarrassing me. 'You're quite plebby, aren't you?' he mocked. 'I bet you say things like settee rather than sofa, and serviette rather than napkin, and toilet rather than loo.'

I didn't really know what he was on about. His class teasing made me afraid to speak for the remainder of the flight for fear of saying the wrong thing. In hindsight what I should have said was 'Hey, stupid name snob, what does that say?' and pointed at the 'Toilets' sign on the plane. 'It doesn't say "loos", does it? Have you got on the wrong flight? This is Pleb Airways, mate. You're fucking with the wrong fake posh boy. Why don't you ask Sam what happened in the boxing tournament?'

When in Corfu, Sam and I were on the hunt for girls or, as Quentin called them, 'top totty' (I think Quentin is probably still a virgin). We both had suntans and Ray-Bans and were feeling confident. Sam's dad rented us a couple of Vespas, and we hit the local town. It was actually more of a historic village. But we weren't perturbed. We had until nine o'clock, our Corfu curfew, and were determined to make the most of it. We scoured the streets. If we had been 'on the pull' for elderly Greek men playing cards, we would have been in luck, but other than them the streets were deserted.

Finally we spotted two similarly aged young girls and devised a carefully thought-out plan of seduction. 'Let's follow them,' Sam suggested. And follow them we did, for about twenty minutes, round and round the village. When they stopped, we stopped. When they continued to walk, so did we. We wanted to be cads but were acting more like private investigators. The problem was that we didn't really have a plan beyond 'Let's follow them.' The two girls then turned and started walking towards us. It seemed like the 'Let's follow them' strategy had worked after all. Sam and I frantically styled our hair as the girls approached. They were surprisingly attractive.

'Bingo,' I whispered to Sam.

The girls halted in front of us and with thick Liverpudlian accents screeched the unforgettable, 'Why the fuck do you think you're following us, you little turds?'

Sam and I had no answer and apologized. 'We're awfully sorry,' we muttered and went home. That was as close as we came to pulling.

Within months, however, I was to experience my first kiss. Doesn't that sound romantic? 'My first kiss.' Well, it wasn't. Sam invited me to a Summer Ball frequented by upper-class-toff teens. It was held at the Hammersmith Palais in London. If you've ever flicked through the pages of *Tatler* magazine and seen the party photos towards the back, you'll know the sort of people who were there. 'Horsey' doesn't come close to describing them. Something happens to your mouth when you speak too posh; it becomes slightly misshapen as if in a constant state of preparation to say something along the lines of, 'Er hillar, jolly good.'

All the Hooray-Henry boys were dressed in black tie, probably in suits passed down through generations of gentry. All the girls were in figure-hugging little black dresses and had names like Arabella shortened to 'Bells' or Pippa shortened to 'Pips'. The object of the ball was to use your odd-shaped posh mouth to 'snog' as many other odd-shaped posh mouths as you could. My mum hired me a suit from Moss Bros and a clip-on bow tie, and I went with Sam and four other cologned young men.

We were dropped off by our parents. 'Have a good time. Don't do anything I wouldn't do,' they hollered, as we disappeared inside clutching our phenomenally expensive tickets. I was nervous and self-conscious. Was tonight the night I would meet the girl of my dreams?

I will never forget the sight that met me when I adjusted my eyes to the Hammersmith Palais lighting. Literally hundreds of under-age upper-class kids with their faces stuck together, 'getting off' with each other. Wow. Maybe it had something to do with them rebelling against their suppressed stiff-upper-lipped lifestyle. Maybe they were just making the most of it until they were carted back to their single-sexed boarding schools. Whatever the explanation my immediate thought was, 'Surely I'm going to pull tonight.'

I turned to express my optimism to Sam only to find him with his tongue already down someone's throat. My other friends also ploughed straight in, mouths open and latching on to whoever was nearest. There are very few things in life as embarrassing as standing next to a kissing couple, so I wandered on to the dance floor and danced, for some time, on my own. Just as I was mid-twist to Chubby Checker's 'The Twist', I saw Sam and another friend, Alex. 'Hey,' I shouted over the music, 'how's it going?'

'Forty-six,' said Alex.

'Fifty-two,' said Sam.

'What? What are you talking about? Fifty-two what?' I genuinely enquired.

'Girls!' they said in unison, now both twisting too.

'You've snogged forty-six and fifty-two girls tonight?' I asked, amazed.

'Yeah,' said Sam.

'Forty-seven!' said Alex coming up for air from his latest conquest on the dance floor.

'How many have you snogged, Michael?' asked Sam.

'None,' I admitted. 'How do you do it? What do you say? Do you say anything? Shall I just start licking someone's face? Help me.'

Sam explained that all he was doing was approaching girls and asking whether they wanted to go and sit down. This was code for 'snog'. They would then take a seat together and he would rack up another digit on his tally.

'Go for it, Michael. Find a pretty girl and ask her if she wants to sit down with you on one of the sofas,' Sam encouraged.

'Really?' I said. 'That's all, just ask if she wants to sit with me on one of the settees?'

'Sofas!' Sam corrected. 'You're such a pleb.' And with that, he disappeared.

I now felt I had more purpose. I saw a space open up on one of the sofas and scanned the dance floor. And there she was, without a doubt the best-looking girl at the ball. 'That's her,' I thought. 'I'd rather kiss her than a hundred of the others.' I twisted over to where she was dancing as Chubby Checker continued to sing. 'How long is this song?' I thought. 'It must be the long version.' She had dark hair and beautiful green eyes and fitted perfectly into her obligatory little black dress. It was as if she was the only girl on the dance floor, the only girl in the world. My heart was pounding. I moved in closer, a bit too close. I moved back a bit. I caught her eye.

'I would like to go and sit down.' I fluffed my line. Rather than ask her to sit down, I had simply informed her of my own movements. She looked at me, puzzled. I quickly tried again: 'Would you like to come and sit down on the sof-tee with me?'

This was better. At least it was a proposition of some kind. However, I had forgotten whether sofa or settee was the correct thing to say and ended up creating my own chair, the sof-tee. I corrected myself again: 'The sofa. Would you like to sit down with me on the sofa?'

There it was, the big question. It was out there. I'm not exaggerating when I say it took her some time to come up with an answer. She literally mulled it over, looking me up and down as I continued twisting to a record I was now convinced was stuck.

'All right, then,' she finally said.

I'd pulled!

Just.

Together we found a vacant slot between two other sets of snoggers. She was gorgeous, smelled wonderful and her perfect lips were attached to a perfect mouth, not like the back pages of *Tatler* at all. We sat down, she took out her chewing gum and within moments we were kissing. In the middle of the Hammersmith Palais surrounded by girls of loose morals, I had finally found one loose enough to kiss me. The sensation of kissing for the first time was extraordinary. Our tongues met with all the passion of a Magimix. Hers was swirling round and round, so mine did the same, chasing it. There was so much swirling that we started to froth a bit and my saliva was in danger of becoming stiff peaks. Then it was over. I thanked her, way too much; she returned the chewing gum to her mouth and stood up to leave.

'What's your name?' I asked, worried I would lose her for ever.

'Izzy,' she said.

'Easy?' I questioned. Just my luck, the only girl I can pull is actually called 'Easy'.

'No,' she said, 'Izzy, short for Elizabeth.'

And then she was gone.

Sam's final total was ninety-one and Alex's eighty-seven. Mine was one. But I didn't care, because I was convinced she was 'the one'. I was in love with her. I told my four friends that I had kissed the most beautiful girl at the ball. They seemed happy for me. 'Her name was Izzy,' I told them through my perma-grin.

It transpired that they all knew Izzy. They'd all snogged her that night. I was just a number on her tally. It was also the common consensus that she wasn't a very good kisser. 'Kissed like a blender,' somebody said. I had to agree. I was deflated, but not for long. I was off the mark. Surely things could only get better now. I had a newfound confidence. I had blender-kissed some chick called Izzy, and now I was a player. I had experience.

The next time I saw Lucy Protheroe sitting on the wall outside my school, I played it super-cool. No problems walking the fifty yards now.

'Hi, Michael, how have you been?' she asked, between hair flicks.

'Good,' I said. As if I couldn't care less.

'Are you going to the disco?' she asked.

The major event on the school calendar was the Arnold

House Disco. All the local girls' schools were invited, and the gymnasium was transformed into a discothèque. I'd been dreaming about this night for ages. But I played it cool.

'Maybe,' I said with more nonchalance than I knew I was capable of.

She seemed intrigued by my cocky persona.

'What have you been up to?' she asked.

'Snogging,' I coolly announced.

'What? In school?' she probed.

'No, me and my friends went to a ball the other night, and let's just say . . . I got a little bit of action,' I said, trying to make her jealous.

'Oh, the one at the Hammersmith Palais. I can't believe you went to that. That's for like, the poshest people on earth. Apparently everyone snogs everyone, it's gross. I know a girl called Izzy went and snogged, like, every boy there. But I'm glad you met someone, what's her name? Where does she go to school?'

My face went bright red as I looked for an excuse to leave. A National Express coach drove past us.

'I'd better go, that's my bus,' and I ran after the coach.

'Where are you going, Michael? . . . That's a coach . . . to Birmingham . . .' she cried as I sprinted after it.

All week the school was buzzing at the prospect of this year's school disco. I was thirteen years old and in my last year at Arnold House. I went shopping with my mum for my outfit and ended up opting for a fluorescent red shirt. I can't remember where we bought it; all I remember is that it glowed in the dark, and I truly believed that my increased visibility would give me the edge over my male rivals. One of my mother's friend's daughters, Jessica Taylor, was also going, so my mother organized her to be my 'date'. Before you get excited and think I may have 'pulled' before I even got to the disco, let me just explain that Jessica was 6 foot 3 inches and had a thick moustache.

Steve had a new 'company car' that David Rosenberg had given him to replace the written-off BMW 6-Series. It was a black Ford Orion 1.6i with 'new car' smell. It was a balmy summer's night, a perfect opportunity to use the sunroof which came as standard. Steve and I picked up my 'date', Jessica, and he chauffeured us to the disco. I sat in the back with my red shirt glowing, and Jessica sat in the front with her head sticking out of the sunroof, her moustache blowing in the warm wind.

It was so weird arriving at school at night. I looked at Lucy's empty wall in the crepuscular (surely the most impressive word I've used so far. It basically means dim) light. I was so over her. As soon as I shake off Jessica, I'll have the pick of all the girls in the Borough of Camden. Jessica and I put our coats away and nervously walked into my school gymnasium, the sound of Wham!'s 'Wake Me Up Before You Go-Go' getting louder with every step. The gym was unrecognizable; there was a glitter ball, flashing coloured lights, and smoke pumped out of a smoke machine. Nobody was dancing. All the boys were camped out in one corner and all the girls in the opposite corner. I looked up to Jessica's face; the lights were reflecting off my fluorescent shirt making her moustache look like it was on fire. Almost in unison we said we wanted to find our friends. So we each took our places on our respective sides of the gym.

There must have been about fifty boys and fifty girls. I hooked up with Sam and my friends. 'What the fuck are you wearing, McIntyre?' Sam said (in fact, everyone said that). 'Who do you fancy?' asked Sam gesturing towards the girls camped in their corner. There they all were. Fifty thirteen-year-old girls of all different colours and creeds and shapes and sizes; it was like an advert for Benetton.

I saw Lucy Protheroe. I could cross her off the list, so there were forty-nine potentials. They all looked pretty in their own way, all dressed up in their new dresses. Even Jessica looked quite attractive until she got her hair tangled up in the basketball net. I had my eye on one girl who was wearing a Madonna-inspired ensemble complete with white lace gloves. When the DJ put on 'Ghostbusters' accompanied by some strobe lighting, she had a mild epileptic fit and had to be picked up by her parents. Down to forty-eight; they're dropping like flies. Someone's got to make a move and ask one of them to dance.

Apparently Rick Astley's 'Never Gonna Give You Up' was what many of the boys were waiting for. By the second verse, the middle of the gym was filled with boys and girls awkwardly dancing with each other. Jessica was dancing with Watson (the smallest kid in the class, who hid behind the blackboard) – that was quite a sight.

But, as usual, I was on my own. My confidence from the Izzy kiss was over, and here I was again, a bundle of nerves. Asking a girl to dance requires a tremendous amount of courage. The fear of rejection is too much to bear. I didn't know if I could take it. There are two different forms of school disco dance. There's the straightforward dancing opposite each other for the length of one eighties upbeat song, or there's a slow dance. A slow dance is, of course, dictated by the tempo of the track playing. A normal dance is relatively trivial, but a slow dance involves bodily contact. Which at that age is quite intense. A slow dance is the Holy Grail of the Arnold House school disco. A girl may accept an invitation to dance to, say, Billy Ocean's 'Caribbean Queen' but refuse a slow dance to Terence Trent D'Arby's 'Sign Your Name'.

Soon the boys' side of the gym and the girls' side were no longer distinguishable. Everyone was dancing with each other and enjoying themselves. I could barely dance. Because we were in the gym, I got confused and started squat-thrusting and doing star jumps, I think at one point I said the Lord's Prayer. There was one girl I liked, but thought she was out of my league – and anyway my old electric-guitar-playing friend Gary Johnson was dancing with her. He was the coolest boy in school – what chance did I have?

Before you give up hope in me, I can tell you that I did pluck up the courage to ask a girl to dance. As the DJ played the Bangles, I walked like an Egyptian until I was standing directly in front of Alison with her dark frizzy hair and welcoming smile. 'Do you want to dance?' I asked confidently.

Just as she opened her mouth to agree, the lights darkened and the music changed to Gloria Estefan's 'Can't Stay Away from You'. It was too late, she'd agreed. My timing was spot on. The dance floor cleared of girls who weren't willing to take their 'dancing' relationships to the 'slow dance' level, leaving just a handful of us.

I'd like to just clarify what a slow dance actually entails. Alison and I were holding each other's hips and stepping from side to side. The song finished, and Gloria Estefan was aptly replaced by 'Don't Stop Believin'' by Journey. Alison wasn't all that keen on me and quickly disappeared, but it didn't matter. I was a hero. Everyone had witnessed our dance. My friends, and boys I barely knew, patted me on the back: 'Nice one, McIntyre.' I was proud that I had found the courage and succeeded, even though Alison may only have been a victim of excellent timing on my part.

There was one person that night who sent every girl in the gym into a flutter. Pulses racing, blushed faces, what a hunk. With timing even better than mine, Steve walked in to collect me as 'The Time of My Life' from the *Dirty Dancing* sound-track played. There wasn't a single girl at the disco (or mother collecting their child) who didn't want to run into his arms and attempt 'the lift'.

My Alison dance was as good as it got for me that night. It could have been worse. I just wasn't one of those boys whom girls had crushes on. I knew I was different. I was a funny kid, in more ways than one. But even from such an early age, I was obsessed with finding my girl. I wasn't inter-ested in all girls. I wanted my one. I always felt incomplete, like I was missing someone, someone to love and to bring the best out of me. I knew she was out there somewhere, just not in the Arnold House School gym.

But she was.

Dancing with Gary Johnson was Kitty Ward. The love of my life, my wife and the mother of my children.

It would be nearly ten years until we met.

10

My teens had begun. I had two dads, two mums, one Date, one Slow Dance, one Snog. My boxing record was one Win and one Loss. I held the Under-9 long jump record, was an experienced voice-over artist and a keen 'fake' guitar-player. Oh, and I was destined for fame and fortune according to a Tarot card reader in a now closed down spiritualist bookshop in Kensington.

I left Arnold House and headed to a public school called Merchant Taylors' in a place named Northwood, outside London in Middlesex. My parents thought it would be good for me to go to a school in the sticks, lots of beautiful grounds, sports and fresh air. It took me ages to get there, and when I got there, I hated it all day, then it would take me ages to get back. Everyone else at the school lived locally in suburbia. There were 150 boys in my year and I couldn't stand any of them. They were all the same to me. Boring. There's a Billy Connolly routine when he mentions how the real characters in life are the very rich and the very poor, but everyone in the middle is dull. That's what the boys at Merchant Taylors' were. Middle. They were middle class and lived in Middlesex and destined to be working in middle management with a middle parting, driving a middle of the range Audi in the middle lane.

The teachers were like they were from another era. They all dressed like Professor Snape from *Harry Potter* and were about as friendly. One of them was friendly though.

Particularly friendly with certain boys; I would say overly friendly. He fancied them. He never did anything improper while I was there; he would just hang out with the students a lot, complimenting them on their work and their bottoms. Years after I'd left I heard that he was fired after his lust finally got the better of him and he lunged for a boy's crotch in the pavilion after a cricket match.

I had no real friends. Not even the paedophile showed an interest. Not a happy time for me, made worse as I was beginning the long and painful transition from boy to man, commonly known as puberty. Why it has to take so many years, I have no idea. There's a classic scene in the film *An American Werewolf in London* when he first changes into a werewolf. He collapses on the living room floor and, while screaming in agony, his body changes shape with hair sprouting out of it. The whole scene lasts about forty seconds. As painful as it looks, I wish puberty happened like that. Exactly like that. Even with the soundtrack. The song 'Bad Moon Rising' by Creedence Clearwater Revival should be cued up on the family stereo of every teenager in the world. As soon as they feel shooting pains in their body, they must rush to the hi-fi and press 'play', then drop to their knees and transform into an adult. That's where the analogy must end; they shouldn't then go on a killing spree and wake up naked in London Zoo.

As it is, this excruciating maturing of your body is spread over several years. I wasn't even aware of puberty. It never crossed my mind that my body had a lot of growing up to do and nobody mentioned it. My mother and father failed to tell me anything at all during this time. I think they left it to each other, but because they weren't on speaking terms, they didn't realize I was still in the wilderness. I never had the chat about 'the birds and the bees'; in fact, for many years, I thought that birds and bees had sex with each other.

So it was a bit of a shock when my body experienced its first changes. Hair appeared under my arm. Not both arms, one arm. I had hair under one arm for almost a year. My left arm. I appeared to be going through puberty from left to right. I was half man, half child. I was all set to become a Greek mythological figure.

Once a week we had swimming. Changing for swimming was a chance for all the boys in my class to catch up with each other's various rates of development. Some kids had experienced no changes whatsoever. I had my hair under my left arm, other kids had hair under both arms, or pubic hair or both, or a little wispy moustache or a small gathering of hairs on their chest. Everybody was at different stages. Everybody except for Panos Triandafilidis, the Greek kid, who was so hairy, it was difficult to see where his foot hair, leg hair, pubic hair, chest hair, facial hair and nose hair began and ended. He had hair in his ears and on his back; I think I saw a couple of strands on his eyeballs. When he walked near soap, it would automatically lather. He looked like early man. Early man, that is, with a girl's voice as his voice hadn't yet broken.

My voice took years to break. For years I sounded exactly like my mother. Every time we picked up the phone at home, callers would get us mixed up. A classmate of mine once called, my mum picked up and they had a five-minute chat about Latin homework. Steve once phoned from work, I picked up and he told me he couldn't wait to come home and have sex with me.

The worst part of all these hormones running around my body was my spots. I would go so far as to say acne. I would get horrendous clusters of spots appearing anywhere on my face. Just when one would leave, another would show up. My face looked like a pepperoni pizza with extra pepperoni. What really wound me up were the products like Clearasil that were supposed to help. The advert would say, 'It gets rid of your spots in just four days.' Just four days? Four days is the amount of time it takes for a spot to heal on its own. Spots last four days if they are untreated. So all Clearasil does is make you stink of Clearasil.

I, of course, made things even worse than that for myself. I chose 'skin-tinted' Clearasil. What you may have noticed from looking at the faces of your fellow human beings is that they all have different-tinted faces. There isn't one skin shade for all. I'm sure there's someone in the world with the exact skin tint as the skin-tinted Clearasil. This product is like a miracle for them; they put it on their face and the spots literally disappear behind this medicinal product that's working hard to rid their face of the hidden blemishes in just four days. Unfortunately for everyone else, and me, the skin-tinted Clearasil makes you look worse than before. I would wipe this beige goo all over my spots, leaving me with what looked like bits of somebody else's face on my face; and it stank.

There was also a dandruff situation. Mine was by no means the worst in the school. There were so many white speckles on school blazer shoulders that when my grandmother came once to watch me play cricket she thought it was part of the design. All this came at a time when I first started to have sexual desires. Before adolescence, girls were soft and made me feel funny inside; now, I wanted to ravage them, a lot.

Unfortunately, these new feelings coincided with me looking horrendous. I would see girls from local schools on the overground Metropolitan Line Tube I took to and from school. I had hair under one armpit, spots covered in skin-tinted Clearasil occasionally with dandruff stuck to it and the voice of a posh girl. I was so embarrassed by my appearance that I would dread any schoolgirls getting on the same carriage as me. I would seriously panic that the species I was so desperate to attract would literally laugh at my appearance.

Every day I took the fast train to school. The fast train missed out certain stations. It was fun to see the other teen-age school kids waiting on the platform thinking the train was going to stop and then jumping out of their skin-tinted skin as we whooshed past. The trains were pretty old and rattly. When the train reached its top speed, the sound of the rails screeching was deafening and the passengers would be bouncing up and down in their bench-like seats. I preferred the fast train, not because it was quicker, but because it didn't stop to let in teenage schoolgirls. The only stop between Finchley Road, where I got on, and the school, Northwood, was Harrow-on-the-Hill.

Sorry, I'm going to interrupt myself because I've just remembered a little story about Harrow-on-the-Hill. I was once trying to get there on a bus and I asked the West Indian bus conductor where the bus was going. 'Herne Hill,' he said. Herne Hill is nowhere near Harrow-on-the-Hill. But if you say Herne Hill with a West Indian accent (try it) it sounds exactly like Harrow-on-the-Hill. So I ended up in Herne Hill.

Anyway, as I was writing. My biggest fear when stopping at Harrow-on-the-Hill was realized one morning when, as I was sitting alone, about fifteen loud, gum-chewing, hair-twiddling, hoop-earring-wearing girls got on and sat all around me in their green uniforms with shortened skirts and green tights. I was so embarrassed I went bright red, which only served to highlight my skin-tinted Clearasil even more. The loudest of the girls had cheap make-up and her hair was pulled back so tight in her shocking pink scrunchy, it looked like she'd given herself a face-lift. She stared directly at me, I immediately turned to look out of the window. 'You're well ugly, intya,' she said while her friends all cracked up laughing at me bouncing around as the train picked up speed. I would have felt more comfortable playing the National Anthem on my guitar on top of Buckingham Palace at the Queen's Jubilee.

My confidence was at an all-time low. Even in sexual matters concerning only myself I managed to fail (brace yourself for this). At some time during puberty, boys start to masturbate. Deal with it. If you're a young boy reading this, thank you for taking the time out of your hectic masturbation schedule to read my book. If you're an even younger boy, this is all still to come (so to speak), and if you're a parent, please knock before entering your son's bedroom. Now, as I have previously mentioned, my parents never discussed any sexual developmental matters with me. I have also mentioned that at Merchant Taylors' I didn't really have any close friends. The net result was that I didn't know what 'wanking' was.

I started, due to nature, to get erections. My fellow students would talk endlessly about 'wanking'. I came to the conclusion that wanking meant to have an erection.

So I was constantly getting erections and doing nothing with them. I thought that I was wanking. My vulgar classmates were often chatting about their own masturbation and borrowing each other's pornography. 'I wanked three times last night', 'Can I borrow your wank mag?', that kind of thing. A classmate once pointedly asked me, 'Do you wank, McIntyre?'

To which I responded, 'Yeah, all the time,' thinking he was referring to getting erections, 'I wake up wanking.'

'You wake up wanking?' he said incredulously.

'Yeah, always. I wanked this morning on the train. I wanked for most of Geography. My mum had people round for dinner last night, and I couldn't stop myself from wanking the whole way through it,' came my shocking response.

Of course, the more I didn't attend to these erections, the more frequent they became, until soon they became permanent. I was walking around with a permanent erection. I telephoned my friend Sam, who now went to Westminster School in central London. Although I was embarrassed, I knew Sam would have some answers.

This was obviously before the days when all teenagers had a mobile phone, but I was lucky enough to have a phone in my bedroom. Although you wouldn't know it was a phone because it looked like a Ferrari. There was a shop on Golders Green Road that sold gimmicky phones, and as a family we embraced them. The phone in the hall was a frog, and the phone in my mum's room was a piano. I should probably update you on the décor in our home and how my mother's taste was developing in the nineties. The house was very colourful. Pastel colours. Every pastel colour there is, clashing with each other. All the rooms had different-coloured carpets from each other and from the hallways and from the walls that had different colours from each other. It was as if she'd looked at the Dulux colour chart and said, 'I can't decide, let's have all of them.' So I called Sam on my Ferrari phone.

'Hello?'

'Hi, Sam,' I said.

'No, darling, it's Sam's mum. Do you want to speak to Sam?'

'Yes, please,' I said.

'Sam! Telephone!' I heard her call.

'Hello?' said Sam, collecting the phone.

'Hi, Sam,' I said.

'Oh, hi, is that Michael's mum?' Sam replied.

'No, it's me, Michael.'

'Hi, Michael, how are you?'

'I've got a bit of an embarrassing problem, and I don't know who to talk to. Can you talk privately?' I asked.

'Yeah, what is it?' Sam said.

'I can't stop wanking,' I confessed.

'Me neither. So what?' said Sam, as if it was no big deal.

'I don't think you quite understand, Sam, I literally cannot stop wanking. I wank all day long,' I continued.

'Michael, it's normal. Don't worry. It's natural. Everyone's doing it, whether they admit it or not,' Sam reassured.

'OK,' I said, starting to feel a bit better. 'But I think I'm doing it more than anyone else. Like when we have swimming at school, I'm the only one wanking in the changing rooms.'

'You wank in the changing room! When you're changing for swimming!' Sam exclaimed. 'What? Like in the loo, while everyone else is changing?'

'Yeah,' I admitted. 'And also when I'm walking around,' I continued, 'and in the pool.'

'You wank while you're walking around! You wank in the pool!' Sam said, revolted.

'That's what I'm trying to tell you, Sam. I can't stop. I'm wanking right now.'

Sam hung up.

My problem only lasted a couple more days before (I'll be delicate) there was an eruption. All on its own, untouched by me. It's how the story of Adam and Eve would have been if there was no Eve. Suddenly it all made sense. My embarrassing mistake was realized, and I am proud to say I haven't masturbated since (this may not be true).

As you can imagine, home life was turning into a disaster. I was hormonal, snappy and ugly. For some reason, rebelling against your parents is part of growing up. Your parents give you life, feed you and clothe you, and then you turn on them in your teens. I would come home from school with my tie half undone, my shirt hanging out of my trousers and my skin-tinted Clearasil smudged on my face.

'Hello, darling, how was school today?' Mum would ask.

'Fuck off, I hate you, I hate you!' I would scream before running upstairs to my bedroom and slamming the door behind me.

I was a nightmare to live with. I committed all the domestic teenage crimes. My mother constantly accused me of 'treating the place like it was a hotel' because I would never tidy my room, I'd leave my clothes on the bathroom floor and steal her towels when I went out.

I was a repeat offender at eating without getting a plate. I would stand at the fridge, grazing on whatever took my fancy, grabbing clumps of ham and dipping them in the mayonnaise jar.

'Michael! What are you doing? Get a plate if you want to eat something,' my mum would demand as she walked into the kitchen.

'Fuck off, I hate you, I hate you!' I would scream as little bits of mayonnaisey ham spluttered on her face, before I ran upstairs to my bedroom and slammed the door behind me.

I feel I need to update you on the relationship between my mother and Steve. While I was skipping my guitar lessons at Arnold House, bouncing around on the Metropolitan Line and walking around with an erection, they were married, and my mum had been pushing out baby boys at an alarming rate. I have three brothers, Nicholas, Thomas and Andre. Technically they are half brothers, so officially I have one and a half brothers. They were like Russian dolls. Not because they were smaller than each other and looked alike, but because they all look like fat Russian girls. That's a joke. They were probably the best part of my teenage life, just like my kids are the best part of my life now. It's wonderful to have innocent new people crawling and toddling around.

I apologize particularly to Steve for my behaviour during these years. If a teenager rebels against their parents, I can tell you, rebellion goes up a notch with a step-parent. Steve made an enormous effort with me, but it was no use, I could barely look at him. Before puberty Steve was a cool bonus dad, resisting my stomach punches and winning at my sports day. Now he was just this bloke living with us, in my face. Get out of my face. Who are you? You're not my dad.

He never reacted to me and I must have pushed him right to the edge. Many lesser men would have reacted. There was one moment when, looking back, he says he was close to breaking point. After months of behaving appallingly, I went down to the kitchen for a drink. This normally involved standing at the fridge and drinking out of a bottle or carton. I was wearing a dirty old T-shirt and my boxer shorts the wrong way round. I opened the fridge and scanned the contents. I couldn't see anything I wanted, so I had a good rummage around. Steve then entered the kitchen to be met with the sight of me bending down. Now, you know that little opening on the front of boxer shorts? Well, that was now at the back and wide open due to my bending.

'Oh, for fuck's sake!' Steve exclaimed.

'There's nothing to drink,' I moaned with my head in the back of the fridge.

'Do you know that your arsehole is on display?' Steve asked in disgust.

'What!' I quickly stood up, knocking my head on the shelf, spilling yoghurt on my hair and covering the back of my boxer shorts with my hands. After countless teenage strops and tantrums, this could have been the final straw. Steve walked out muttering to himself about how he couldn't take much more. But he didn't (for want of a better word) crack, and he never did. Not with me anyway.

As I've previously mentioned, Steve is a remarkably good-natured man. My teenage shenanigans weren't enough to derail his passive personality. He never even raised his voice. But it soon transpired Steve did indeed have a breaking point. One average summer's day he was driving my mum in the BMW 3-Series with their two toddlers Nicholas and Thomas (Andre wasn't born yet) in baby seats in the back. I should mention the car is the same 3-Series as before and was now so old that actual grass was growing on the floor. Grass. Growing in the car. I don't know if this has ever happened to another car. I remember the day when my mother announced the phenomenon and the subsequent debate over whether to cut it or add an herbaceous border.

Anyway, so Steve was driving to or from a spot of shopping in Temple Fortune when a car full of yobs pulled up alongside our moving garden. They started hooting to get attention, and making lewd gestures and suggestive remarks to my mum. Make no mistake, these thugs were wild-eyed and dangerous. My mother told them to fuck off, but Steve calmed her down, not wanting to encourage them. He tried to manoeuvre the car away from the ruffians but ended up directly behind them in traffic. My mum was rattled, but luckily the kids in the back were pretty much oblivious to the unsavoury incident.

The traffic started to move, and Steve began to pick up speed when the hoodlums in front braked suddenly, deliberately forcing him to do the same. He screeched to a halt. My mother reached in front of Steve to hoot them, but Steve again felt it would only encourage them to respond. The traffic moved once more, and again the villains in front braked hard, forcing Steve to do the same. This time the whiplash hurt one of the kids, who started crying. The yobs in front were swearing and laughing. The situation was getting tense. They had to get out of there.

My mum was hysterical and scribbled down the licence plate of the ASBO wannabes and told Steve to drive immediately to the police station, for their own safety as much as to report the incident. Steve remained ice-cool. He managed to drop back in traffic and reach the police station without further trouble. They got out of the BMW. My mum, still shaken, lifted the kids out of the car. Steve then spotted the culprits sitting in traffic a little further down the road.

'There they are,' said Steve methodically.

'Quick, Steve, get in the police station!' my mum implored.

'Wait here,' Steve said in an unfamiliar voice and with a look in his eyes she'd never seen before. Only one person had seen this look before, the bully who locked him in the cupboard on his first day at school. My mother screamed for him to come back, but it was no use. Steve sprinted down the road at fathers' race-winning pace.

There were four of these youths in the car. Late teens/ early twenties. They were hoodies in the days before hooded tops. Their eyes lit up at the prospect of a fight as Steve knocked on the driver's window. The driver rolled down the window: 'Yeah! What the fuck do you want, mate? Do you want me to get out of this car and beat the shit out of you?' threatened the driver, with the rest of the car chipping in with similarly articulate intimidation. But Steve wasn't there to engage in macho posturing. Steve had reached breaking point and, although they didn't know it yet, that was bad news for them.

Steve grabbed the driver by the throat and ripped him out of the car window. He then lifted him up off the ground and issued a few basic suggestions about how he might wish to behave in future. The three other thugs got out of the car but, rather than confront a man who pulls other men out of car windows with one hand, made a run for it. Steve dropped the driver on to the road and received deserved applause from fellow drivers and elderly Jewish ladies who had abandoned their Danish pastries to come outside and witness the kerfuffle.

From then on, I was a little bit more respectful around the house and always made sure my boxer shorts were the right way around when bending.

My real father and Holly also married, a lovely summer wedding with the reception at Drayton Wood. And they too produced children of their own, Billy and Georgina, another half-brother and half-sister for me. Bringing my total to one sister, one half-sister and four half-brothers (the equivalent of one and a half sisters and two brothers).

But their love affair with the English countryside soon ended and they moved to Los Angeles. They sold Drayton Wood with its 35 acres of land, swimming pool, tennis court, stables and two paddocks. They sold the Range Rover, their wellies, their Barbours, their two dogs (a Great Dane called

Moose and a sheepdog named Benjie), two cats (Marmalade and Turbo), three horses (Nobby, Dancer and Lightning), two cows (Bluebell and Thistle), no partridges and several pear trees. And my dad sold his BMW 635 CSI.

I can understand the lure of LA. Holly had been living there, the sun shines every day, and it's the home of show-business. England, however, was the home of his children and leaving us was heartbreaking for Dad. I tried to convince him not to leave England's green and pleasant land and sung the National Anthem (unaccompanied this time) as he packed his suitcase. I remember him telling me over and over again how he loved me and how leaving Lucy and me was the most difficult decision of his life. In truth, I didn't feel abandoned. You can't miss something you never really had in the first place. We led separate lives. We only saw each other every other weekend – that was simply not enough time for us to have a proper relationship.

The plan was for Lucy and me to spend our school holidays Stateside with our dad. The first time I went to California, I had to agree it had the edge over Hertfordshire. My dad and Holly bought a beautiful Spanish house in the Hollywood Hills. It had an enormous swimming pool, a guesthouse, a trampoline, a grand piano and celebrity neighbours. Holly drove a Chrysler Station Wagon, and my dad bought a new Jaguar. My father started a video production company making music videos, and Holly opened a children's clothes shop called Lemonade Lake. Lucy and I loved it. We went to Universal Studios, Disneyland and Sea World, rode the biggest rollercoaster in the world at Magic Mountain, but best of all spent quality time with our dad. For the first time since Hampstead, it felt like we lived with him.

I want to get across to you how special a time we had

together on these trips to America, so I'm going to write it as a cinematic comedy montage. Cat Stevens's 'Father and Son' plays as we see:

Scene 1: We're bouncing on the trampoline together, giggling. Dad bounces into the sitting position, which leads to me being bounced high into the sky and landing in a tree. We both laugh hysterically and I cling to the branches.

Scene 2: We're cruising down Rodeo Drive in my dad's Jaguar. He opens the sunroof. I squirt the windscreen fluid which projects through the roof and into his face. We both laugh hysterically.

Scene 3: We sit next to each other on Colossus, the highest rollercoaster in the world. The car slowly ascends to its full height and then tears downwards, twisting and turning at high speeds. It comes to a halt. We both vomit and then laugh hysterically.

Scene 4: We're playing ball in the garden. He's wearing an American football helmet and throws an American football, cut to me dressed as a cricketer. I hit the ball into next door's garden. It hits a sunbathing John Travolta in the head. We laugh hysterically.

Scene 5: We're sipping hot chocolate with marshmallows and watching a movie before bed. I'm in my pyjamas and he's in a dressing gown with the word 'Dad' written on the back.

Cat Stevens fades out.

During my trips across the pond, I really embraced the American way of life. I became an all-American kid overnight. I loved baseball, I told everybody to have a nice day and I put massive amounts of weight on my arse. I actually became obsessed with baseball. I passionately supported the LA Dodgers. I watched all the games on TV and can still name all the players, who invariably had names tailor-made for the over-the-top American commentators, my favourites being Darryl Strawberry, Pedro Guerrero and Orel Hershiser.

The highlight of my first trip was when my dad and I went to Dodger Stadium to watch a game. The Dodgers were clinging on to a 1-0 lead when it was the turn of Danny Heep to hit. Danny Heep wasn't a regular in the team. I had never seen him hit the ball once. In my three weeks of following baseball, I had concluded that Danny Heep was useless. I turned to my dad and said, 'Danny Heep is shit.'

To which my dad said, 'Heep of shit.' He then proceeded to chant, 'HEEP OF SHIT, HEEP OF SHIT, HEEP OF SHIT.' Before long the crowd surrounding us started to join in, 'HEEP OF SHIT, HEEP OF SHIT.' My father's unsupportive jibe was spreading around the stadium. Soon the entire Dodger Stadium was chanting, 'HEEP OF SHIT', including the other players, children and even Danny Heep himself (I may be exaggerating). Heep naturally struck out and returned to the dug-out. My dad and I laughed hysterically.

My father continued to smoke constantly. As any wife would be, Holly was worried about his health. Her idea to stop him smoking was to start smoking herself. Her theory was that he would be so worried about her health that they would both quit. This, of course, backfired, and she too became a heavy smoker. But when they weren't coughing, they seemed deliriously happy, and so were Lucy and I on our visits.

One of the most powerful memories of my early teenage years was how I felt when I returned to England knowing it would be six or nine months until I saw him again. This was the first proper pain I had experienced in my life. I didn't feel heartache when my parents got divorced. I didn't miss my dad when I only saw him at weekends. I didn't even feel particularly upset when we said our goodbyes in Los Angeles. I was excited to get home to see my mum and little brothers. But when I got back to Golders Green and I was wide awake in the middle of the night with jet lag, I yearned for him. I missed him so much.

My bedroom was in the converted loft, and I would creep downstairs to find Lucy in exactly the same state as myself. Crying and longing for our dad. There was a lot of talk by both our parents through the years about how decisions were made for the best – logical, reasonable arguments about how life would be better this way – and most of the time I agreed. You just get on with life, that's how you survive. But in the small hours of the morning, after every visit to America, the true raw reality of my parents' separation broke my heart.

Wow. That was a little heavy. Let's lighten the mood and turn our attentions to the loss of my virginity. Strap yourselves in. So as I've already told you, I wasn't the most attractive teenager. Girls didn't fancy me, they laughed at me on trains. By the time I was sixteen I still hadn't added to my one blender-kiss at the Hammersmith Palais. I didn't know how to pull girls; for a while I didn't know how to pull myself. Opportunities were limited. I had no real friends at Merchant Taylors' but had remained close to my Arnold House friends.

Like everyone else at that age, Sam was totally obsessed with sex. He was, however, more overt about his obsession than most. He had a library of pornography. His bedroom walls were covered in pictures of tits. I, on the other hand, had no pornography. I was too embarrassed to borrow any or, God forbid, buy any. The most titillation I got was watching Felicity Kendall bend down to do some weeding on *The Good Life*.

That was until we became one of the first households in the country to get Sky TV. When we had Sky TV, they only had one advert on it, for Eagle Star Insurance, which they played over and over again. (It worked, incidentally, as I now have my home insured with them.) The satellite receiver was in my mum and Steve's room, and they ran a cable to my room so that I could watch the cricket from the West Indies through the night. This set-up meant that the channel could only be changed from the receiver that was in a cupboard next to Steve's side of the bed. The thrill of early satellite television for me was not the Test Match, but the German gameshow *Tutti Frutti*, which featured girls stripping between standard fingers-on-the-buzzers Q and A. It was in a language I didn't speak and the picture quality was poor, but *Tutti Frutti* was the best show I had ever seen.

Getting to watch *Tutti Frutti* was not easy. I had to sneak into my mum and Steve's bedroom while they were asleep, open the cupboard that was less than a foot from the sleeping Steve. The channel would invariably be on number 11 as they tended to fall asleep watching Sky News. I had to change it to 47, RTL. I couldn't just press 4 and 7; that sophisticated channel changing technology was still at the prototype phase. I had to flick individually through all the channels, 12, 13, 14, 15, 16 . . . until 47. The tension was unbearable, but the thought of German tits kept me focused.

Occasionally Steve or my mother would stir or there would be a noise from the street outside. I would be startled and rush back to my bedroom, only to find I had not yet reached the magic number 47. I may only have reached number 22, the History Channel, or even 46, the National Geographic Channel; interesting, informative and educational they may be, but not the visual stimulus for what I had in mind. So I would return later to complete my mission. I did this every night. I think I watched every episode of *Tutti Frutti* ever made. I even started to enjoy the game play element, and when Hans Schneider was crowned champion, I was genuinely chuffed for him. Hilariously, after a few weeks an engineer came round to look at our Sky Box because Steve had complained to customer services that there was a fault. 'It keeps changing itself to some weird German channel during the night.'

'I'm sorry, sir, it's a mystery,' said the engineer. Well, the mystery ends here.

Sam and I had tried following girls in Corfu without success, but now we had a new plan. We would go to a night-club. We scanned the clubbing section of *Time Out* magazine and selected a trendy hotspot just off the King's Road. The major stumbling block was that we were two years underage. I was sixteen and looked younger. My most adult feature was the hair under one armpit. I thought of trying to comb it across to the other side or cutting one sleeve off a shirt to reveal my manliness, but it would be no use. There was just no way we could pass for eighteen. Sam looked even younger than me.

'Sam, there's just no way we'll get in. You've got to be eighteen,' I said, deflated.

'That's not a problem. I know somewhere we can get fake ID,' Sam replied confidently.

This was a tremendously thrilling and illegal prospect. Fake ID could open up the entire adult world to me. A world I was desperate to gain entry to. Thank God for Sam, he's so cool, so well connected. We'll hook up with his contacts at MI5 who will furnish us with new passports, new names, new identities. Identities of eighteen-year-olds, eighteen-year-olds who have sex, I'm going to have sex as a fake eighteen-year-old with a new name.

Maybe I could select a name that might help me seduce women, like Don Juan or even David Juan, Don's older brother who taught him everything he knew. I could choose the name of a dynasty synonymous with wealth, like Kennedy or Getty or Rothschild. I could choose a family name that has become a successful brand, like Cadbury, Ford or Guinness. I could be a Freud or a Von Trapp. The possibilities were endless and exciting. After much deliberation, I decided to keep my first name. Michael was a name I was used to. I liked it and I was worried that if I changed my name to, say, Jake, I might confuse myself unnecessarily. I imagined myself dancing in a nightclub just off the King's Road when a gorgeous eighteen-year-old girl approaches: 'Hi, it's Jake, isn't it? I want to have sex with you.'

'No, I'm Michael, I think you've got the wrong guy,' I reply. 'No, wait, I actually am Jake, look, look at my fake ID, I mean ID.' I couldn't risk it.

So it was decided my new name would be Michael Casio-Sony. I decided to take advantage of my oriental looks and pretend to be heir to both the Casio and Sony empires after my mother, Kati Casio, married my father, Ray Cameron Sony, in a ceremony that started precisely on time and where the music for the first dance was listened to on Walkmans.

'Where are we going to get the fake ID from?' I asked Sam.

'The YHA,' Sam said.

'The what?' I questioned.

'The YHA, the Youth Hostel Association,' Sam explained.

'What is that?' I asked.

'It's the association of youth hostels, what do you think it is? You just join up and fill in your details and apparently they then give you a card with your details on,' Sam explained.

'How does that help us?' I was genuinely confused.

'You don't give them your real details, you give them a fake name and date of birth, and then they give you a card with whatever you told them written on it. Bingo, fake ID.'

It might not have been the passport issued by Q from James Bond that I was hoping for, but it seemed worth a shot. Although I was worried that even if the nightclub bouncer believed we were eighteen, did he really want to let in people who were members of the Youth Hostel Association, was that really the kind of clientele this trendy hotspot was looking for? I wanted to look like someone who was going to be drinking cocktails and chatting up girls, not someone seeking shelter.

Sam and I headed down to YHA headquarters in central London and joined the massive queue of foreigners lugging enormous backpacks. I bought my passport-size photo and filled out my form with the key lies. Name: Michael Casio-Sony, D.O.B: 21/2/1974. When I finally reached the front of the queue, I handed over my false information and, just as Sam had said, it was instantly processed with no questions asked. Within minutes, we were both fully fledged YHA members. With a bit of luck, we would be handed cards to use as fake ID to get into nightclubs, and as an added bonus, if we pulled, we could take the lucky ladies to over 20,000 youth hostels worldwide.

We were indeed handed official-looking YHA memberships that displayed our photos, our new names and ages. So far, so good. Unfortunately, the membership card was an enormous piece of paper, about A4 size. It was basically a certificate. But we had queued for most of the day, we'd come this far, it was too late to back out. We went home to freshen up and negotiate our curfew with my mum. We checked *Time Out* magazine; the club opened at 9 p.m. and closed at 3 a.m.

'Mum?' I asked within moments of arriving back. 'Can Sam and I go to the cinema tonight?'

'Sure. What's on? Do you want me to drive you?' helpfully asked my mum, forever trying to be nice to her bolshie, hormonal sixteen-year-old.

'No, thanks, we'll take the Tube,' I said.

The word 'thanks' was a mistake. I don't think I'd used it since the first hair appeared under my left armpit. She knew something was up.

'It's quite a long film, so we might be home quite late, please.'

Please? What was wrong with me? I was completely malfunctioning. That 'please' didn't even really fit into the sentence.

'What time?' my mum asked sceptically.

'I don't know, midnight, maybe later,' I said, pushing my luck.

'Michael, you have to be home by eleven. That's the rule. That's more than enough time to see a film, and if it isn't, see another one. I know you're up to something, so whatever it is, be back here by eleven o'clock.'

'Fuck off, I hate you, I hate you!' I screamed before running upstairs to my bedroom and slamming the door behind me.

Sam and I plotted our evening. It takes forty-five minutes to get back home from the King's Road, so we would have to leave the club at 10.15 p.m., which leaves us with one hour and fifteen minutes of clubbing time. We'll have to make them count. I perused my wardrobe. What to wear? What will make beautiful King's Road chicks fall at my feet?

I knew nothing about fashion. I still don't. If I had done, I would have known that my outfit selection was putting me at a severe disadvantage in the pulling arena. My grandma had bought me a beige T-shirt covered in prints of African elephants. I knew it was expensive, so I thought it must be cool. Just the kind of thing the heir to two electronics empires would wear. Jeans have never suited me; in case you're wondering why – then imagine me in jeans. Go on, do it now . . . See what I mean? So I opted for cords. Brown ones. Little did I know then, but it has since been scientifically proven that it is impossible for a woman to be attracted to a man wearing brown corduroy. So with my brown cords and African elephant T-shirt, what better way to complete the ensemble than with a pair of black loafers? Believe it or not, I did look in the mirror before I went out and thought I looked good.

We were concerned about the club being very busy, so we arrived half an hour early so that we might be first in the queue. We needn't have worried. Nobody, literally nobody, apart from Sam and me in 1992, has gone to a nightclub at the opening time. Most clubbers show up at midnight or later, but there we were loitering on our own at the entrance at 8.30 p.m. It was still light. At 9 p.m. our big moment came. Two burly bouncers (is there any other kind?) were standing outside as Sam and I confidently strode up to the entrance.

'Are you open?' Sam said, his voice breaking on the words 'are' and 'open'.

The bouncer couldn't help himself from chuckling as he saw the pair of us.

'Do you want to come?' he asked.

Nerves overcame me, which, as you know, results in me becoming extremely posh.

'Yes, please, we want to come into this night establishment,' I said.

'Night establishment?' the bouncer asked. 'How old are you two?'

'Eighteen,' we both said in unison, practically before he'd finished asking the question.

'Have you got any ID?' the bouncer pressed.

This was the moment we had been preparing for all day. We instantly whipped out our A4 YHA certificates. The bouncer scrutinized them. He didn't seem to be perturbed by the size or nature of them, he just checked the information. Sam's name and birth date on his fake ID were both strokes of genius.

'That's today's date. It is your birthday today, David?' the bouncer asked Sam.

'Yeah, it is, mate,' Sam replied in an odd cockney accent.

'Happy birthday,' the bouncer said, seemingly genuinely. 'David Kray, any relation?'

'Yeah, leave it will ya?' Sam confidently revealed.

Now, in my opinion, there's no way on earth that the bouncer believed him. I think he just admired his audacity – so much so that he let us both in. Sam and I got into the hottest club in London with our fake IDs, at 9 p.m. We paid the exorbitant entrance charge and took a look around. What we found was an empty nightclub. The music hadn't even started yet. There was a barman cleaning glasses and another man mopping the floors. We took further advantage of our fake IDs and drank a Malibu and lemonade each, but the scene in the club hadn't changed by the time we had to go. We were the first to arrive and the first to leave.

Our clubbing adventure did not produce the results I was hoping for. Although I think even if we had stayed until three in the morning, Michael Casio-Sony wouldn't have had much luck with the ladies. The problem was the clothes on my body and the spots on my face. But, as if by magic, these problems would disappear. On holiday. On holiday you don't really wear clothes. As long as you don't wear Speedos, and I didn't, it's difficult to go too far wrong. Also the sun had a miraculous effect on my skin. It cleared my spots up almost entirely and made me much better-looking. In fact I tanned quite well, which would bring out my blue eyes. I had been doing endless sit-ups in my bedroom, a bit like Robert De Niro when he was incarcerated in *Cape Fear*. So I was in good shape, the best shape of my life, it would turn out. Put simply, after three or four days on holiday, I was gorgeous.

That summer Lucy and I were not visiting our dad, as we would be spending Christmas with him instead. So I organized some serious summer vacationing. It kicked off with a two-week family holiday in Malta with Lucy, my mum, Steve, Nicholas and Thomas (Andre still not born). Then Sam and I were Interrailing around Europe. Our itinerary was as follows: London to Paris, Paris to the South of France, where Sam had relatives and we had friends, South of France to Monte Carlo to meet up with my grandma (Helllo, daaarling) and Jim for a few days, South of France to Switzerland, where Sam had a royal relative living in a castle, Switzerland to Italy, where we also had a friend to stay with, and then Italy to home. I set off with my rucksack, my passport, my Interrail ticket, some travellers' cheques and my virginity. During that summer I lost my rucksack, my passport, my Interrail ticket, some travellers' cheques and on the very last day I lost my watch. I'm kidding. I lost my virginity. Unfortunately, losing my passport was about as pleasurable.

It came to the last day of my summer. I had visited four countries and one principality without closing the deal. But now on the final night of our adventure, I was odds-on for some nookie. I had met a French girl in Malta; her name was Sandrine and she was reasonably attractive in the right light, more attractive still in no light. We shared some passionate moments at night on the beach in Malta. We'd reached second, maybe third base, using the popular baseball analogy. Continuing the baseball analogy, I would say that both of our techniques were as accomplished as the hitting skills of

Danny Heep. She was also a virgin. Not ideal. I've always felt that life would be so much easier if boys were shown the ropes by an older, more experienced woman. I would actually make it compulsory, like jury duty. Single women in their late thirties should be assigned a teenage boy each. They would be sent a name and address in the post and they have six months to have sex with him or face jail time. This is probably a bit extreme (although I bet there are some single women in their late thirties totally up for the idea).

Anyway, after a lot of nocturnal fumbling in Malta, we said an emotional goodbye and exchanged details. It turned out she lived in Calais. Who lives in Calais? Does she live in the port? Is she a ferry driver? Regardless, this was good news for me, as I would be passing this port, with my passport, twice over the coming weeks. So when it came to the last day of my trip and my virginity was intact, Sam and I decided to stop off at her Calais residence. Sam provided me with sexual tips. Embarrassing as it may be to admit, he even drew me a diagram on a napkin of areas to aim for on the female form. 'Make sure you talk to her, girls love it. Tell her how beautiful she is, compliment her,' Sam advised.

'But she isn't really,' I admitted.

'That's not the point, this is your first time. You have to start somewhere, and girls need to be coaxed, they need to be turned on. Listen to me, or it will be a disaster,' Sam continued.

When we arrived at Calais train station to be picked up, the scene was tremendously awkward. Sam and I spoke GCSE French, and Sandrine and her parents spoke Baccalauréat English. This worked quite well at the beginning, but we soon used up all our phrases in the car journey.

'Hello, how are you?', 'What is your name?', 'My name is

I'm so glad we dug up this photo. Here is Steve, rag-rolling his way into my mother's heart.

Lucy and me hanging out with Patrick Swayze (Steve) on a summer's day, reading magazines and killing ants.

Grandma preparing me for my audition to play Damien in *The Omen*.

In the Arnold House school gym in my boxing prime, about to unleash my silky skills on a helpless Sam Geddes.

Now that's how you're supposed to wear swimming trunks.

Lucy, Dad, me and our camera-loving Great Dane called Moose at Drayton Wood, my dad's countryside abode in Hertfordshire.

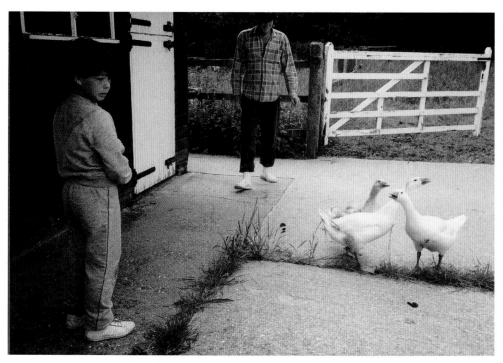

The ill-fated 'watchdogs' preparing for their one and only night at Drayton Wood.

My father and me in his BMW 635 CSI. As much as I loved his car, notice my subtle hints for an upgrade.

Me and my dad after he moved to Los Angeles.

A trip to Disneyland while visiting our dad in Los Angeles. We were having so much fun with him that we failed to notice the couple behind us lose their child in the ravine.

Me and Lucy with our little brothers Nicholas and Thomas in our Golders Green garden.

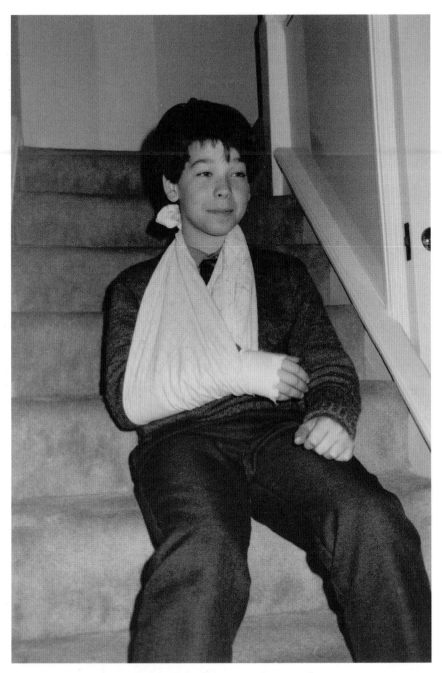

A few weeks after I discovered masturbation.

I genuinely don't understand why I never had a girlfriend.

Sam and me in the South of France during our Interrailing trip, scouring Europe trying to lose my virginity.

Michael', 'How old are you?', 'Can you tell me the way to the train station?', 'Why? We've just come from the station', 'What time is it?', 'I would like some bread.'

The last ten minutes of the journey passed in silence until her father said, 'This is our home.'

To which I said in French, 'Where do you live?'

Waiting for us was Sandrine. She was hairier than I remembered. I wondered if she might be related to Panos Triandafilidis from Merchant Taylors'. She was pleased to see me, she liked me; I just wished she liked deodorant as much. She had a friend with her who was much better-looking. Sam swooped instantly. Sandrine showed me around her sweet home. Strangely, her parents went out, encouraging me to take their daughter's virginity. Sam also disappeared, with the hottest girl in Calais. 'I told you I had a girl in every port,' he said as they left. 'Remember,' he whispered, 'compliment her.'

She showed me to her bedroom. It was neat and tidy and had views of the Channel. We sat on her bed, with my diagram in my pocket, and shared a bottle of duty-free wine and giant Toblerone from the local booze-cruise supermarket. I was a little freaked out by a shrine she had constructed in her room. It was a shrine to the few days we spent together in Malta. It was a bulletin board that had the note with my address on it as well as the tickets from a disco we went to and photos of us together. This was obviously the moment. I couldn't not close this deal. She had a shrine. To me. In her bedroom.

I don't want to go into too much detail, but by the third mountain of giant Toblerone I made my move. We started kissing and undressing. Sam had briefed me on the potential stumbling block of the bra strap. Rather than risk an awkward hiccup, he had equipped me with nail scissors which I subtly removed from my back pocket and cut clean through the strap behind her. Bravo. It worked a treat. I went swiftly though first, second and third bases, but I was nervous, so I then went back to second base, then back to first base, then to third. What kind of a baseball game was this?

This was probably the most nervous I had ever been in my life, which, of course, made me super posh when I followed Sam's advice to compliment her. 'You have quite the most beautiful . . .' I scanned her for her best feature. She had pretty good legs. I was all set to say 'legs' when I noticed this enormous birthmark on one of her thighs. So I decided to say 'leg'. But then I thought, 'I can't, I can't say, "You have the most beautiful leg."' I ended up saying 'room'. 'You have quite the most beautiful room.' She didn't seem to mind that I'd overlooked everything about her and commented on the scenery.

In fact, she loved it. 'Merci, merci, Michel.' It really got her going.

This encouraged me. 'I'm particularly fond of your lamp; is it antique?' Things moved swiftly from here. Before I could comment on her rug (the one on the floor), I found myself at home base. I'd scored. It lasted no more than about three minutes (still a record for me) and afterwards I felt like a man. At last.

I lit one of her duty-free Gauloises cigarettes and looked out of her bedroom window as the sun set over England.

'I'm coming home. I set sail tomorrow. Lock up your daughters!'

In retrospect, I think saying this out loud was disrespectful.

I2

My main priority on my return home was not to lose my tan. I was a tanned, sexually active man, and I wanted it to stay that way. Nature dictated that my tan would gradually fade. Every day I was becoming paler, and my spots were returning. My newfound power to attract girls who make shrines to me in their bedroom was leaving me. However, I was determined to fight nature and purchased some Clarins fake tan. I now had a fake tan and fake ID. I was the real deal. Unfortunately, my application of the Clarins fake tan was far from expert and, in my haste to darken my face, I forgot about my neck. This was OK while I still had the remnants of my real tan, but when that disappeared, I had a face that looked like it had just got back from two weeks in the Caribbean and a neck that looked like it had just got back from two weeks in Glasgow. To say that I was teased about this at Merchant Taylors' would be an understatement. I claimed that I fell asleep sunbathing in a polo neck, but nobody believed me, and I was soon forced to admit that my bronzing was fraudulent. I then seemed to have even fewer friends there than the zero that I had before.

Unbeknownst to me, my days at Merchant Taylors' were numbered. I was in my first year of A-Levels and, despite my failure to connect socially with anybody there, I was settled. I had worked hard and done well in my GCSEs (five As and four Bs) and was studying Biology, Chemistry and Geography for my A-Levels. I didn't particularly enjoy these subjects, but I was pretty good at them. They weren't vocational; I didn't plan on becoming a doctor or a weatherman. I opened the batting for the cricket team and was top scorer in the hockey team. I had less than two years remaining, and then I suppose I planned on going to university like everyone else. But then, totally out of the blue, in the middle of term, in the middle of the week, my father telephoned. We normally spoke on Sundays, so his phoning was irregular.

'Hi, Dad, what's up?'

'Are you sitting down?' my dad said, seriously.

It seemed like such an odd question. Nobody had ever said anything like that to me before. He was going to tell me something that could potentially make me fall over. What could this collapse-worthy news be? Anyway, I wasn't sitting down.

'No, I'm not, I'm not sitting down. Shall I sit down?' I was intrigued by this whole sitting-down thing.

'I think you should,' my dad confirmed, keeping the same serious tone.

I was speaking on the frog phone in the hall. There was nowhere to sit.

'There's no chair here. Shall I sit on the floor?' This conversation was getting weirder and weirder.

'If you want, Michael, sit on the floor,' my dad agreed.

I sat cross-legged on the carpet.

'OK, I'm on the floor now, Dad, I'm sitting on the floor. What is it?'

'Michael, I'm very sorry but you have to leave your school. I'm in serious financial trouble, and I simply can't afford to pay the fees any longer. I'm so very sorry, I know you're happy there. I've tried very hard to find a solution, but I can't.'

When my parents split up my father had agreed to pay

school fees for Lucy and me. Lucy went to Henrietta Barnet, one of the best state schools in the country that was conveniently located less than a mile from our home, but my dad still had to fork out a small fortune to send me to a school nowhere near my home so that I could be surrounded by characterless, suburban twats and one suspected paedophile.

At this point my dad had been in America for about five years. His explanation for things not working out was that in England he was a big fish in a small pond but in the States he was a small fish in a big pond. When you also consider he had to cross the pond to get there, you can see the kind of nightmare he was having. He had been ripped off by one of his partners at his video production company in LA and Holly's shop, Lemonade Lake, hadn't been as profitable as hoped. They had downsized in LA before moving north to the breathtakingly beautiful state of Vermont. There they had opened another Lemonade Lake, this time selling toys, and lived a much simpler life. So there was little income. The Range Rovers, BMWs, Jaguars, swimming pools, tennis courts, farm animals and trampolines were over. Showbusiness is tough and unforgiving and my dad was now in his early fifties. If only he had stayed in London and been a comedy exec at the BBC – but he chased a dream in America and it backfired.

I wasn't devastated at all. I needn't have sat on the floor. In fact I wished I hadn't, as I got quite bad pins and needles and when I moved I cried out in pain. My father misinterpreted this and thought I was taking the news very badly. The only thing that did upset me was that his paying my fees was one of the few links I had to him. I had an argument with him the previous year when he suggested that I went to a state sixth-form college. 'You'd have to give me the money for the fees,' I said. He was unbelievably upset by this remark, but it was not born out of greed. I didn't want his money; I wanted to feel like he was giving me something.

I hated my school, and the prospect of taking my brown face and white neck out of there seemed quite exciting. My mum and dad had apparently been in cahoots over this for a while. This wasn't a maybe, it was happening, now. Merchant Taylors' were aware of the situation, and I had an interview the following day at a local state sixth-form college in Finchley. I was moving to state school. I wish it had been filmed, as it would have made for a hilarious Channel 4 fly-on-the-wall documentary.

Let me tell you a bit about the school life I was accustomed to. I wore a uniform with a tie representing my 'house' called Hilles. There were school 'houses' who played each other at sport and had meetings and such. When the teacher entered, we had to stand up and say, 'Good morning, sir' or 'Good afternoon, sir.' The teachers wore black cloaks that wafted behind them as they walked. The headmaster wore all the gear. He had several cloaks and a big hat, so his authority was in no doubt.

I had no idea what was appropriate to wear to the interview at Woodhouse College. I suggested to my mum that I wear my Merchant Taylors' uniform without the tie. She told me to look smart, so I donned my elephant T-shirt, cords and loafers. My brother Nicholas was at nursery, but Thomas was still a baby so he had to come with us. Our appointment with the headmaster was at 11 a.m. We arrived in good time with Thomas conveniently sleeping in his pushchair.

The college was a lateral, not unpleasant Georgian building. Inside, it was much like you would expect, modern, sterile, functional, cheap. My mum and I sat on seats not designed for comfort outside the headmaster's office. I was nervous. Waiting outside any headmaster's office is nerve-wracking.

At five minutes to eleven, the headmaster's door opened. My heart skipped a beat. False alarm, it was a man in a track-suit top. It must be the gym teacher.

'Hello? Michael, is it? If you're early, then we might as well start,' he said, kindly.

Good Lord, it was the headmaster. In a tracksuit top. What kind of a place was this?

My mother and I stood up to the shared relief of our bottoms. Thomas was still soundly asleep in his pushchair. I decided to break the atmosphere with a joke. 'I hope you don't mind,' I said to the headmaster, 'but I brought my wife and child along.'

This, I repeat, was a joke. I thought that was obvious. Apparently not for the headmaster of a state school that teaches sixteen- to nineteen-year-olds.

'That's absolutely fine, Michael,' said the headmaster, 'many of our students have kids here.'

Unbelievable. Where was I?

The interview went so well that at the end he said he was not just happy to accept me into the college, but also offered me the position of English teacher.

So within days of taking my father's phone call while sitting cross-legged on the carpet, I was starting at a new school. This time nervousness did not make me posh, it made me mute. Everybody else had started at the college about six weeks earlier, they had made friends and formed cliques. I was a late entrant, the new guy. I took the same number bus I used to take, but this time in the opposite direction. When I arrived for my first day, the scene was a far cry from the samey Merchant Taylors' pupils. The major difference was that the lack of school uniform meant the students could express themselves at a time in life when they were extremely keen to express themselves. Every fashion statement ever made was being made by someone, and every race, creed and colour was represented. When I got inside the main building, it resembled the departures lounge of an international airport.

I kept my head down and kept quiet. I was terrified, but already enjoying it more than Merchant Taylors'. The exciting difference from what I was used to was girls. Girls, girls, girls, everywhere. Small ones, big ones, white ones, black ones, brown ones, tall ones, short ones, blonde ones, brunette ones, ginger (strawberry blonde) ones, a bald one (what's going on there?), too-much-make-up-wearing ones, not-enough-make-up-wearing ones, and one with the biggest breasts I had seen in my life. Wow. I was mesmerized by them. These were knockout knockers. They were attached to a long dark frizzy-haired beauty. I was lost. Asking directions is an ice-breaker. It could lead to something.

I opened my mouth to speak, but as I hadn't spoken for so long my throat was dry and no words came out, just this bizarre croak. She looked at me, bemused. I cleared my throat and tried again.

'Hi, I'm looking for room 42,' I said finally with the clarity I'd initially hoped for.

'Room 42?' she said with a voice that seemed to perfectly match her tits. 'Just down the hall and I think it's the second left.'

Our exchange did lead to something. It led to room 42. I'd hoped for more, but, hey, I had plenty of time. I went to school here, with hundreds of girls. This knowledge suddenly gave me a rush of confidence, and I decided to take our relationship to the next level.

'What's your name?' I asked.

'Tina,' she said.

I stood there for a few moments waiting for her to ask mine. She didn't. I headed to room 42.

I found room 42. My classroom. When I entered, the scene was so rowdy that nobody noticed the new boy. It was a large class of about thirty-odd. People were laughing, play-fighting, chewing gum, throwing bits of paper, smoking, breastfeeding. I took a vacant seat right at the back next to a stocky bloke with two gold earrings in one ear and a shaven head.

'All right, mate?' he said in a voice that seemed to perfectly match his hair and earrings.

'Yes, mate, I'm fine, dandy.' I had never used the word 'dandy' before in my life. What a time for it to make its debut.

'You're posh, innit?' he asked.

There's really no answer to this question. So I decided to ask one of my own.

'What "house" are you in?' I asked, referring to the school 'house' system at public schools.

He just stared at me, trying to make sense of my question before saying, 'Yeah, I like a bit of house, but mainly hip-hop and ragga.'

At that moment, the teacher walked in. I had met him briefly when I came in for my interview. I immediately bolted to my feet and exclaimed at the top of my voice, 'GOOD MORNING, SIR!'

Nobody else in the class reacted when the teacher walked in. But they certainly reacted to me. They all stopped laughing, play-fighting, chewing gum, throwing bits of paper, smoking, breastfeeding and turned to stare at me.

I was baffled why they weren't standing to attention and presumed they hadn't noticed the teacher had entered.

'Sir's here,' I whispered to my new classmates.

'Who?' a few of them mumbled.

'Sir!' I repeated, motioning towards the teacher. At this point, even the teacher looked behind him, wondering who I was referring to.

So this tremendously embarrassing misunderstanding is how I introduced myself to the class. People were confused by me, as if I was an alien from the Planet Posh. That didn't really change much as people got to know me. Woodhouse was all about cliques. The mass of differences I witnessed arriving on my first day soon turned into groups. There were probably more, but the ones I remember are: 'The Goths', 'The Asians', 'The Jews', 'The Rockers', 'The Greeks', 'The Geeks' and me. Initially I joined 'The Asians' (maybe it was my Clarins fake tan).

They auditioned me for their clique by inviting me out to lunch. At lunch, most people went to North Finchley High Road. I suggested PizzaExpress. They laughed. We went to the kebab shop and bonded over doners. A week previously I was at a school like Hogwarts but without the magic, and now here I was eating kebabs with Dilip, Chirag, Ammet and Jeet on North Finchley High Road. I felt out of place in both settings. I always felt out of place, but at least I was in a new place, and the kebabs were amazing.

Not long after I started at Woodhouse, it was Valentine's Day, the day for lovers and for wannabe lovers to make their intentions known. Valentine's cards are traditionally sent anonymously, signed with a question mark. Great lot of use that is – you have no idea who fancies you; for all you know it's the Riddler from *Batman*. My new college was filled with posturing boys and blushing girls waiting to make a move on each other. This was the perfect opportunity.

An internal post bag was set up for students to send each other cards. I wasn't particularly hopeful of receiving any, but when the bag arrived for my class on Valentine's morning, it was so overflowing I thought I might be in with a shout. As it turned out, every single card, and there must have been close to a hundred, was addressed to the same guy. The school stud, Karim Adel. He accepted his teen heart-throb status with nonchalance and even handed out some of the cards for his fellow classmates to open on his behalf. I opened a few and they didn't just contain question marks, they were shockingly graphic essays of desire.

I didn't understand it. I looked closely at Karim; I needed to be like him. What did he have that I didn't? Well, for a start, he was Iranian. There was nothing I could do about my heritage. We were of similar height, similar build, I definitely had better teeth, but the main difference was his shoulder length hair. In fact, one of the saucier cards I read made several references to Karim's hair. So I decided to grow my hair and imagined myself one year on when the next Valentine's postbag was delivered. Karim and I would be sitting next to each other with our long hair intertwining and bathing in a sea of Valentine's cards addressed to us.

Growing your hair isn't easy. Because hair grows upwards, you have to wait until it reaches a certain length and weight before gravity kicks in and it falls nicely over your shoulders – 'Because I'm worth it!' Before that, it will look unkempt and unattractive – 'Because I'm not worth it!' During this difficult middle phase, I bought a cap and squashed my overgrown hair inside. Soon the cap couldn't contain the growing locks and they would sprout out of the back and on the sides.

When I removed the cap, my hair would shoot up vertically.

While I was waiting for my hair to grow, a new opportunity to attract girls presented itself. I had started driving lessons and on one of her Sunday visits, my grandmother announced she wanted to give me some money to buy my first car. She was like a fruit machine: every once in a while you'd hit the jackpot. She gave me £2,000 to buy whatever car I wanted. I was so excited. My own car. Freedom. Every day I scanned the pages of *Loot*, *Autotrader* and *What Car?* to find my dream set of wheels.

Quite a few of the students had their own cars and drove to college. They would park adjacent to the school in a parade of the worst vehicles on the road, like a queue for the crusher at the car pound. I wanted a car that would stand out and turn heads. In particular the head of Tina, the girl I met on my first day who had her own airbags to compensate for the lack of extras on whatever car I could afford.

What is the coolest car you can buy for £2k? It was like a challenge on *Top Gear*. I stumbled across the 'Classic Cars' section of *Loot*. I hadn't been checking there as I assumed classic cars cost a fortune. But there she was. There was no photo but the particulars sounded amazing: Triumph Spitfire Mark IV, Royal Blue, convertible, reliable, 6 months' MOT. It belonged to a man in Kent and as soon as I saw the price, I wanted it. £1,999, perfect, I could even use the pound change for the Dartford Tunnel on the way home.

I bought my Spitfire, and she sat proudly in our Golders Green driveway while I learned to drive. Meanwhile my hair continued to grow, upwards, refusing to drop. I had to buy a bigger cap to contain it. I looked like an idiot, awful, invisible to the Woodhouse girls. But I waited patiently, knowing that soon I would remove my cap and, like a plain secretary taking off her glasses and releasing her pony-tailed hair in slow motion, I would be transformed. At home, I would take the cap off to assess my progress, but still my hair would ping upwards.

After about six months, I had to admit defeat and booked a haircut. But I didn't want my six months of suffering to go to waste and asked the hairdresser if there was any way to keep the length and give me a style. So he cut the front and left the back long. The net result was a mullet. This was a totally inadvertent mullet. It's not like I went in the hairdressing salon and said, 'I want a mullet, please. I want to look like Glenn Hoddle and Chris Waddle when they sang "Diamond Lights" on *Top of the Pops* in 1987.' I did not say that, but I may as well have.

'Why did you keep your mullet?' you are surely asking. Well, I didn't know what a mullet was, my mullet was accidental, and the fact is my hair looked a lot better than it had for the last six months squashed under various caps. So, believe it or not, I thought it looked good.

This is a recurring theme of my youth. I was desperate to be attractive, so that I could attract attractive women, but I did myself no favours whatsoever. However, I still had my next throw of the dice waiting: my Spitfire. Surely when I parked this car in the parade outside Woodhouse, nestled among the Nissan Micras and Fiat Pandas, girls would see that I'm different, interesting, classy.

When I passed my driving test, I was wildly excited about my new life on the road. On my first drive into college, conditions were perfect. The skies were blue and my little sports car was sparkling in the morning sunshine. After a quick breakfast, I put the roof down and set off, slowly. I could sense the car may have some mechanical issues. There was an unidentified rattling, the distinct smell of petrol, and when I braked, it took quite a while to stop. But there was no denying my Spitfire looked splendid and was turning heads.

As I approached college, my heart raced and my engine struggled, but we were going to make it. I had timed my arrival to perfection, it was the busiest time, the road was filled with students, and every one of them stared at me in my convertible classic car as I parked directly outside college. It was like I was pulling up on pole position at the Monaco Grand Prix. It was exactly how I'd imagined it would be. All the cliques of Woodhouse froze, open-mouthed, staring at the new me.

I shut the car door; the rearview mirror trembled from the reverberation, but clung on. I swung my rucksack over my shoulder and walked towards the school gates in what seemed like slow motion. My self-conscious walk to Lucy Protheroe on the wall outside Arnold House did not return. I felt surprisingly confident and strode purposefully. Then I saw Karim Adel, typically, surrounded by groupies. They were all staring at me in amazement. Karim opened his mouth to speak. He had never spoken to me; already I was being noticed, accepted.

'Niiiice . . .' he said slowly. I was so sure he was going to say 'car' that I started waving and nodding like the Queen in her motorcade. But then the real reason for all the open-mouthed staring became apparent. '. . . mullet!' Karim finished, to giggles from his groupies and lots of laughing and pointing from what felt like everybody else in Finchley.

The only positive from this latest humiliation was that Tina didn't witness it. My new mobility meant that I could drive to the hairdresser in my lunch break and immediately remove my mullet. After a false start, the mullet-less me was now on a mission. I was desperate for Tina to see me in my hot wheels. Every day when I drove in, I looked for her. Finally, one morning I spotted her. But what was I supposed to do? I couldn't hoot, I didn't know her. I couldn't exactly call out to her, 'Hi, it's me, the guy who was looking for room 42. Look how cool I am, do you want a lift somewhere, like my bedroom?'

So I decided to rev the engine in the hope that the sound would make her turn around and see me cruising with my roof down and my conventional hairstyle blowing in the summer breeze. But for all the Spitfire's sporty looks, the engine size was only 1300cc, like a Mini. I had noticed that when I dropped down a gear the engine made a growling sound. So I whacked the car from third to first gear for maximum effect. It worked, and the car erupted with a magnificent roar. However, the sound did not get Tina's attention. Nor did the crunching sound that followed, the sound of the gearbox breaking.

I now couldn't get the car into any gear, so I just sailed in neutral for as far as the momentum took me, then stopped in the middle of the road. The cars behind me started hooting and shouting at me to get out of the way. Thankfully, this still did not get Tina's attention. I put my hazard warning lights on (only one worked so it actually looked like I was indicating) and got out of the car apologizing profusely to the traffic behind.

I had seen people pushing cars to the side of the road when they had broken down, so I started to push my car. But I forgot that there should be someone in the car, to steer it. So when I pushed my car, it just rolled away and crashed straight into the side of a parked Mercedes. This did get Tina's attention. I had fantasized endlessly about Tina behaving like a girl in a Diet Coke advert as I bombed past her in my sports car, but here was the reality. She watched me push my car into another vehicle while being abused and sworn at by commuters.

It seemed that every time I envisaged a scenario whereby I was cool, it would backfire. But I never got disheartened. I was young, filled with optimism, exuberance and hope. I was seventeen, on the threshold of officially becoming a man. I had my whole life ahead of me.

But before my eighteenth birthday my life would be changed for ever.

13

My dad had started to come to London regularly to generate some income. It wasn't easy as time had passed and the faces in the industry had changed. He was an older big fish in a small pond that now had new fish in it (I think I'll leave the fish and pond analogy alone now). He was searching for an idea or a show that could resurrect his career. He contacted Kenny Everett, Barry Cryer and others he used to work with, but they had moved on.

I remember being with him in the flat he borrowed in London when he visited. He was on the phone to Barry saying, 'Let's make magic again, Baz.' I was seventeen years old and wrapped up in my own nonsense (as laid out in the previous chapters), but I knew that the magic he and Barry had created was over, and he probably knew it too. It must have been soul-destroying for him trying to go back, but he was desperate.

My dad had left London at the height of his powers, and now he was returning to a changed landscape. His tea boy when he worked in the record industry was now running a major label. From when my parents got divorced to when he left for America, he had had a personal assistant, Pete. Pete was a kid then, eighteen years old. He was always around my dad, driving him, buying his cigarettes, doing his washing. Now Pete was running a successful music video production company.

Lucy and I were so excited to see our dad on these fleeting

visits. We would go to the cinema and out for pizza. We argued a bit because I was a teenage pain in the arse, but it was a joy to see him. He seemed optimistic about his new ideas and projects, but I could sense his unrest and worry. He talked a lot about money, mistakes and bad luck. He was still smoking constantly. I watched him puffing away on his little borrowed patio and he looked distracted and frail. He made an effort with Lucy and me, but seeing him alone with his thoughts, it was clear that he was deeply troubled.

Just when it seemed hopeless, it looked like the show that got him started in comedy would return to save him. *Jokers Wild* had last aired in the seventies, and now twenty years later the show was to return. My dad was to produce a modernized version called *The Hecklers*. It was a pilot for the BBC, but if it went well it would be good news for everyone. My dad would be working again, and if a series was commissioned, he would have to move back to London. For Lucy and me, this was a wonderful prospect because, although he was visiting regularly, we were also saying good-bye regularly, which was always painful.

The Hecklers was to feature new comedians, so my dad, who was now totally out of touch with the UK comedy scene, had to go talent-spotting at London's comedy clubs. I didn't know anything about stand-up comedy. I had only seen three comedians on TV, and although I enjoyed them, I didn't have an epiphany or anything. I saw the American Steven Wright, who delivered a stream of monotone one-liners ('I bought some batteries, but batteries weren't included'). I'd also seen Lee Evans and Lenny Henry in their live shows, but my mum and Steve were laughing so much I didn't catch many of the jokes.

When my dad came to London, he went out every night

to comedy clubs to unearth the stars of tomorrow. Lucy and I would spend the day with him before he'd drop us off in his rented car and say he was off to the Comedy Store in Leicester Square or riffling through an *A–Z* to locate clubs in Greenwich, Balham and Battersea. I had never heard of comedy clubs, I had never even heard of these places in London, but one day I would. He was going to a club called Up the Creek in Greenwich, the Banana Cabaret in Balham and Jongleurs in Battersea. In the years to come I would play these clubs hundreds of times, and I don't think there was a time I set off in my car that I didn't think of my dad setting off to the same place.

This was an era when Eddie Izzard was the king of stand-up but refused to appear on television, and Tony Slattery refused to do anything that didn't involve appearing on television. So after extensive scouring for talent, my dad finalized the line-up for the pilot. The unknown comedians would be Mark Steel, Steve Coogan and Richard Morton, and the host, you guessed it, Tony Slattery.

My dad bought himself a new black jacket for the pilot. This became my first experience of live comedy, and I had never laughed so much in my life. Each comic performed a few minutes to introduce themselves to the audience, and they were all hilarious. Tony Slattery, in particular, was hysterical.

Everybody seemed thrilled with the pilot, but, as with all pilots, Dad would have an uncomfortable wait before the powers that be made their decisions. While he was waiting, he continued to come to London to drum up business. In November 1993, Lucy and I said goodbye to him on the steps of the flat he borrowed in Maida Vale. We weren't upset, as he already had another visit scheduled for soon after Christmas.

That Christmas he sent Lucy and me our presents, and we

got up early together before the rest of the house awoke to open them. We didn't want to open them with Mum and Steve because our relationship with our dad was very separate and personal to us. We knew he was struggling financially so didn't expect much, but his presents were lovely and thoughtful, especially the book about how to fix classic cars. We spoke later that day to wish each other a Merry Christmas.

That would be the last time we spoke.

Since I had my driving licence, I was barely at home. On the evening of 27 December, I was in Highgate at the house of a friend whose parents were away. There was a group of us, including Sam and some girls, most of whom I fancied. We had been larking about all day, watching movies, smoking cigarettes, eating junk food. This was prior to the days when everyone had a mobile phone, so my mother was clueless as to my whereabouts. I remember the phone ringing and being told it was for me. 'Hello?' I said.

'Michael, it's Mum. I've been trying to find you all day. You need to come home immediately.'

'Why? Has something happened?' I asked, not overly concerned.

'You just need to come home now. I can't tell you over the phone,' my mother said coolly. Her voice seemed relatively normal. I didn't sense that anything terrible had happened.

'Why can't you tell me now? Is it something bad?' I pushed.

'Michael, don't worry. Just come home now, OK?'

'OK,' I said, hanging up.

Because of my mother's tone, I was intrigued rather than panicked. As I drove home I wondered what might have happened. Might it be to do with one of my brothers or Lucy or Grandma or Jim or Steve's parents? All I knew was that it couldn't be that serious. My mum's performance on the phone was too convincing. As I neared Golders Green, the thought suddenly entered my head: what if it is something serious? That's exactly how my mum would behave on the phone. It was like when my dad asked me to sit down when he told me I was leaving Merchant Taylors' – people don't like to deliver bad news on the phone. I was so consumed with mucking about with my mates and my various teenage crushes that I hadn't really thought this through. Something bad had happened. To whom? As I drove alongside the park towards my house, my father's face popped into my mind. A chill came over me.

I turned the corner into my road just as the panic in my mind was reaching a crescendo. The front door of my house was open, my mother was standing outside, her body buckled with pain, tears streaming from her face.

I jumped out of my car. 'What is it?'

'Your daddy's died.'

It was strange because I felt like I knew before my mother opened her mouth to tell me. I knew, I knew my father had died.

'Where's Lucy?' I said.

I ran upstairs to find Lucy in my bed waiting for me, crying. Through all the changes in my life, my parents divorcing, remarrying, moving home and school, having new half-brothers and sisters, Lucy was the constant in my life. We experienced everything together. Our dad had a new life, a new family, and so did our mum, and as hard as everybody tried for it not to feel this way, Lucy and I were stuck in the middle. But we had each other, and at this moment we needed each other more than anybody else.

The previous day, Boxing Day, my dad had complained to Holly about chest pains in the night. He went out for a walk and some fresh air, had a heart attack and died on the side of the road. It destroyed me to think of him on his own, strangers trying to help him. He was fifty-three years old.

Holly lost her husband, their children Billy and Georgina lost a dad they hardly got a chance to know. His first wife, to whom he was married long before I was born, held a memorial service for him. A death affects so many people in so many different ways. For me, I lost a future with my dad. I felt that our relationship had been dominated by circumstance and distance, but that we were cut from the same cloth and that we would become closer and I would learn from him. But that was not to be.

The months following were a bit of a whirlwind. My dad was cremated, and Holly brought his ashes over from America. We didn't really know what to do with them. Holly, Lucy and I decided to go to Scotland, where his parents were originally from before emigrating to Canada. We went to Edinburgh and walked up Arthur's Seat, which is the main peak of a group of hills that overlook the city. It was a typically blustery, chilly Scottish day. We climbed as far as we could, Holly clutching the solid brass urn containing my father's remains. It was surreal and ultimately comical. We selected a spot. Dog-walkers kept passing by. 'Good morning!' they would say in their thick Scottish accents.

We waited for some privacy, and then Holly tried to say a few words, but they were blown downwind so Lucy and I struggled to hear her. Then it transpired there was no way to open the urn. There was no lid; it was solid brass all the way around. We'd taken a five-hour train journey, booked hotel rooms and climbed a small mountain only to find we couldn't get it open. The only solution was to try to smash it open against a rock. So Holly repeatedly banged the sealed-shut container against the largest rock she could find. After a period of denting, she finally broke through at a moment that coincided with a large gust of wind, which blew my father's ashes all over her face and hair. She was covered in grey soot, she could barely get her eyes open. Another Scottish dog-walker passed saying, 'Good morning', before noticing Holly's appearance and scuttling off encouraging her dog to follow: 'Come along, boy, hurry up.'

'Your dad would find this hilarious,' Holly said as she shook his remains out of her hair.

We all laughed at the absurdity of the situation.

Holly then changed her position, the ashes caught the wind once more and now flew freely along the hilltop, billowing in the cold morning air and then disappearing.

Goodbye.

The sudden nature of my dad's death was shocking, and made it especially hard to deal with. One day I was chatting to him on the phone, the next he was gone. Little things freak you out, like his voice on the answerphone or his unmistakable smell on his clothes. I kept replaying our final goodbye at his borrowed flat in Maida Vale over and over in my head. I drove there in my Spitfire and sat outside. I drove to our old house in Hampstead and walked around the block, a walk I used to do with him as a child. He had just gone. Vanished.

But a few weeks later, the most extraordinary thing happened. I received a letter from him, seemingly from beyond the grave. My dad had been on a turbulent plane journey on which the captain made the passengers sit in the crash position amidst panic and praying. It made him think about his mortality and the possibility of dying without being able to say goodbye to his family. So he wrote letters to his children that he planned to update over the years. It's an extraordinarily thoughtful thing to do. Most people avoid the subject of death altogether, not wanting to tempt fate. Maybe my dad had this foresight because his own father also died young and suddenly, also in his early fifties. Or maybe he knew somewhere deep down that he was nearing the end. Whatever made him write it, I was so grateful. This letter was the most wonderful and thoughtful gift I have ever received. I have cherished it and kept it in my desk ever since.

The letter starts with: 'If you are reading this, it means the worst has happened.'

It was like he spoke to me one last time. He apologized for the time we spent apart and advised me as best he could. It was poignant and from the heart and helped me to move on.

He ended it with:

You've got good stuff in you, so go get 'em! You've got your whole life ahead of you, and I want it to be as full of happiness as possible.

I believe in you, Michael, always be the best you can be.

I'll love you always.

I had experienced a terrible loss. There were things left unsaid, but my dad addressed them and left nothing unresolved between us and me in no doubt of his love for me, allowing me, in his words, to 'go get 'em'.

14

I returned to Woodhouse to find that just when I thought things couldn't get any worse, Tina had had a breast reduction. I had never even heard of such a procedure. That should be illegal, this is a man's world, we can't be having that. Tina's shrinking tits were the talk of the college. Apparently her assets were giving her back pain so she was medically advised to reduce their size. If I was her doctor, I would have recommended back exercises or perhaps finding a hobby that involved lying down. Why didn't she come to me? I would have helped her support them, taken some of the strain off her back, that's the kind of guy I am, always thinking of others.

The world was suddenly a very different place, but I had no time to dwell, my A-Levels were rapidly approaching. This was the culmination of school life. Everything would come down to three grades, three letters that defined my academic abilities. A peculiar thing that happens before A-Levels is that teachers predict what grades students are going to gain. Despite displaying no psychic abilities before this point, they suddenly start to predict the future. These predictions are then put to universities, who may or may not make offers to students.

I simply wasn't prepared for my exams. Not only had I lost my father but I had changed schools mid-term and the standard of teaching at Woodhouse was a lot poorer than at Merchant Taylors'. In Biology, for example, the 'teacher' copied the textbook page by page on to the white board without saying a word. We then had to copy from the white board into our pads. At the end of the two years, we had each compiled handwritten versions of the textbook.

The net result was that I was 'predicted' low grades and subsequently rejected by every university. This annoyed me. I thought the 'prediction' procedure was scandalous. They had no way of knowing how I would perform in my exams, and if they accepted 'predictions', couldn't I tell them about the Tarot card reader? Maybe that would have helped my cause.

The atmosphere at college was dominated by revision for the exams. Suddenly everybody was studious. The kebab shops were empty and the library was full. It was suggested that Tina had worked her tits off. This, after all, was the reason we were there. I got my head down and started cramming, but feared it was too late.

My exam results were exactly as predicted. I got a C in Chemistry, a C in Biology and a D in Geography. This meant two things: my future was in turmoil and my teachers may actually have been psychic. Most of my friends were taking a 'gap year' between school and university. I told everybody I was taking a gap year, but in truth I had no place at university, so the rest of my life was lining up to be a series of 'gap years'.

I had no money, and my grandma was in no mood to reward me for failing my exams. So I started working as a labourer for some builders who had installed my mum's new kitchen. I was told to wear 'something you don't mind getting ruined', so I put on my elephant T-shirt that had so far helped me pull precisely zero girls. I arrived for my first day in my Triumph Spitfire, which was surprisingly still working, although the fuel tank was leaking petrol into the car. Believe it or not, I was oblivious to petrol being flammable (I was lucky to get that C in Chemistry) and was lighting up cigarettes while driving.

You might be questioning why I took up smoking, given my dad's struggles with cigarettes. Well, as with everything else I did, it was another attempt to pull the opposite sex. Seasoned seducers advised me that 'Have you got a light?' is a wonderful chat-up line. I tried it a few times when I was a non-smoker, and it didn't have quite the impact I'd hoped for.

I would sidle up to a hotty and ask, 'Have you got a light?'

To which she would say, while fluttering her eyelashes, 'Yeah, sure.' So far, so good. She would get out her lighter and spark up a flame.

And I would just stand there awkwardly.

'Don't you have a cigarette?' she would ask, confused.

'No, I don't smoke,' came my baffling reply.

So I started smoking, and guess what, they're really addictive.

I started my building career on a family house in Hendon. It seemed that one of the occupants was a person called Jeremy who had also just done his A-Levels as there were cards scattered all over the mantelpieces. 'Dear Jeremy, congratulations on your exam results, good luck at uni' was the general theme. I spent my first two days sweeping the driveway before being promoted to painting one of the bedrooms. It appeared to be Jeremy's bedroom as congratulations cards dominated the room. This wasn't a high point for me. Whoever this Jeremy was, he had passed his exams and was off to university, and here I was painting his bedroom. I was up a ladder rolling eggshell emulsion on the walls when Jeremy himself walked in.

'Michael?' said Jeremy.

Shit. I knew Jeremy. He was in my class at Woodhouse. What an unfortunate coincidence.

'Jeremy! You're Jeremy, this is your room,' I said, stating the obvious and struggling to keep my balance on the ladder.

'Are you a painter now?' Jeremy asked, confused.

'Yes, at the moment I'm doing some painting,' I replied honestly, before trying to jazz up my responsibilities, 'and . . . sweeping.'

'How weird . . . running into you . . . in my bedroom . . . painting it,' Jeremy correctly pointed out. 'Oh, OK, well, see ya.'

Jeremy then ran off to celebrate his exam results while I finished decorating his bedroom.

He was embarrassed for me, but I wasn't. I found it funny. I could see the comedy in the situation. I enjoyed telling people the story of how I had done so badly in my exams I was now painting the bedrooms of my former classmates. I was starting to make people laugh with little anecdotes and stories from my life. People were beginning to refer to me as 'the funny guy'. I would mimic people and do impressions. I was constantly riffing on life to others and even to myself. I started to look for comedy in every situation. I would stand on my terrace in Golders Green at night, smoking cigarettes and chatting to myself, making myself laugh. Funny was starting to be my thing.

My dad's old personal assistant, Pete, offered me a job as a 'runner' at his production company off Ladbroke Grove. It was a lovely circle of life that I should be working for him at the same age he was when he worked for my dad. It was good to get a little razzmatazz back into my life. Showbiz had been sorely lacking since my dad was making *The Kenny*

Everett Show. Steve's job in 'computer-aided design' just didn't have the same ring. Pete's company was called Partizan, and they made music videos for the likes of Björk, Radiohead, Annie Lennox and Massive Attack.

I was basically a dogsbody. Making tea and coffee for the producers, delivering things around London, doing whatever needed to be done. I worked alongside two other 'runners', Jamie and Steve, and the receptionist, Zelda. Being a runner is the entry point in the media – most successful people in film and television start out as runners. I was fortunate to land the job; every day we received CVs from well-qualified graduates desperate to make the tea that I was making. In fact, I'm sure they could have done it better – my tea-making was appalling. My toast-making was so bad, I had a tutorial from Pete on how to 'Butter all the way to the edges'. I think if it wasn't for nepotism, I would have been fired pretty early on.

Jamie and Steve were desperate to become directors, and Zelda was desperate to become a producer. I was just having fun. I was discovering my sense of humour and becoming addicted to the sound of laughter. It seemed to me that the whole of life was just there so that I could try to make it funny. I was also trying to impress Zelda. She was a 22-year-old bubbly blonde with a wicked sense of humour of her own. Despite her being in a long-term relationship with her 'drummer in a band' boyfriend, she became the latest unrequited love of my life. We pranked and laughed our days away. My time would be spent working in the office or on set when there was a shoot.

The first music video I worked on was for the *Big Breakfast* puppets Zig and Zag. Some savvy record producer called Simon Cowell thought he might be able to land a hit single with a novelty record. The song was called 'Them Girls' and the video featured a club scene with a few boys but predominantly sexy girls dancing around Zig and Zag, as they sang, 'Them girls, them girls, they all love me.' I was the runner on the shoot, which meant I was literally run off my feet from very early in the morning until very late at night. My job was to be on hand to help everybody from the director to the caterers.

My Spitfire was now not only leaking petrol but also brake fluid, so I would have to fill up on both several times a journey. The studio was in Bow, and I was running so late that I didn't have time to fill up the brake fluid. When I arrived the brakes were so soft I sailed fifty yards past the crew entrance and finally stopped at the artists' entrance. There were about a hundred models arriving, and I was mistaken for one. I think it was more the car than my face, or maybe my coat. My grandmother had given me one of my grandfather's old coats. It was a very expensive black pure cashmere overcoat. I loved it and hardly ever took it off. I certainly didn't look like your average 'runner'.

I should really have said something. I was late, I was in trouble, there would have been people looking for me, I was badly needed on the shoot, but before I knew it, I was whisked into a communal dressing room surrounded by naked models. NAKED MODELS! Naked models who seemed to be flirting with me a bit. One girl asked me to help her out of her dress! She moved her long dark hair to one side as I unzipped this gorgeous woman from behind.

'Michael!' cried Jenny, one of the production assistants who was organizing the extras. 'What are you doing? Everyone's looking for you!'

'Sorry, I was just helping . . .' I scooted out, leaving behind a half-zipped beauty and returned to my actual job of production slave.

News of my indiscretion travelled throughout the production, and all but a few found it hilarious, and most of the male crew congratulated me on being a bit of a stud. But my out-of-control antics were soon to jeopardize my job.

Partizan was becoming quite successful, mainly due to one of their directors, Michel Gondry, who was and is a phenomenally creative Frenchman. He would go on to direct one of my favourite films, *Eternal Sunshine of the Spotless Mind*, starring Jim Carrey, and indeed win an Oscar for it. So the company started to diversify and produce commercials directed by Michel. For me, this only meant that I would be delivering and picking up packages from advertising agencies as well as record companies. Very kindly, Pete occasionally allowed me to drive his company Mercedes when on these deliveries.

On the day in question, I was delivering a package to the agency Saatchi & Saatchi. Saatchi & Saatchi was run by brothers Charles and Maurice Saatchi. While sitting in traffic, en route, I heard on the radio that Maurice Saatchi was leaving the agency. 'That's interesting,' I thought, 'I'm on my way there now.' So I listened closely to the news about how he was being ousted from the company and would probably start a new one. The big question seemed to be, would his major clients like British Airways follow him.

When I arrived at Saatchi & Saatchi, it was a media circus. Outside the main entrance were cameras, news teams, reporters. I was only dropping off a package, so I double-parked the car and ran in unnoticed. On the way out, however, all the cameras, lights and reporters focused on me, standing on the steps of Saatchi & Saatchi in my expensive cashmere coat.

'What do you think the future is for Saatchi & Saatchi?' I was asked, mistaken for an advertising exec.

Well, you see, they asked me a question, so I chose to answer it. I was filled with all the information I had just heard on the radio and said, 'I don't think there is much of a future.'

Obviously, everybody else had been saying, 'No comment', because as soon as I spoke, there was a media scrum surrounding me, microphones were thrust into my face from all angles, BBC, Sky News, ITN, etc.

'Maurice was the lifeblood of this agency,' I continued, repeating exactly what I had heard a commentator say on the radio just minutes previously. 'I think many of the major clients will follow him out, certainly British Airways will.' This was massive news; they were scribbling, jockeying for position around me.

'What do you do here?' somebody shouted at me.

'Well, nothing now, I've just resigned,' I said then, cool as a cucumber. I beeped open Pete's double-parked Mercedes, jumped in it and sped off.

I was exhilarated by my latest joke and told everybody in the office. Pete summoned me and told me in no uncertain terms that what I had done was very funny, but if it came back to him and Partizan in any way, he would have to fire me. I nervously watched the news that night, but nothing was on it. My job was safe, I could continue with my reign of mischief.

One reign that was about to come to an inevitable end was that of my Triumph Spitfire. My car struggled to stop in perfect driving conditions, so when snow and ice entered the equation, there was little hope. Driving home from work in wintry conditions, I applied the brake and skidded serenely. While skidding, I couldn't remember the advice I had been given; was it to brake, not brake, pump the brakes? By the time I'd remembered, I'd crashed into a parked Volvo Limousine.

I have honestly never seen a Volvo Limousine before or since. Volvos are renowned for their strength and limousines are renowned for being long. So it was hard for me to avoid this long strong car. The result was that my car crumpled into an unsalvageable heap, offering no resistance whatsoever. It was almost as if the car committed suicide, like it had been waiting for the right car to crash into and spotting a Volvo Limousine was too much to resist. I was unhurt, as was the Volvo. I may not have remembered the skidding rules, but I did remember being told that if you're involved in an accident, do not accept responsibility. The fact that the car I crashed into was unoccupied didn't seem to affect my denial of blame.

The limo was parked directly outside its owner's house on West End Lane in West Hampstead. He heard the impact and came rushing outside.

'What do you think you're doing?' he cried.

'What do you think you're doing?' I said, leaping out of my wreckage.

'Have you been drinking?' he accused me.

'Have you been drinking?' I asked.

'Yes,' he said, 'but I'm having dinner with my family. Are you insane? I'm allowed to drink and eat. Have you been drinking and driving?'

We exchanged details, he returned to his dinner and I awaited rescue. I had lost my car, but I had another funny story to add to my expanding repertoire. The next morning when I went to Partizan, I wasn't depressed to be on the bus. I couldn't wait to tell Zelda and everyone else how I'd hit the only Volvo Limousine ever made and blamed it on a man who was eating dinner at the time. The story got big laughs and that made me happy.

Making people laugh made me happy.

15

As my 'gap year' neared its end, I had no idea what my next move would be. 'Clearing' is a process whereby universities advertise places they still have available and the grades you need to be considered. So I found all the courses that accepted A-Level grades of C, C and D and they tended to be at former polytechnics or working as a janitor or security guard at one of the more prestigious universities.

Then, surprisingly, I found a course at Edinburgh University that only required C, C and D at A-Level. Edinburgh is a top-notch seat of learning. I'm not really sure what the course was; I know it was either Biology or Chemistry or maybe a bit of both. All I knew is that after a few phone calls I was accepted. I was off to Edinburgh.

I packed up my belongings and, after an emotional farewell, I left home. I was fleeing the nest and heading to a student flat where I would be living with two unknown flatmates. When I arrived, they were already there. We said hello awkwardly, like at the beginning of *Big Brother*. It was immediately obvious that my new flatmates were partial to smoking marijuana. One of them was wearing clothes made of hemp and the other one only packed a guitar. They both needed a good bath but weren't going to get one as the flat only had an out-of-service shower. They became the best of friends following this exchange:

'Have you got any Rizla?' asked the guitar one.

'Yeah,' said the hemp one.

We were each given a 'starter pack' containing leaflets, spaghetti hoops, loo roll and a condom. I joked that maybe it was a leaflet telling you how to have sex with the spaghetti hoops and then clean up afterwards. They didn't laugh, then both wolfed down their spaghetti hoops straight from the tin, unheated when it clearly states 'best served hot'. Shocking.

I unpacked and burst into tears. I now had to fend for myself, in the big bad world. Well, that's what it felt like. In reality I was in student accommodation with a pretty healthy allowance from my grandmother. But like a baby, I missed my mum. 'You take me for granted,' she had been shouting at me for years – well, now I would realize that for myself. I had no idea how to look after myself. I smoked several cigarettes, also ate my spaghetti hoops cold and straight from the tin (actually not that bad) and fell asleep in my clothes.

In the morning, I headed off to a laboratory on campus for some kind of induction to my course. Well, for everyone else it was an induction. For me, it was an opportunity to find out what course I was studying. I assembled with about thirty other similarly nervous and self-conscious students. I scanned the lab for the most attractive girl and settled on this cute blonde in the Kylie Minogue mould. I was then handed a lab coat and safety glasses. This is not a good look for me, for anyone. I don't think any girl in history has uttered the words, 'Who's that guy with the long white coat and the massive plastic glasses?'

I think the course involved Biology and Chemistry in the first year and then you specialized in one after that. The good news for me was that in Scotland university courses are four years as opposed to the three years in England. So everything that we were taught in the first year, I had already studied for at A-Level. So I decided to take the rest of the year off.

Later that day I ran into several of Sam's friends from Westminster. They were a close-knit bunch of public school boys and girls who had been friends for years. I sort of tagged along with them and during my tagging along ran into a friend from Woodhouse, Jonas, a Swedish gentleman whom I had always liked. Jonas tagged along also. So now there was the ex-Westminster mob, Jonas and myself, and we never really separated for the remainder of that year. I soon left my student flat (I don't think Hemp and Guitar noticed), and we all rented a flat together on Blair Street above the City Café, a hang-out for Edinburgh's grooviest residents.

My flatmates were a lovely couple, Will and Poppy (posh), a lovely couple, Nicky and Mellow (posh), Ben (posh), Jonas (Swedish) and myself. The flat was ex-council and in relative disrepair. It had a unique design. A central kitchen surrounded by five bedrooms. Home improvements were first on the agenda, so we each painted our own bedrooms. I purchased some silver spray paint and sprayed everything, including my television. I had a silver television. I also painted around my bed, which was positioned against the wall. I didn't see the point in moving the bed and painting behind it as nobody would see that bit. I have the same theory today when ironing shirts – because I always wear a jacket I tend to only iron the visible 'V' on the front.

I was already living with two couples. This is what was happening, people were getting together and having serious relationships. Will and Poppy ended up getting married and now have three kids. I still hadn't had a girlfriend. Nothing. I had been obsessively trying to meet somebody since Arnold House and had nothing to show for it. I remember thinking that statistically there must be someone who never ever has a girlfriend just through bad luck, and I thought that might be me. At university I was surrounded by young couples in love, and I found some of their relationships unfathomable. I would chat and giggle with girls, make them laugh until they were wiping tears from their eyes: 'You're so funny, Michael, you're the funniest guy I've ever met.'

I'd be thinking, 'Great, let's have a relationship', but they always had a boyfriend, some guy back in Leeds or Southampton or wherever they'd come from. Or sometimes the boyfriend was sitting right next to them, not saying a word, with a hairstyle hanging over one eye, so he couldn't see out of it. 'This guy? What are you doing with this guy?' I would want to say and occasionally did. Nobody wanted to be with me.

Before long, my two other single flatmates, Jonas and Ben, also found girlfriends, meaning that four of the bedrooms surrounding the central kitchen contained couples. One morning I woke up, opened my silver bedroom door to the kitchen and put the kettle on. I heard noises from the bedrooms surrounding me. Every single couple, that's four couples, were having sex. I sat there sipping my morning coffee on my own surrounded by four couples having sex. When was my luck going to change?

But when they weren't enjoying the love and intimacy that I wasn't, we had as much fun as you would hope to have when you're a student. Edinburgh is a wonderful city. It had already played a very sad part in my life with the scattering of my father's ashes, but now it was a party town. We were out almost every night and when we weren't out, we were slobbing out back at the flat, drinking and smoking and watching movies. In fact, our lifestyle in the flat was so lazy that we purchased a fleet of remote control cars to pass things to each other without having to get up. We strapped ashtrays, lighters, beers, tobacco and crisps on top of the cars and navigated them to each other by remote controls.

Now, I've just come off the phone to Bill Clinton, who tells me my career shouldn't suffer if I tell you about a particular incident involving marijuana. Experimenting with drugs is difficult to avoid at university, it's part of life, part of growing up. One of my flatmates managed to get the details of a drug dealer who lived in the depths of Leith. If you are unfamiliar with Leith, then watch the film *Trainspotting*. I volunteered to go and buy it, trying to impress my new friends. I regretted my decision almost immediately.

I headed down to Edinburgh's most deprived area in a taxi at about 10 p.m. I was off to visit a drug dealer by the name of Scott. Why did I agree to this? I was terrified. I rehearsed what I might say to him, but everything sounded so wrong coming out of my mouth:

'Hello Scott, any pot in the house?'

'Scott, would I be correct in assuming you are the possessor of skunk?'

'Yo, Scott, I'm here to score some weed, dude.'

'Scotty, baby, it's Mikey, here for the herb.'

I liked the fact that he was called Scott and from Scotland. I thought it must make form-filling a bit easier when the answer for 'Name' is the same as 'Nationality'. I thought of making this joke to him as an ice-breaker, but correctly decided against it.

It was freezing cold as always. I arrived at Scott's tenement block in my buttoned-up cashmere coat from my grandfather. I looked up with trepidation at Scott's building glowing eerily in the moonlight. The main door was ajar so I pushed it open. It seemed to be colder inside than outside. He lived on the top floor. I climbed the four flights of stone stairs, getting more tense with every step, preparing for my illegal transaction. I reached the door and knocked.

Within moments, I was being viewed through the peep-hole, as I heard a Scottish voice from the other side of the door holler, 'It's Hugh Grant, but he's all Chinesey.'

The door opened to reveal a man with a tattoo of the map of Scotland on his face. This was worse than I could have expected. 'All right, pal?' he said before walking away. I followed him. I followed a man with a Scotland tattoo on his face. I arrived in the living room. The décor of the living room was minimal. Not minimalism which is a design statement involving clean lines, Scott just didn't own anything. There was a nail in the wall. Maybe a picture had fallen off or he was waiting for the right print to go with the room. There was a brown sofa, a chair, a top-of-the-range television and a coffee table on which sat an overflowing ashtray. Needless to say, the room reeked of spliffs.

The tattoo-faced chap sat on the chair and on the sofa sat a man who was the spitting image of Skeletor from the eighties animated children's series *He-Man and the Masters of the Universe*. Next to him on a side table I saw the strangest thing. A toaster with the front ripped off exposing the hot grills. There was no toast in it, but it was burning hot.

'All right, mate, I'm Scott,' Scelator said, friendly, smoking a joint.

'Hiya, I'm Michael, your name must make form-filling a bit easier when the answer for "Name" is the same as "Nationality",' I said. Why did I say that? I panicked.

Scott laughed unexpectedly. He really laughed. I laughed too.

'That's hilarious,' he said in a Scottish accent that nearly required subtitles. 'You're hilarious. Are you lookin' to buy some weed?'

This was going really well. I didn't need to ask after all, he had asked me. Tremendous.

Then the toaster popped up, with no toast in it. Scott nonchalantly pushed the toaster button down again. Odd.

'How much do you want?' Scott asked.

'I don't know, whatever is the done thing. Will you take a post-dated cheque?' I said.

This was not a joke; this was my level of naïveté.

'Are you fuckin' jokin'?' Scott said.

I froze. This was an error. I knew I should have brought some cash, but nobody had any. Shit. Then the toaster with the exposed burning grills popped again. Scott popped it back down again.

'I'm not joking. I have a guarantee card,' I said, potentially making things worse.

Scott just stared at me, his scalding toastless toaster next to him.

'I tell you what, you've got balls comin' in here with your post-dated cheque. Student bastard. That's hilarious. Sit yourself down and have a toke on this.' He then passed me his joint as I took a seat alongside him on the big brown sofa. This was not something I had envisaged. I had never done this before, I didn't even know if I planned on doing it later. I was buying the marijuana for my flat to appear cool. I couldn't say no. I took a puff on the joint. It didn't take long for the effects to take hold, and I relaxed and slumped into the chair.

'It's good innit, pal?' Scott said.

'Marvellous,' I said, honestly.

Then the bizarre toaster situation occurred again. It popped up, and he popped it down with no toast. I was now stoned and feeling more confident.

179

'Scott, you must tell me, what's going on with that toaster?'

'Heating's broke,' Scott said, matter of factly.

His stoned mind had created a heater out of the toaster by peeling off the front panel and popping it down every three minutes. Priceless.

I sat with Scott and the man with a tattoo of Scotland on his face for about an hour telling them all my funny stories. I told them about crashing my car by pushing it into a parked Mercedes, painting Jeremy's wall and pretending I worked for Saatchi & Saatchi. We were all in hysterics. I wrote Scott a post-dated cheque, did the deal and stood up to leave. The tattooed man asked, 'Where are you staying in Edinburgh?'

'Would you like me to show you on your face?' I said. We all rolled about laughing again.

I was in a right old state. I could barely see in front of me. I kept laughing to myself about the toaster as I trundled down the stairs. When I reached the bottom, the door was now closed. I pushed and pulled but it didn't budge. I realized it must be one of those doors where you buzz yourself out. I searched for a buzzer and found one. Bingo. I pushed the buzzer and then the door, but it still wouldn't open. I pushed the buzzer and pulled the door, still nothing. I then repeated this, kicking the door. As successfully as my Scott visit had gone, I didn't plan on returning, ever. So I kept buzzing and kicking until the door finally opened.

It transpired I was actually on the first floor and not the ground floor. My scrambled brain had not completed the final flight of stairs. The door I was buzzing and kicking was somebody's front door. The door swung open to reveal an overweight Scottish man in his boxer shorts, not dissimilar to Rab C. Nesbitt.

'What the fuck are you doin' bangin' on ma door?'

I ran for my life. I realized instantly that my explanation would sound absurd and he looked about ready to kill me. So I bolted down the stairs and out of the ajar main door. I sprinted as far as I could before looking behind me, terrified at the prospect of seeing a near naked Scotsman chasing me, but thankfully the coast was clear.

I decided there and then that maybe this drugs malarkey probably wasn't for me. But I continued to drink and smoke and not attend my lectures. I wasn't rebelling; I just had no interest in Biology or Chemistry. I received a letter from the department head summoning me to a meeting. I told him I was struggling to adjust to university life and assured him I wanted to be a biologist . . . or chemist.

At some time during my first year, I watched a Woody Allen film. I had never heard of Woody Allen, but this was the epiphany I had been waiting for. It wasn't even one of his better films – I think it was *Crimes and Misdemeanors* – but I was transfixed. I then rented every one of his films every day until I had seen his entire body of work. Nothing had resonated with me as much as Woody Allen. It wasn't just that he was hysterically funny, it was where the comedy was coming from. He was confused about life and love, he was a loser, a funny loser, like me. I know there is a great deal of difference between this neurotic New York Jew and myself, but I could relate to his insular outlook on the world.

After I watched all Woody Allen's films, I immediately realized what I was put on this earth to be. I am a writer. I'm going to write a film. For the first time in my life, I worked at something with a passion. I had worked hard on occasion at school, but then it was because I had to, it was expected. Now I was driven and excited. I bought every book about screenwriting I could find and devoured them. As soon as I understood how to structure and lay out a screenplay, I sat down at my computer, a hand-me-down from Steve, and wrote and wrote and wrote until I passed out, then I woke up and carried on. The words and story just gushed out of me, I was so engrossed in it, I felt so creative, so switched on.

The film was a romantic comedy set in Edinburgh. It was called *Office Angels* and was about a student, Marty, who was a loser in love (ring any bells?). The premise of the film was that everybody has his or her own angel. Angels work in regular offices with phones and faxes and canteens; their job is to find true love for their client. They negotiate with other angels until they have built up enough of a romance file to make a presentation to the Love God (ideally played by Sean Connery; I would have accepted Billy Connolly), who decides whether they have found true love. If they have, their work is done; if not, their clients break up and the angels go back to work. The film jumped between the lives of characters in Edinburgh and how they are affected by the work of their angels. The problem with Marty was that his angel was lousy and lazy, and his mistakes lead to Marty's appalling love life, but, you guessed it, he gets his girl in the end.

What I enjoyed most about the script was that it was an opportunity for me to create the happy ending that my own life wasn't providing. I created a fantasy girl, Sasha, well out of my league, and wrote a story where she and I end up together. Real life wasn't panning out for me, so I created a fantasy. That's basically what this script was. It was a fantasy of how I wanted things to work out for me, with jokes. I was thrilled with the result and like any writer managed to convince myself I was on for an Academy Award. I gave it to a few select people to read and they all reported back positively. I then packaged it up and sent it to various local producers. I wanted to send it to all the big boys of the British film industry like Working Title, Film4 and Fox, but they didn't accept unsolicited scripts. This meant I needed to have an agent, although due to my naïveté at the time I thought I needed a solicitor.

Initial feedback was good, but the readers didn't seem to share my conviction that it was Oscar-worthy. The consensus seemed to be that it was funny, but there were various comments regarding the plot. 'What do these people know?' tended to be my overconfident reaction to opening these rejection letters. 'Idiots.' I had read stories about successful film scripts being rejected for years, so I wasn't disheartened; I genuinely believed I was sitting on a goldmine. I missed most of another term writing, rewriting and flogging my script. Again I was summoned to see the department head to discuss my poor attendance and again I assured him I wanted to be a biologist . . . or chemist.

I sent *Office Angels* to Scottish Screen in Glasgow. They developed screenplays and are an entry point into the film industry. They enjoyed the script and I travelled to Glasgow for a meeting with them, but again they weren't overly interested, just encouraging.

Then I had a bit of a breakthrough. There was a show on BBC2 called *Scene by Scene* hosted by the Northern Irish film maker Mark Cousins. I watched his show on Sunday nights every week. The show consisted of one-on-one interviews with directors and actors. I watched avidly, recorded and re-watched again and again as he interviewed the likes of Martin Scorsese, Steve Martin and the highlight, Woody Allen. While drinking with friends in a bar in Edinburgh, I spotted the man himself, Mark Cousins. Outside of the Edinburgh Festival, you don't tend to see TV faces around (although nowadays everybody seems to claim to have sat next to J. K. Rowling in a café), so I had to double-take. But it was him, the man who had met Woody Allen. I wasn't going to let this opportunity slip by and immediately made my way over to him.

'Hello, you're Mark Cousins,' I said.

This is the kind of nonsense people say when they meet people from the telly. People say it to me now all the time. 'You're Michael McIntyre.'

What am I supposed to say? 'Thank you, I've been having these bouts of amnesia where I forget who I am, your reminder has been a great help to me.' Thankfully Mark was more polite.

'Yes, I am,' he said in his very trademark Northern Irish accent.

'I'm really sorry to disturb you, but I've written a screen-play, and, well, I was . . .'

I didn't really know what I was asking, but before I could finish my ramble, he said, 'Sure, I'll read it. Have you got a pen and paper and I'll give you my address?'

'Really, oh, thank you,' I said. I didn't know it, but Mark Cousins was a bit of an industry player. He was the head of the Edinburgh Film Festival and had access to all the produc-ers I needed to get at. I just wanted to ask him what Woody Allen was like. But I left the bar that night aglow, clutching Mark Cousins' address. I couldn't believe I had met Mark Cousins from the TV, and he was going to read my script.

I packaged it up along with my covering letter and sent it special delivery the next day. Meanwhile, I had end-of-year university exams. I didn't care; I had found my vocation. University was actually becoming successful for me; I was socializing and working incredibly hard for my future. The problem was that I wasn't working hard at the course I had signed up for. I was concerned about being kicked out, and my department head told me he was interested to see how I would perform in the exams. I started to revise; I didn't see that I had a choice. It was during my half-hearted revision of chemical equations that the phone rang. It was Mark Cousins. He loved the script and wanted to meet. I slammed shut the textbook, which was never to be opened again. He loved my film, I knew it, I knew it was good. I was so thrilled to have that vindication, from a professional, who had met Woody Allen.

I met him in the Dome Restaurant that was one of the locations in the film. He was so generous to give up his time to help a young aspiring writer. He couldn't have been more complimentary about the script and wrote me a list of producers to send it to and said I could use his name in the covering letter. Well, that A4 piece of paper with Mark Cousins' handwriting was all that I felt I needed to move to London to make it as a writer. I had my final meeting with my department head.

He looked me straight in the eyes and said, 'Are you sure you want to be a biologist . . . or chemist?'

I replied, 'No, I'm going to write comedy films, like Woody Allen. I'm moving to London!'

16

I wouldn't be moving back home in London. Not because I was an adult now, determined to fend for myself, but because my mum, Steve, Nicholas, Thomas and Andre (now born) had upped sticks and moved to France. My mother had always dreamed of living in the sunshine, so she sold the house in Golders Green, and with the proceeds in cash drove to the South of France and bought another one. So my grandmother rented a tiny studio flat in West Hampstead for my sister and me to stay in.

Lucy was also heading up to Edinburgh University but was rather more studious and academic than myself. She got eleven As at GCSE and three As at A-Level so the world was her oyster. She didn't require 'clearing' to get into Edinburgh; nor did she have to wait until she got there to find out what her course was. She was Little Miss Perfect: outgoing, social, she had a huge circle of friends and a charming boyfriend. She could have perceived me as her loser university dropout older brother, but she believed in me and she loved my script. She read it and improved my writing significantly. I would have been lost without her input but mostly her support, especially when I started to receive rejection letters on a daily basis.

I sent the script to everyone on Mark Cousins' list with hope and optimism. In fact more than that: I fully expected a bidding war. But the returned scripts would land on my doorstep. Many of the covering letters were standard, copy and paste: 'Thank you for sending in your screenplay, which we read with interest, blah blah, blah. Good luck with placing it elsewhere.' One script was simply returned to me with the word 'NO' in big red pen on the front. Not a good day. I was also struggling to write another script. My first one had been such a breeze, but I had difficult-second-album syndrome. The problem, of course, was that my first album wasn't a hit.

My sister was spending a lot of her time at her boyfriend's flat, leaving me to struggle with my new script and start working as a barman at All Bar One in St John's Wood to help make ends meet. She came to witness me pulling pints and excitedly told me she'd met an actress who was perfect for my film.

'Have you been casting for my film?' I asked while serving up a lager with an overflowing frothy head. 'I love that you've got so much confidence in it.'

'She's a friend of Joe's,' she said, referring to her boyfriend. 'She's just hilarious and ditzy, a real character. I kept thinking she reminded me of someone, and then I realized it was Sasha, the girl in your film. She's an actress, and her dad is a really famous actor. You're going to love her.'

I was already approaching actors for the film. A film script always has more weight with 'talent attached'. I was waiting to hear from (still am, incidentally) Sean Connery, Billy Connolly and Anna Friel. To give you an idea of the extent I was residing in cloud cuckoo land at the time, I wanted to play the main character, Marty. So a meeting was set up with me and potentially my leading lady.

She did indeed come from good acting stock. Her father was a major star in the seventies, playing Winston Churchill in Richard Attenborough's *Young Winston*. Her sister was also an actress and had starred in *Return to Oz* and Steven Spielberg's *Young Sherlock Holmes*. The signs were good. My sister said she was twenty years old and beautiful, a femme fatale with a string of men obsessed with her (including, awkwardly, Lucy's boyfriend, Joe). She sounded exactly like the character I had created in the film, my fantasy girl.

We arranged to meet Lucy and Joe in a pub in Belsize Park called the Sir Richard Steele. I wore my grandfather's cashmere coat, even though it was the height of summer. I walked into the pub in work mode, pretending to be an up-and-coming screenwriter, but as soon as I saw her I completely forgot about my film. There she was. I'd sat in my smoke-filled flat in Edinburgh and created her, and now my dream girl had come to life.

The last time we'd been in the same room as each other had been the Arnold House disco.

Her name was Kitty Ward. She was the girl I had been looking for. My girl.

In the romantic comedy that was my life, this would have made a good ending. We would fall madly in love and live happily ever after. Within moments of seeing her and chatting to her, I was totally up for that ending. Unfortunately, she wasn't. It turned out we were actually at the beginning of a romantic comedy that might or might not have a happy ending.

I may have written a story about a fictional hot young blonde bombshell who came to life, but she didn't write one where she falls in love with a bouffant-haired university dropout with one sexual experience. As had been the theme of my youth, I just didn't do myself any favours. My cashmere coat may have been exquisite and expensive, but it was also several sizes too big for me. It dragged behind me. When

I sat down on the stool in the pub, it draped on the ground like a rug. When I saw other people with my hairstyle I would say, 'What a twat!' but for some reason continued to have it myself. And I was never myself, never relaxed, when I was attracted to someone. I always tried to do an impression of the kind of man I thought girls would be interested in, but as previous results had indicated, it wasn't working.

But I had one thing on my side. Destiny. When I asked for Kitty's phone number, she gave it to me; I'm not sure she even knew why. This was only the second time a girl had given me her number. The first had been very recent. The night after I met Mark Cousins, I hooked up with my friends at a bar. I was feeling very confident after my high-powered showbiz tête-à-tête, so when I got chatting to a psychology student, I asked for her phone number, and she handed over her digits no problem.

The following day I telephoned. 'Hello, it's Michael,' I said, jovially, 'we met last night.'

'Who?' she said.

'Michael, you gave me your number last night,' I said, realizing she hadn't exactly been waiting by the phone.

'Did I?' she said, hardly engaged in the conversation at all.

'Yes, that's how I called you,' I explained, and then there was silence.

She said nothing, so I said, 'OK then, bye,' and hung up.

This was actually the most success I had with women during my stint at university. The condom from my university 'starter pack' was still in my wallet when I met Kitty in the Steeles pub. My prospects of using it were so slim, I thought I might have to leave it to someone in my will.

The only thing that made me feel better about not having a girlfriend at university was my friend Robbie. Robbie had also never had a girlfriend. Like myself, he never pulled. Robbie was a virgin; it was common knowledge. At least I had some sexual experience. I always felt better about my situation because of Robbie. It eventually transpired, however, that Robbie was having more sex than anybody at university. He was a closet homosexual who was shagging every Tom, Dick and Harry and Sebastian and Craig and Jerome and Alfredo and then Tom again and then Sebastian with Alfredo . . . you get the point.

So that just left me with my appalling record. But here I was in London holding the phone number of a girl I had connected with, a girl I had fallen for instantly. We had talked and joked in the pub about trivial things, but I could see what my sister meant. She was a real character. She was confident, opinionated, but her most noticeable characteristic was that she was smouldering. It was easy to see why men were falling at her feet. She wasn't just beautiful with her blonde hair and English rose complexion; she worked it, she knew what she was doing. Men are pretty simple beasts, and she knew how to make them fall at her feet, how to make everything revolve around her. Oh, and her favourite film was Woody Allen's *Play It Again, Sam*. I was in love.

Scarred by my previous disastrous 'phoning a girl the next day' experience, I felt sick with worry when I dialled her number. I typed it into my new BT phone with caller ID. Caller ID had just come out, and it was genuinely quite thrilling to know who was calling before you picked up.

It was ringing. I was nervous. I cleared my throat. After taking advice from my sister, my plan was to ask her out for coffee.

'Hello, it's Michael,' I said, jovially, 'we met last night.'

'Who?' she said.

I couldn't believe it. Exactly the same as before. Why am I so forgettable?

'Michael, you gave me your number last night,' I said, like I did to the girl in Edinburgh.

My heart sank. I thought we had connected. She was definitely flirting. There were signs. How could this happen? Why was this always happening?

'I'm joking,' she said. 'How are you?'

She was joking. Funny. I nearly killed myself; but funny.

'I'm fine,' I said.

'So shall we go out then for dinner and talk about your script and stuff?' she asked.

Wow. Things had really turned around here. She sort of just asked ME out; to dinner. Not a coffee; dinner! The big one. The most romantic meal of the day, there's wine and candlelight. Wine relaxes you, gives you confidence and helps you lose your inhibitions. Coffee makes you tense, uptight and talk too quickly, and gives you bad breath. Dinner was great news as was the other thing she said: 'To talk about the script and stuff.' 'Stuff'! That's good, that's a good word. This wasn't just about the script, it was about stuff too. Stuff could mean anything.

'Yes, that's a great idea, when are you free?' I asked, revealing too much eagerness. I was hoping for that night, maybe the next day, certainly that week.

'Let me see, I can do two weeks on Friday,' she said, leafing through a diary.

Two weeks on Friday? What? How can anybody be busy that many nights in a row? The only things I had in my diary were the things already printed in it, like St George's Day, First Day of Spring and Christmas.

So we arranged to meet in over a fortnight at PizzaExpress

in West Hampstead, at 8 p.m. People who are having a dinner in a restaurant always book for 8 p.m. if they can. 8 p.m. is 'dinner in a restaurant time', although at home you never eat dinner at 8 p.m. Odd.

In the two weeks leading up to our date, I thought only of her. I'd only just met her. A few days previously I didn't know who she was, but now I was consumed by her. During this painful wait, I found out that I wasn't the only one with these feelings for her. It seemed she had several suitors with much the same level of infatuation as me. On one level the news was good, she didn't officially have a boyfriend. Men were in love with her, but she wasn't in love with them. They are not me. I have a date booked in, for dinner, to talk about 'stuff'. But then I panicked. Is that what she's doing every night? Is she having dinner with different men every night? Is that why she couldn't squeeze me in? Am I in some kind of auditioning process, like *The X-Factor*?

When the night finally arrived, I put on my cashmere coat and walked to PizzaExpress just around the corner. She wasn't in the restaurant, so I decided to wait outside for her, to greet her, and there she was jiggling to a halt in her sky-blue Mini Mayfair, looking stunning in a camel coat. 'Get in!' she shouted across the road.

I was standing in front of PizzaExpress. Why does she want me to get in the car? 'The restaurant is here,' I said, motioning towards it like a model revealing a prize on *The Price is Right*.

'Get in!' she repeated.

I crossed the road and squeezed into the smallest car on the road. We kissed on the cheek with predictable awkwardness. I went for one cheek, she went for two, there was a small headbutt.

'I thought we were going to PizzaExpress,' I said.

'No, I thought we'd meet here. We're going to Odette's in Primrose Hill, you'll like it.'

OK, fine. We're going to another restaurant. I, of course, hadn't heard of Odette's, mainly because I was not a multi-millionaire. I thought twenty-year-olds went out for pizza – not this one, she went to Odette's. She was sophisticated and classy. The bill was more than my rent.

I had never been to a restaurant like this before. The waiter offered me 'an apéritif'.

I had no idea what he was talking about, so I said, 'No, we'll just have a drink to start.' Kitty asked for a gin and tonic, so I asked for the same.

The waiter said, 'Would you like it on the rocks?'

'No,' I replied, 'I think we'll have it here at the table.' After the meal started, the waiter gave us each a sorbet. How was I to know it was to clear our palate? My palate had survived for twenty years without being cleansed between courses. I didn't even know what a sorbet was. 'I'm sorry, we haven't had our main course yet, this is dessert,' I said quite firmly, 'and anyway we didn't order ice cream!'

When I wasn't being naïve, we hit it off. She was wild and fun. I was relaxed with her. We talked easily to each other, we laughed and flirted. We didn't mention the script, the script was history. She didn't know what she wanted to do with her life; she had fallen into acting because of her family. She wasn't really an actress, and I wasn't really a writer. I had tried to write another film and couldn't. My writing started me on the road in comedy and led me to her.

After dinner, we got into her Mini and I kissed her. I think the size of the car helped. I was practically sitting on her lap as it was. I think if she'd had another car, like an American-style station wagon, I might not have been so bold. We shared our first kiss on Regent's Park Road outside Odette's restaurant. She dropped me home, and I watched her chug off as only the old Minis can.

It was the perfect night. I was smitten.

She liked me. We had had a wonderful night sealed with a kiss. If I played the right moves now, she would be mine. I needed to be cool, mysterious, maybe not call for a few days. But I didn't know anything about playing it cool. I didn't even know 'playing it cool' was an option, it never crossed my mind. I didn't want to waste any time whatsoever. In my opinion, we had found each other – let's go, let's start making a life together. So over the following days, I phoned her so many times that my behaviour could only be described as 'creepy'.

I didn't know it, but I was undoing all the good work of our night together. After days of harassing her for another dinner, Kitty suggested we meet for coffee. I was being downgraded. I was expecting an upgrade to the bedroom of my studio flat (which also happened to be the living room and kitchen), but only coffee was on offer. So we met for coffee, which served to add hyperactivity to my stalker-like behaviour. She seemed so different. I didn't understand it. I continued to smother her, making things worse for myself. She didn't even finish her coffee before making an excuse to leave. I tried to kiss her again and rather than turning her cheek she actually pulled away.

I went home devastated. My sister explained to me how I had played it all wrong and that I absolutely had to leave her alone for a while otherwise risk losing her for good. I felt sick. She left her hairclip on the table of the café in her haste to get away from me and I sat in my bedroom/living room/kitchen holding it, pining for her.

I followed my sister's advice and waited, for nearly an hour, before calling Kitty. I had already installed her number as Memory Preset 1 on my new BT phone. It rang and rang but went to the machine. After several times of calling, I started to withhold my number. I was now officially a stalker. How did this happen? A week ago we were relaxed, giggling and flirting in Odette's, and now I had ruined it. I tried her number intermittently over the next few days before she finally picked up.

'Hello,' she said.

'Hi, it's Michael,' I said, still clutching her hairclip.

'I know it is,' she said, coldly.

'You seemed a bit weird the other day, is everything OK?' I asked, wishing I could turn back time.

'Listen, Michael, I don't know if I gave you the wrong impression or anything, but I'm kind of busy at the moment and, you know, I am sort of seeing someone.'

Whoever she was seeing, it can't have been that serious because last week she was with me, kissing me. I had had my chance and I had monumentally blown it.

'Oh, OK, really, who?' I asked, defeated.

'It's complicated. I've got to go, OK?' she said, winding up the conversation and ending my life.

'But I thought,' I pleaded, 'I thought we had something, I thought, I just thought . . .'

'Well, you thought wrong,' she declared and hung up.

For all the heartache of unrequited love in my life, this was the lowest my heart had ever sunk.

H4E1N1D2

'"Hend", dat's only eight, I hev terrible letterrrs,' my grandmother said, trailing me for once in one of our Scrabble
games that were now supporting me financially. I was her
friend. She had favoured me since I was a little boy, she cared
for me, looked out for me and loved me. But she was cruel,
cold and judgemental to just about everybody else. Jim had
died while I was at university. Her living alone had accentu-
ated her eccentric behaviour. She had stopped talking to Lucy
for literally no reason; she was never that keen on her and
seized any excuse to 'cut her off'. She couldn't stand Steve,
wasn't all that keen on learning the names of my little brothers, and when it came to my mother, her daughter, she was
constantly disappointed. Her treatment of my mum was very
damaging and unnecessary. She continued to wield her purse
like a light sabre and change her will on a weekly basis. I was
torn. I could see that my grandmother was unkind, unpredictable and destructive, but she was old and my visits seemed
to make her genuinely happy. So I stuck it out. But what I
wasn't going to accept was the word 'hend'.

'There's no such word as "hend", Grandma,' I said.

'Don't be zo ztupid, put it down, eight points, "hend",
"hend"!' she said while waving her hands around.

'That's "hand", Grandma. I should know – I'm a writer,'
I corrected.

'OK, I vill do another one, but you're not a bluddy writer. I don't understand vot you are doing. You say you are a writer, but nobody is interrrested in your vork. You are a vaster and ven are you goin to get a girlfriend? Vot is wrong with you? . . .'

Just as she was mid-rant, her new Polish cleaner, Marta, entered, dusting and polishing. My grandmother had a remarkably high turnover of staff. This one had been on the scene my last few Scrabble visits. She had the body of a gymnast and seemed to be wearing some kind of white catsuit. She reminded me of Princess Aura, from *Flash Gordon*, who was responsible for my earliest sexual stirrings. I couldn't help but enjoy the view as she contorted herself while cleaning. As my grandma continued to rant, Marta caught my eye and licked her lips suggestively and blew me a kiss. I had been waiting years for a girl to do such a thing, but the setting wasn't ideal.

My mouth must have dropped open because my grandmother stopped her criticisms in mid-flow. 'Vy are you staring at Marta?' Then she turned to her Polish cleaner. 'Marta, daaarling, go and do the kitchen now, vill you, please?'

My grandmother then turned to me and uttered a sentence I will never forget. She said, 'Do you vant to fuck Marta?'

Now I'm sure as you're reading this, you might be thinking of your own grandmothers. Sweet little old ladies with black-and-white photos, who make tea and have biscuit tins and make their own jam. My grandmother was part-pimp.

'No, what are you talking about?' I said, horrified.

'She's alvays talking about you, ven are you coming round, Michael dis, Michael dat. She's after ze money, don't flatter yourself, but you can fuck her, because I know you are desperate. You never hev a girlfriend – are you virgin?' She was unstoppable.

'Grandma, please can we change the subject? If you must know, I have met a girl.' My grandmother's reaction to this was unexpected. I thought she would be pleased. This after all was what she said she wanted for me. But her face dropped.

'Really? You hev a girlfiend?' she asked, sceptically.

'No. But I have met someone, and she's the one. I can't stop thinking about her,' I admitted.

'She's not right for you,' my grandma concluded, based on no evidence whatsoever.

The thing with my grandma, and I suppose I was realizing it then, was that she wanted to be the most important person in my life. It was the same for my mother. My grandma never liked my dad or Steve, because she felt, in her warped way, that they were stealing her daughter from her, and now I was going to be on the receiving end. She wouldn't accept anyone as my girlfriend.

'Well, she's not interested in me. I blew it, but I'm going to get her. I'm in love with her,' I confessed.

'Don't vaste you time,' my grandma replied, nastily, 'she's only after ze money.'

I wanted to say, 'What money? My Scrabble winnings?' but it would have been no use. I felt sorry for my grandma; all she wanted was to play Scrabble with me every day. But that wasn't quite the future I wanted. When I got home, I took off my oversized cashmere coat that she had given me. It was a weight on my shoulders. It was symbolic. I wasn't really my own man. I was surviving on £50 notes from my grandma, I was wearing all these odd clothes she was buying for me. I had dropped out of university, I didn't have a job, nobody had committed to my script, I couldn't write another one, and I actually really wanted to have sex with Marta.

I was twenty-one years old. What was I going to do? Who

was I? But I already knew; I always knew what I wanted to do. I was already doing it unofficially. My whole life revolved around making people laugh. Every time I went out, I would come home and judge my performance. A good night for me was when I was funny. The only positive reactions to my script were to do with the jokes. I would hear people laughing when they read it, laughing out loud. Comedy was what I did. I'm a comedian. I'm going to be a stand-up comedian.

I announced the news to everybody. Here is a selection of their responses:

Lucy: 'Brilliant, Mike, that's brilliant. You're so funny, I'm so pleased for you.'

My mum: 'Oh my God, Michael, I'm so worried about you. That's a very difficult thing to do. Your father said it was the hardest job in the world.'

Sam: 'I'm funnier than you.'

Grandma: 'Don't be so bluddy stupid, vot kind of a job is dat? You vill starve if you do dat. Now, whose turn is it?'

Kitty: 'I can't talk right now, but please leave your message after the tone and I'll get back to you.'

At this point, I had never seen any live stand-up comedy. So Lucy and I headed to the Comedy Store in Piccadilly Circus and also booked tickets to see Jerry Seinfeld at the London Palladium in his only London performance. It was so wonderful to witness live comedy. I loved how instant the reaction was. I was used to packaging up scripts, sending them off and a month later being rejected. In stand-up, you spoke and if it was funny, people laughed. Bang, no argument. The comedians had their own points of view, their own styles and their own outlooks on life. The audience either enjoyed it or didn't. I had my own point of view, my own style and outlook on life, and I knew it was funny; I made people laugh every day.

I had been nervous going to see live stand-up. I was nervous because I thought that maybe I was kidding myself and that although I was funny in the pub, professional comedy might be another league of funny. However, I left the Comedy Store and the Palladium having laughed my head off, but confident that I could do it. When my sister and I went to an open-mike night at a club called the Comedy Café off Old Street, the new acts were awful, cringe-worthy apart from one, the host. He was a few years younger than me, had a beard, thick glasses and a stutter. He was called Daniel Kitson and he did worry me. Jerry Seinfeld hadn't, but this teenage misfit did. Seinfeld delivered wonderful word-perfect routines, but Kitson was just so natural and creative. He wasn't just funny, he had a stage presence that belied his awkward looks. I realized then that there was more to this business than just saying funny things. You need to have gravitas, the audience has to believe in you, you have to be a performer. I knew I could be funny, write funny, but would I connect with an audience? Well, there was only one way to find out.

The booker for the club, Hannah Chambers, went to Westminster School, and we had friends in common. So despite there being a long wait for a slot, she booked me in the following week for my first gig.

That week I was so terrified, I could barely eat or sleep. I wrote joke after joke of mixed quality, some bad, some worse. I was trying to write jokes in the style of Woody Allen or one-liners like Steven Wright. I didn't have a style, I had never done this before. I compiled my five minutes and rehearsed it endlessly in front of the mirror, holding my pen as a microphone (I've never owned a hairbrush, perhaps you've noticed). The jokes were forgettable, which is why I can't remember most of them. Here are the ones I can remember:

'I remember when I was born because it was the last time that I was inside a woman who looked genuinely pleased when I got out.'

'I have a car, it's a good runner. It gets me from A to B, except I live in Kew.'

'There are a lot of gay politicians. It gets confusing when they're in the closet, then they're in the cabinet, then they're in the closet and in the cabinet, then they're out of the closet but still in the cabinet, then they're out of the closet and the cabinet . . . and on to the back bench.'

I was mid-rehearsal when the phone rang. I flicked my eyes at my state-of-the-art caller ID. These were the digits I had been longing to see displayed for weeks.

'Hello?' I said.

'Hi, it's Kitty,' came the reply I thought I might never hear again, 'I heard from Joe that you were trying stand-up and I just wanted to wish you luck.'

We chatted for over an hour, like old friends even though we'd met only three times. I was elated after she had phoned. I suddenly felt that my life was now full of ambition. I had goals to be a stand-up and to make Kitty fall in love with me. I knew they might be long roads, but I was on them. I was at the beginning of the roads, the two long roads (I'm struggling with this analogy); it was a dual carriageway.

Wednesday night was my big night. My five minutes of jokes were spinning round and round in my head. I went with my sister and her boyfriend. Lucy had helped me so much that week that she knew my act word for word. On the Tube, I asked her if she could perform it for me. When we arrived at the club, I thought I might vomit. The Wednesday new-act night has free entry, so the audience was packed with people who don't like to pay for entertainment. I made this remark to my sister and she laughed. I should have mentioned that onstage, that's the kind of comedy I should do, that I do best, just say things that made me laugh.

Instead, I kept rehearsing my act, the keywords of which I had scribbled on my hand. There were ten of us on the bill, each doing five minutes. It was easy to spot the other acts loitering about, pacing nervously, biro all over their hands. I was on third. Daniel Kitson was again hosting and was just as hilarious as the previous week. He was enjoying himself and doing far too long between the acts. The audience were in the palm of his biro-free hand. He would introduce each act almost as if he was apologizing for the interruption to the Daniel Kitson Show, and it wasn't an interruption the audience appreciated because he was significantly funnier than everybody else.

The first two acts were decidedly amateurish. They got a few small laughs but nothing like the sound of the laughs Daniel was getting. I was next. My sister squeezed my hand, 'Good luck.' She left me waiting in the wings and took her seat. Daniel started bantering with the audience, who were rolling about with his every word. He had hit a goldmine with a character in the audience and wasn't about to pass over the reins. Occasionally, it would seem he was about to bring me onstage, but then something else hilarious would occur to him.

'OK, ladies and gentlemen, it's time for our next act.' He took out the list of acts from his pocket and read out my name, beginning my comedy career: 'Michael McIntyre.' The audience applauded as I walked towards the stage and took the

With my grandma in my Triumph Spitfire. Unfortunately she was the only female
I picked up in it.

I look quite good here with Lucy. I'm thin, I have a tan, but of course I have to
ruin it with those glasses and that 'I'm on my gap year' necklace.

Mr and Mrs McIntyre
on our big day at Combe
Florey in Somerset.

This is one of dozens of photos we have of the horses at our wedding.

One of the many photos Kitty and I took of each other on our honeymoon in the Maldives.

The poster from my first Edinburgh show in 2003 that enticed precisely one person to buy a ticket, and it was a 2-for-1 deal. The quote from the *Sun* was made-up.

PAUL DUDDRIDGE MANAGEMENT PRESENTS

Michael McIntyre

'The best new comic in the English speaking world'
THE SUN

9.30pm PLEASANCE 0131 556 6550
1–25 AUGUST (NOT 13TH)

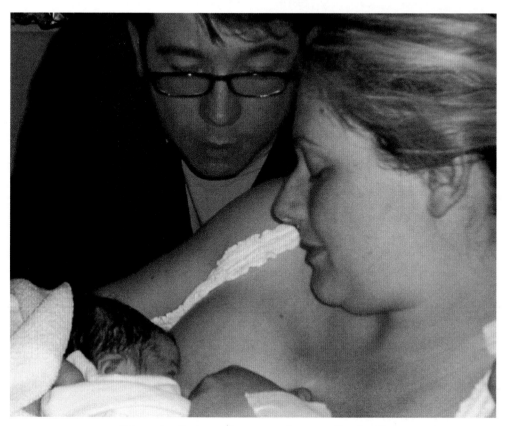

'How the fuck am I supposed to pay for this?'

With my gorgeous wife
at the *GQ* Men of the
Year Awards.

Comedy legends Ronnie Corbett, Rob Brydon and Billy Connolly with
'The King of Comedy' himself.

Whatever Prince Charles said, it can't have been THAT funny.

An advert for my DVD at Piccadilly Circus. It looks very cool but was actually revolving with several other adverts. I went to see it with Kitty and we had to drive around the block twelve times before we caught it!

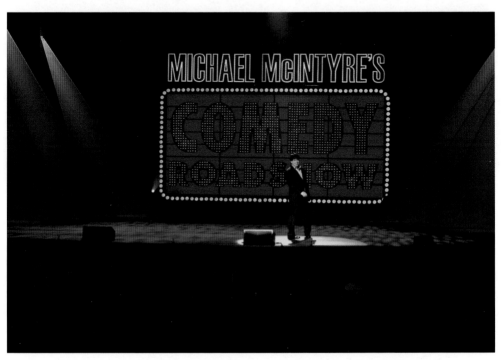

In action on my *Comedy Roadshow* in my favourite city of them all.

Basking in the spotlight during the recording of my second DVD, *Hello Wembley*.

microphone out of its stand. I had been advised to look into the middle distance. As I'm writing this I can see that there's a routine just in looking into the 'middle distance' as opposed to the 'long distance' or 'near distance', but then I was a comedy virgin with no instinct as to what might work onstage. So I looked for the middle distance, and gazed into it.

The view from the stage was surreal. Nothing can prepare you for all the expectant faces staring at you. I can't remember what I opened with, but I remember hearing the sound of laughter. It was amazing, I felt like Jerry Seinfeld. 'I'm a natural,' I thought, 'this is a breeze.' Unfortunately, I then proceeded to struggle for the remaining four and a half minutes. I walked offstage to lacklustre applause, and within moments Daniel had them back laughing at full volume.

But I was away, off the mark. Technically the gig was a disaster, but I did get one laugh, one solitary laugh, something to build on. I was so relieved that it was over and proud that I had cleared the most terrifying hurdle of my life so far. I sat in the audience at the Comedy Store and the Palladium confident in my ability to succeed as a stand-up, but now I knew that was because the comedians made it look easy. It wasn't.

I had been bitten by the comedy bug. I booked myself into several other new-act nights and I was now on the road, but what about the other lane of my road, the Kitty Lane? (Sorry, I genuinely thought I'd left this analogy behind.) Well, we started talking on the phone regularly. I had learned my lesson from before and eased off a bit. She and her friends, including my sister's boyfriend, would go to the Lansdowne, a pub in Primrose Hill. I would head down there to run into her accidentally on purpose. My natural instinct every time I saw her was to drop to my knees and ask for her hand in marriage, but I just about managed to hold it together. We were becoming friends. I was one of her many friends, an alarming number of whom were men with a similar yearning look to me. There was no doubt about it; I faced a lot of competition.

My days revolved around writing jokes, wondering whether to phone Kitty and hoping she would phone me. My state-of-the-art BT caller ID phone was playing a huge part in my life. To see her number flash up on the display was the highlight of my day. When my lease ran out on my studio flat in West Hampstead, I took my obsessive behaviour to the next level. I found a small one-bedroom flat two roads from the flat she shared with her parents. My new residence was in a 1930s block called Stanbury Court that overlooked her local pub, the Steeles, where we first met. She seemed to welcome my being local, and we started spending evenings together, drinking and laughing. At regular intervals, she would remind me that we were just good friends; either by saying the words 'We're just good friends' or telling me about other men in her life. Although this was like a dagger in my heart, I played it cool.

I once tried to make her jealous by telling her about a fictional girl I had met. Unfortunately, she seemed genuinely pleased for me. Not only that, but she really wanted to meet her. She was also very keen to come to one of my gigs, but that was out of the question. After my Comedy Café debut, I had had about five further gigs and still hadn't really added to my tally of one laugh.

The holy grail of stand-up for a new act is playing the Comedy Store in Piccadilly Circus. The Comedy Store has an amazing history. Everyone starts out at the Store: Lee Evans, Jack Dee, Jennifer Saunders, Dawn French, Eddie Izzard, Clive Anderson. Robin Williams has played there.

For me, just walking around the Store as a punter was magical. There are photos and press cuttings of its illustrious history adorning the walls. It's underground, the ceiling is low, the audience are packed in, surrounding the comedians, no more than a few feet away, the atmosphere is electric. It's the perfect comedy club.

The Store is owned and run by the legendary Don Ward, 'The Don'. Don could easily sit back and rest on his laurels. His club is the hottest comedy ticket in town. But Don has always supported new talent. On every bill of the best stand-ups around, he will give an 'open spot' a chance. It's part of the tradition of the Comedy Store and fun for the audience to see how a rookie fares; but for the new acts it's an incredible opportunity to test themselves at the highest level and potentially get a leg up in what my dad called 'the toughest business there is.'

Having spoken to other new acts during my first five ill-fated gigs, it became apparent that competition for 'open spot' places at the Comedy Store was fiercer than for the stool next to Kitty in the pub. Apparently, it was at least a six-month waiting list to get a five-minute spot. This was perfect for me; I needed those six months to prepare. My plan was to work every day and gig as much as possible. Then I would take my big chance at the Store with the big boys and under the watchful eye of Don Ward, who would then set me on the path to glory. I daydreamed about this sequence of events repeatedly. The audience would be whooping and cheering as I took my triumphant bow and then I would call for Kitty like Rocky calling 'Adrian' having defeated Apollo Creed in *Rocky I* (Adrian? Apollo Creed must have thought he'd been beaten by a homosexual). Kitty would run into my arms as the audience gave me a standing ovation.

This dream was a long way off. I had only received one laugh as a stand-up. Kitty had no romantic interest in me and thought I was seeing a fictional girl. Also the Comedy Store has a strict policy about the audience getting onstage. Enormous bouncers are poised throughout the show, so Kitty would have been physically removed from the club before she made it to my arms.

I telephoned the Comedy Store and got a date, in one year. Although it seemed like too long, I felt that at least I'd be ready. I took a deep breath when I hung up the phone. I had one year to make this daydream a reality. Rather than getting straight to work, I decided to have the daydream again. Just as I reached the bit where the audience were whooping and cheering, the phone rang. My heart leapt at the prospect of Kitty's numbers lighting up the display but it simply read 'Unavailable'. 'Unavailable' is a gamble, but my life was at the stage where I had to gamble, I had to pick it up.

'Hello?'

'Hi, is that Michael?'

'Yes.'

'It's Charlotte from the Comedy Store. We've just had an open spot drop out of the show tonight. I can't get hold of anyone, and your number was in front of me. So do you want to go on?'

'Tonight?' I said in disbelief.

'Yes, I'm sorry it's such short notice.'

This was a split-second decision. I wanted six months to prepare, I thought I had a year, now I had an afternoon.

'OK, I'll do it.'

18

I had been going to the Comedy Store with my sister regularly since I became a stand-up. I watched the acts thinking, 'I'm going to be on that stage one day.' It was an exhilarating feeling. The best comic I had seen there was Terry Alderton. He was sensational, a powerhouse who had the whole audience on their feet at the end. It was inspiring to see a man reduce an audience to tears of laughter.

As I headed out on the Tube with my sister to make my Comedy Store debut, I thought about Terry's performance and realized I had made a terrible mistake. I was totally out of my depth. I was going to ruin everything. I was so nervous and panicked, I was struggling to speak in sentences to my sister as the Tube rattled along the Northern Line from Belsize Park to Leicester Square.

'This was a mistake,' I announced dramatically. 'Don Ward is going to see me and think I'm shit. Because I am shit.'

'Michael, you can do this. I think deep down you know that, which is why you took the gig. Don't think about Don Ward,' Lucy encouraged.

'Yes, but I should have been more prepared for when he sees me for the first time. You don't get a chance to do impressions.'

What I was trying to say was 'You don't get a second chance to make a first impression', but due to the stress my brain was malfunctioning. Lucy tried to make sense of my remark, leading to a bizarre conversation that almost ended up with me trying impressions at the gig.

I was a mess.

When we arrived at the Comedy Store, the queue was enormous. The club holds 400 people. A line of 400 people seems to go on for ever. I took my place at the back of the queue, with the audience. I checked in at the box office and was pointed towards the dressing room behind the stage. My sister found a seat at the back of the club and crossed her fingers.

I don't remember the other comedians on that night apart from Terry Alderton. I wanted to tell him how much I enjoyed his performance the other night, but rather than get the words in the wrong order, no words originated from my mouth whatsoever. In fact I couldn't even get my mouth open. I wasn't just nervous, I was in danger of passing out. The dressing room of the Comedy Store is tiny. There is a white board with the bill listed on it, and there was my name.

'Michael MacIntire (5 mins).'

The 'McIntyre' had two spelling mistakes, but there it was, my name in marker pen, on the bill at the Comedy Store. Just a few months after I had realized that maybe all the laughs I get in my everyday life could actually lead to a career as a stand-up comedian, here I was at the home of stand-up to find out.

What I didn't know then, as I paced around the dressing room with my heart beating out of my chest, is that the Comedy Store is actually the easiest gig on the circuit. The five gigs I had done were for small audiences of people who hadn't paid for entertainment. They knew you were a new act and had low expectations. Often most of the audience at these 'open mike' nights are made up of the other 'open spots' and their friends. The gigs are poorly lit, the sound is bad, it's just some bloke standing in the corner of a pub function room. But at the Comedy Store, conditions were perfect. When the 'open spots' are introduced, the compere doesn't tell the audience they are a new act until afterwards. All the comedians are introduced in the same way. So when the compere says, 'Ladies and gentlemen, are you ready for your next act of the evening?' they are expecting a seasoned professional when they cheer their encouragement. 'Please welcome Michael McIntyre . . .'

I walked onstage with the audience whooping and cheering encouragement. This time, when the first thing I said got a laugh, it was the most magnificent sound I had ever heard. The Comedy Store laugh is like no other, it reverberates in the bunker-like room and smacks you in the face. The deafening sound of the audience laughter washed away all my nerves, and I didn't just tell my jokes, I expressed them, I shared them with the audience and remembered why I thought they were funny. I left the stage to appreciative applause. The compere then told the audience it was one of my first gigs, and as I re-entered the dressing room, I received another round of applause. Terry Alderton was eating a plateful of food; he applauded by banging his fork on his plate and with his mouth full said, 'You were really funny, mate.'

I barely had enough time to take a breath and digest the feeling of my first successful gig when the door swung open to reveal The Don. Like Clint Eastwood swaggering into a saloon, the room went quiet as the other comedians' heads bowed with respect. He shook a few hands before making his way over to me. 'Michael, well done,' said The Don, as we too shook hands.

My daydream was coming to life, although an aspect of

this meeting that hadn't appeared in my fantasizing was that my sleeve then became caught on his jacket. I tugged at it, but it wouldn't free itself. I didn't want to spoil this moment by pointing out this fabric faux pas.

'You were very good,' Don said. 'How long have you been going?'

'This is my sixth gig,' I said. He was suitably impressed. I subtly fiddled with my sleeve, but it remained caught.

'Follow me, we'll book you back in for a ten-minute spot.'

Don walked out of the dressing room and I followed, although in truth I had no choice as we were connected to each other. We walked through the audience who were milling about in the interval; people were patting me on the back and congratulating me. I should have been lapping up this newfound adoration, but I was mainly concerned with the issue at hand, or rather sleeve. He took me to his little office at the back of the club.

'Take a seat,' Don said, opening up his big red diary in his office. He pencilled in another gig for two weeks' time, we shook hands and then we both left the office. This was my moment to leave and enjoy my wonderful night, one of the best nights of my life, the moment to find my sister and celebrate, to watch the rest of the show and hang out with the other comics. But I was physically attached to Don Ward.

Don walked back towards the dressing room, and I was forced to go with him. He looked at me, puzzled as to my continued presence. He then stopped to chat with some staff, and I remained by his side. I continued tugging at my sleeve, but it was no use. I started to panic that I was going to ruin everything. He gave me a look that confirmed my fears that my enforced hanging around was starting to annoy him. He then walked around the club seemingly trying to shake me off. The show restarted, he stood at the back to watch with me uncomfortably close by his side.

'You can go, you know,' Don eventually said with more than a hint of annoyance.

I gave my sleeve a final yank and thankfully freed myself from The Don. I think I just about got away with it. Don thought I was funny, a bit clingy maybe, but funny. I had a booking for two weeks' time. I would play the Comedy Store twice in a fortnight, I was up and running, I felt like a comedian for the first time.

The saying goes, 'You're only as good as your last gig.' Well, in my mind that meant I was now a sensation. My first success in stand-up went straight to my head. I informed everyone I met that I was a comedian. I recounted the story over and over again: '. . . and then they called back and said we've got a spot tonight . . . and I was like . . . TONIGHT? OK, I'll do it . . .' Another thing I did in my overexcitement was to invite everybody I knew to come to the Comedy Store in a fortnight to witness at first hand my rising stardom.

The person I most wanted to watch me at the Comedy Store was Kitty. I was convinced that the dream I had had was about to come true, in just two weeks. All I had to do was repeat my performance with her in the audience, make sure my clothing didn't become attached to Don Ward and she would fall helplessly in love with me.

The only problem was that Kitty said she wasn't available on the night of my Comedy Store booking. Not available? My dream is coming true here and she's unavailable. It transpired that the news was even worse than that. She was going out with somebody else that night, this other guy, the 'it's complicated' one. I couldn't believe it. I knew she was seeing someone, but I also knew that we were talking on the phone every day and when she wasn't with him she was with me. This was my big night, she should be there for me even if we were 'just good friends'. But I had to face the reality that she was more than 'just good friends' with 'it's complicated' guy, and when it came down to it, she chose him. When I put this to her, she denied it and said it was just due to timing, this was a longstanding arrangement.

I was starting to lose my 'playing it cool' strategy. 'Just cancel him, this is important to me,' I pleaded.

'I can't, Michael,' she said, adamantly.

'This is a massive night for me and I want you to be there, you should be there,' I continued.

'I don't understand why. Why can't I just come to another gig? I've been asking to come to your gigs before and you wouldn't let me, what's so special about this one. What's the big deal? You're overreacting,' she said.

She was right. I was overreacting. I was in love with her and I was pinning my hopes on this one night that I had fantasized about so much that I had convinced myself it was becoming a reality. But it wasn't reality. The reality was obvious. She liked me, but not enough, and not even as much as this other guy. Seeing me have a triumphant gig at the Comedy Store wasn't going to change that. I was wasting my time here. I realized that just like every other girl I had feelings for while growing up, she just didn't quite feel the same way. I wasn't going to give up, I couldn't, I loved her. But after that conversation, I stopped dreaming.

I had a job to do. This Comedy Store night was massive for me. I had invited friends to see me and if I had another good gig, Don Ward could catapult me up the comedy ladder. In my desperation to make this happen, I made a terrible decision that reflected my lack of experience. I decided to perform a completely new set. Don had heard my jokes. I thought that performing a brand new ten minutes would be the most impressive thing to do. So I went on with untried and untested material and died a thunderous death onstage, in front of all my friends. It's one thing dying on a bill of 'open spots' because most of them are having a similar experience. But at the Comedy Store, where the standard is so high, it's horrific. It was just as painful for the audience as it was for me.

Even today, if I tried to write a brand-new ten minutes and perform it at the Comedy Store, I would struggle, guaranteed. So imagine how awful it was. The only salvation was that Kitty was out with 'it's complicated' guy. Suddenly I was thrilled that she had another man in her life and we were 'just good friends'.

Oh, and I nearly forgot, somebody in the audience shouted, 'You're shit.' Like I needed confirmation from this arsehole. I'm losing all my dignity, humiliating myself in front of 400 people, but this guy felt that wasn't enough. Welcome to the world of stand-up comedy: when it works, there's nothing better, and when it doesn't, there's nothing worse.

This time when I returned to the dressing room, the other comedians ignored me entirely. The door opened a few times, but it wasn't Don. Don wasn't coming this time. I couldn't bear to face my friends, so I just slipped out. I had no future bookings and no chance of any – maybe in a year, if I was lucky. What a dramatic turnaround. My dad said this was the toughest job there is, and I had just found out why.

You're only as good as your last gig.

It was important to get back in the saddle as soon as possible, so I performed at a series of open-mike nights with varying success. I just couldn't make myself nearly as funny onstage as I could offstage. Having blown my big chance at the Comedy Store, my opportunities to progress were now limited. I telephoned Jongleurs Comedy Club. Jongleurs is a chain of clubs throughout the UK; they have open spots at their London clubs in Camden and Battersea. Again, I was given a spot in a year at their Camden club. This time I hoped I wouldn't get a phone call back. So I had that in the diary to work towards, and I also had the new-act competitions. I entered four competitions, the Hackney Empire 'New Act of the Year', the *Daily Telegraph* 'New Act of the Year', the BBC 'New Comedian of the Year' and 'So You Think You're Funny?' run by Channel 4. Over the years the winners of these competitions have included the likes of Peter Kay, Alan Carr, Rhod Gilbert, Lee Mack and Dylan Moran.

To give you an idea of the standard of comedy I was producing at this time, I was knocked out in the first round of the Hackney one, the *Telegraph* one and the BBC one. My final chance was the aptly named 'So You Think You're Funny?' This was the competition that Peter Kay won with his first few gigs and that set him on the road to National Treasure. The unfortunate thing for me was that I wasn't so sure I was that funny when I headed out of my flat to the first round at Madam Jo Jo's in Soho. But there wasn't a competition called, 'I'm not so sure if I am funny any more', so off I went to try my luck once again.

Walking out of my flat, I saw Kitty's blue Mini parked outside the Steeles pub. I considered not popping in, fearful of finding her in the arms of 'it's complicated' guy, but thought I had little to lose at this point. It had been six months since the Comedy Store gig, and we were now genuinely friends. My pursuit of her had been curtailed. I couldn't keep it up, especially as she offered me no signs of hope. I had also had a few mini-romances of my own. I had no real feeling for these girls, but I was starting to become more self-assured – getting rid of my cashmere coat certainly helped. So when Kitty suggested she came with me to the gig, it wasn't a big deal. It was natural.

I wasn't trying to impress her, we were just two people sharing an evening together. Friends. I wasn't particularly nervous about performing for her because I wasn't performing for her; I was performing for me and for the judges.

Stephen K. Amos was the host. He was warm, funny and generous to the other acts. He introduced me as looking like Hugh Grant. It was a relaxed atmosphere. I didn't have to tell myself I had nothing to lose; I genuinely felt that way. The result was a very comfortable and naturally funny gig. It was effortless. I had lost my air of desperation in both my performance and the way I was behaving with Kitty.

It was almost as if I had given up trying. Trying to be funny onstage and trying to make Kitty like me. I had started to be myself. We were inseparable for the next few days. Something had changed, something natural and wonderful was happening between us. I wasn't overexcited by this shift in our relationship. I didn't have to play it cool, I felt cool. She asked me to take her out for dinner as she had something she wanted to say to me. I booked her favourite restaurant, Villa Bianca, an Italian in Hampstead. She picked me up in her Mini as she had done two years before, the last time we had been out for dinner. We held hands as we walked from the car to the restaurant.

'So what is it?' I asked, confident that what she was about to say was what I had been waiting for. Waiting for two years and longer, much longer. Nothing was as important to me as her, nothing meant more. I was prepared to just be her friend, just to know her. But it seemed my backing off had allowed to happen what I always felt was inevitable.

'I think I'm falling in love with you,' she said.

At last.

19

Finally I got my romantic comedy ending. The credits would roll over snapshots of our future together, on our wedding day, sipping cocktails on our honeymoon, cradling our newborn in the delivery room, that kind of thing. Although there was some unfinished business to attend to, the situation with 'it's complicated' guy.

'I'm going to meet him tonight and tell him,' Kitty said a few days later, waking up in my undecorated untidy one-bedroom flat.

'Meet him?' I said. 'Call him, text him, why do you have to meet him? Can't you just not return his calls? He'll get the message. Or leave him a message – in fact, I think this is a good idea. Why don't you leave an outgoing message on your answer phone telling all other men in your life that you're with me now? "Hi, I'm sorry I can't take your call, I'm in love with Michael. Please leave your congratulations message after the tone, and I won't call you back."'

'Michael, stop worrying. I should meet with him out of respect. We are very close, and I'm not going to see him any more, so I think I should tell him in person,' she reiterated.

'He's not your boyfriend, you're not a couple, there's nothing to break off. I don't get the relationship between you two,' I said, refusing to back down.

'It's complicated,' she repeated for the millionth time.

It seemed I had little choice but to trust her as she went out that night with 'it's complicated' guy. I suppose I understood.

I had to trust and respect her. I just didn't trust him. I know what men are like; I am one. He was going to try everything to make her change her mind about me and that really pissed me off. She might think she's saying goodbye to him, but she's actually giving him a final chance.

After she left my flat for the first time in days, I spent the afternoon amplifying my fears to fever pitch. I asked her to come back to me later that night, but she said I was being 'Silly, and it'll be late. We'll talk tomorrow.' I knew I couldn't stay at my flat alone that night, counting the minutes until morning, so I went round to a friend's house. He lived just up the road in Belsize Park, equidistant from my rented flat and the flat Kitty shared with her parents. I continued to worry, panic and work myself up while getting steadily drunk on cheap white wine. Repeating myself again and again, slurring my words, belching, ranting like a madman:

'Why does she have to meet him?'

'Why can't she come back to my flat?'

'I thought she loved me, she's supposed to love me.'

'What does she mean, she'll be home late, how late? Why late? How long does it take to tell someone to fuck off? Let's time it . . . "Fuck off" . . . how long did that take?'

At about 1 a.m., I stumbled to my feet and said goodbye to my friend, who must have been thrilled to see the back of me. Standing on his doorstep, I could have turned left to my flat or right to Kitty's. My judgement clouded by alcohol, I concluded that I should go down Kitty's road to see if her blue Mini was there, to make sure she was back. She should be back; it was 1 a.m. As long as I knew she had returned, I could take myself home, pass out and then wake up and hopefully spend the rest of my life with her.

I staggered up her road towards the substantial Victorian

house where she lived in the ground floor flat, but there was no sign of the Mini. There were also plenty of available spaces. She wasn't back, it was one in the morning, and she wasn't back. I was starting to despair, and then just at the moment I was walking past her front door, I heard a car. I turned around and caught an unmistakable glimpse of her Mini chugging up her road.

'Shit!' She can't see me here. This looks awful! So I quickly dived behind a bush in her front garden. Luckily, it was a bushy bush so I was pretty well hidden.

I heard her park her car. In the dead of the night only her sounds broke the still atmosphere. Her turning the engine off, shutting the car door and locking it, her high heels clicking on the pavement getting louder as she approached. I was confident she hadn't seen me.

But then her footsteps stopped. She was standing directly in front of the bush. I remained motionless, trying to suppress my breathing. What a mess I had got myself into this time. I'm convinced that only I could have created such a surreal moment. I have found the girl of my dreams, she has pronounced her love to me and within our first week together here I am, hiding in a bush in her front garden at one o'clock in the morning.

'Michael?' she said to the bush, tentatively.

I had no choice. I bolted upright from the shrubbery and tried to act as normal as possible.

'Hello, darling,' I said, just like a husband to his wife coming home from the office.

'What the fuck are you doing hiding in my garden? Have you been here all night? Are you insane?' she shouted.

This was a key moment in our relationship. The fact is, I am slightly unhinged, otherwise how would I have found myself in this mess? As I tried to explain how I came to be in such a compromising situation, Kitty (as she told me later) stood there looking at me popping out of the bush and had to decide if she was up for this. Could she cope with this badly dressed, floppy-haired comedian-wannabe, riddled with anxiety?

'Do you want to come in or are you planning on sleeping in the garden?' she said. The answer was yes. She loved this badly dressed, floppy-haired comedian-wannabe, riddled with anxiety. I stayed the night, and the next day I moved in while we looked for a place of our own. We would live together from that day on. I asked her how her evening went.

'It's complicated,' she said. I deserved that.

The following night it was time to officially 'meet the parents'. An informal evening drink was planned for the four of us in the living room of their modest two-bedroom rented flat. Despite having known Kitty for two years, I had never met her parents. This was a big night for me, I knew her parents would be analysing me. It didn't help that her mother, Alexandra, was an actual psychoanalyst. Her father is Simon Ward, the esteemed actor.

As soon as I met them, I was put at ease. I walked into their living room and Simon, who had been reading *The Times*, jumped up to greet me. He was exceptionally charming and welcoming. Alexandra looked lovely and had obviously made a real effort for the occasion. Her hair had that 'just walked out of a salon' look. She seemed nervous, more nervous than me. I was so flattered by this. I thought I was on trial at this meeting; it never crossed my mind that they might feel the same way.

After the introductions, Kitty and I sat down on a sofa flanked by her parents sitting on comfy chairs. I treated it a little bit like a job interview, trying to convince them with my answers that their daughter had chosen well. Rather than saying that I had dropped out of university, I simply said, 'I read the sciences at Edinburgh.' Rather than say I had never been paid as a comedian, I said, 'I'm a stand-up comedian. I play the Comedy Store, are you familiar with it?' Simon seemed to be warming to me, although he might just have been acting, and launched into several highly entertaining theatrical anecdotes.

Alexandra, however, treated the occasion as if I was interviewing Kitty. She spent the whole evening selling her daughter to me. Not only had I been pursuing Kitty for two years, but I thought it was obvious to anyone that she was well out of my league.

'I love your home, Alexandra, have you lived here long?'

'Kitty's a wonderful swimmer,' she announced, 'she enjoys reading and travelling and speaks GCSE French.'

It was like she was reading from a CV. I didn't know how to respond.

'Great news,' I said. 'My mother lives in France. That will be useful, and she has a pool, too. There will be many opportunities to swim and speak French.'

Alexandra ploughed on. 'Her cooking is improving all the time, and she has an excellent backhand. She wears a size four shoe, the perfect size, I've always thought.'

Meanwhile, Simon continued telling his stories. On several occasions Simon and Alexandra were speaking at the same time, over one another. They were eccentric to say the least. Simon would be mid-story about performing with Laurence Olivier, while Alexandra revealed how Kitty mastered the yo-yo at a surprisingly early age. They had been married for over thirty years, and it was apparent that Alexandra had heard all of Simon's stories several times before. Every time he started a new one, she would mumble, 'Oh no, not that one again.' Towards the end of the evening, Simon told a story that he had told towards the beginning of the evening.

'For God's sake, Simon,' Alexandra interrupted, 'you've already told that story tonight. Now, Michael,' she said, turning to me, 'have I told you about Kitty's needlework?'

I had a wonderful evening with them. They were personable, charming and entertaining, and I've loved them from that moment on.

The family introductions were off to an excellent start. With my mum now living in France, next up was my grandma. We arranged to go out for lunch, but Kitty had to cancel, as she was unwell. It was clear from my grandmother's reaction to this cancellation that my suspicions about her not actually wanting me to have a girlfriend were valid.

'Vot do you mean, she can't make it?' she said.

'She's not feeling well, we'll have to reschedule.'

'I don't like the sound of this girl, Michael, she not right for you, she's verry sickly, she's always ill. You're too young to settle down, play ze field a bit. Vot about Marta? My cleaner?'

So it was with some trepidation that I took Kitty with me the following week to my grandmother's plush flat in Putney. Kitty was naturally very nervous, but I genuinely believed that, despite her reservations, my grandma would fall in love with her as I had.

The signs weren't good when she opened her front door and – rather than say hello to Kitty – she asked first about the milk she had requested me to bring.

'Oh fantastic!' she exclaimed with a beaming smile when she saw us, giving me false hope. 'You rememberred ze milk.'

'Grandma, this is Kitty,' I said, with my girlfriend smiling beside me.

'I know, you better come in,' my grandmother said, now with her back to us and scuttling along her luxurious corridor.

When we finally settled down with drinks – that I had to offer and pour – my grandmother proceeded to take the opposite approach to Alexandra. Rather than try to promote me to Kitty, she set about discrediting me.

'Kitty, daaaarling, do you know zat Michael is a universiity dropout? He has no qvalifications, nothing.'

'He's doing well though now, as a comedian,' Kitty said.

'Daaarling Kitty, listen to me, I hev known Michael his whole life, never hes he made me laugh. He is meny things, but not a comedian. The funniest thing he hes ever said to me vas "Grandma, I vant to be a comedian." He is a lozer!'

'Anyone want any more drinks?' I asked, interrupting, but Grandma wasn't to be stopped.

'I buy everything for him. I bought a car, do you know about this? He crashed it, this is his life, a car crash, a pretty girl like you could do better.' Then she turned to me, as if Kitty wasn't in the room. 'What about Marta? You have feeling for her, yes?'

'Grandma, what are you talking about?' I said, jumping to my feet, 'I've never even spoken to Marta! I'm going to get us some more drinks, let's change the subject.'

'Who's Marta?' I heard Kitty saying as I left for the respite of the kitchen.

While I was getting the drinks, my grandma said something to Kitty that we still laugh about today.

'I'll tell you something else, Kitty daarling, when Michael comes here to wisit, he teks the most enormous shits, he has the smelliest shits, like nothing I hev ever known, the whole place stinks for days, I hev to fumigate. Is dis the kind of life you vant, Kitty?'

It was funny, but it was ultimately very sad. My grandma was jealous of my girlfriend. It was a bizarre and unhealthy situation. She was spiralling out of control and over the next few months became increasingly rude to and about Kitty. She created an untenable situation. She would stop at nothing to get Kitty out of my life. She was forcing me to make a choice between them, so I did what was right. I split up with Kitty so that I could play Scrabble with my grandma and inherit her millions.

I'm kidding.

My grandma and I had a flaming row, and true to form she cut me out of her will. I was deeply hurt that my grandma could turn her back on me. She had fallen out with so many others that perhaps it was only a matter of time, but I thought our relationship was different. As unhappy as I was, I was also pleased that I could spare Kitty from the same manipulative unpleasantness that had dominated my mother's life. I wanted my life with Kitty to be free from all that rubbish. I had hoped my grandma would change, but it wasn't to be. So Kitty and I started our life together away from her shadow.

My grandmother had always been my safety net, she was always there to look after me and bail me out of any financial trouble. Now it was time for me to be my own man. Something I wished I had become years earlier. I didn't have a penny and neither did Kitty. All my stand-up comedy was unpaid, and Kitty had decided not to pursue an acting career. So when we moved into a £190-a-week flat in Fleet Road, just down the road from Kitty's parents, we had no means of paying for it, let alone eating.

The next nine months were my first experience of real life.

It was tough. Kitty got work as a nanny with horrendous hours, and I sold mobile phones for a telesales company. I worked for a company called Dial-a-Mobile, maybe you've seen their adverts in the back of newspapers. I sat in a vast call centre with my headset on surrounded by hundreds of other sales people all nattering away about free minutes, off-peak call charges and free in-car chargers.

I took it remarkably seriously, unlike when I was working at Partizan in my gap year. I desperately needed money. I don't know what happened to me. I think I became slightly hypno-tized by all the jargon and rhetoric from my Dial-a-Mobile supervisors. I became obsessed with selling mobile phones. I went from living my life for laughs to living my life for sales targets. The pay was appalling, but the more mobile phones I could sell, the more money I could earn. I was like a robot.

About a million times a day, I would pick up the phone at work saying, 'Hello, welcome to Dial-a-Mobile. Are you call-ing about the new Nokia 3310, with 600 free minutes per month and free weekend calls to landlines?'

After a while I started picking up the phone like that at home by mistake. 'No, Michael, it's your mother, what are you talking about?'

It was embarrassing, although I did sell my sister Lucy a phone that way.

Our flat was unfurnished, so Kitty and I would spend most weekends browsing the showroom of IKEA in Wembley. I spent countless Saturday afternoons clutching my IKEA half-pencil and paper tape-measure, discussing the relative merits of beech veneer and birch veneer surrounded by couples having similar conversations.

Everything looked such good value in the IKEA show-room. I would constantly be amazed by the price. 'Forty quid for this Aneboda coffee table – wow, that's unbelievably cheap!'

Then I'd get downstairs to the warehouse and the Aneboda coffee table turned out to be just a pile of wood and some Allen keys.

'Forty quid for this? Are they joking? They may as well have given me an axe and directions to a forest in Sweden. What a rip-off!'

My first man drawer contained about a thousand Allen keys. Who is Allen Key? I bet he's amazing at self-assembly.

My favourite trip to IKEA was when we were looking at beds and the sales assistant asked, 'Have you decided whether you want the bed?'

And I said, 'I'm going to sleep on it.'

Neither Kitty nor the sales assistant laughed, but I found that hilarious.

'So you don't want it?' asked the sales assistant.

'No,' I said, 'but can I interest YOU in a new Nokia 3310, with 600 free minutes per month and free weekend calls to landlines?'

Apart from IKEA, Kitty and I also searched the classifieds in the local paper for bargain furniture. We found a sofa bed for £50 belonging to a gentleman in Highgate. We went round to his flat, spending most of the journey convincing ourselves he was a murderer. He showed us into his office, and we both sat on his for sale navy blue two-seater sofa bed for about ten seconds before agreeing to buy it. If only we had sat on it for longer, because after thirty seconds it starts inexorably to turn itself from a sofa into a bed. You would sit on it and gradually lie down until you were flat on the floor.

It was the early days of eBay, and I found a gorgeous sofa

at the unbelievable bargain price of £20. 'Perfect condition
. . . As new', the blurb went. The photo made it look stunning. The sofa arrived a week later, in a jiffy bag; it was for a
doll's house. I put it opposite the 'sofa that turns itself into
a bed after thirty seconds' with the Aneboda coffee table in
the middle, and our living room was complete.

Our bed was Kitty's old one from her parents' flat. The
good news was that the bed was King size; the bad news was
that the bedroom was Queen size. The bed only just fitted
into the room and had to be wedged at a slight angle, meaning each morning Kitty and I would wake up squashed against
the wall. You know the popular expression, 'Did you get out
of the wrong side of the bed this morning?' Well, I couldn't
get out of either side of the bed; I had to roll through the
door at the end of the bed.

The kitchen was bogey green with appliances from the
Middle Ages, and we mainly ate blue-and-white-striped Tesco
value food. In fact, we had so much Tesco value food I
suggested to Kitty that I painted the kitchen with blue and
white stripes, but Kitty said it was an unnecessary expense.
There was a door in the kitchen housing the toilet. The toilet
was in the kitchen. Who would design a flat with a loo in the
kitchen? Kitty would come home from a hard day at work,
kissing me in the kitchen and saying, 'Hi, darling, something
smells good?'

'Oh no, that's peach air freshener. I've just been to the loo,'
I would say.

The only asset we had was Kitty's Mini, which would probably have fetched about £500 in *Loot*. When Kitty had a small
collision in Hampstead Garden Suburb that dented the front
bumper, the front right wheel was blocked against the bent
metal of the car. The result was that the wheel would not

turn to the right, as the tyre was blocked. The car was no longer capable of turning right.

Unfortunately, we only had third-party insurance and no means to pay for the repairs. But not wanting to lose our only asset, we continued using the car only turning left. I would carefully plan each journey with an *A–Z*, so that we could navigate to our destination without having to turn right. We survived for two weeks until I was pulled over by the police for driving the wrong way around a mini-roundabout. Years later I told this story on the BBC panel show *Would I Lie to You?*, where one team has to tell unlikely stories and the other team has to guess if they're true or not. I won.

I may have been struggling at this time in my life, but I was gathering material for my later career in television. After my *Would I Lie to You?* tale, our next car, a white Austin Metro Princess that set me back £395, provided me with several stories for my *Top Gear* interview in 2009. The petrol gauge was broken, so I had to check the milometer and mentally calculate the miles per gallon to know when I needed to refuel. This worked pretty well until the milometer broke as well. Then I had to drive along guessing how many miles I had driven and then calculate the miles per gallon. This worked less well. Needless to say I ran out of petrol several times and spent a lot of time filling up my jerrycan at petrol stations. The first time it happened, I didn't have a jerrycan and totally forgot that they were called jerrycans. I said to the petrol station attendant, 'I need a . . . oh what's it called? A . . . you know . . . thing you put petrol in . . .'

And the attendant said, 'Car?'

The closest I got was 'petrol suitcase'. Jeremy Clarkson and the *Top Gear* audience all had a good laugh at the nightmare that was my life at the time.

But, for all our financial woes, Kitty and I were happy, deliriously happy together and in love. We lived on the philosophy that 'love is all you need', until the bailiffs knocked on the door and refused to take 'love' as payment. Then we realized we would also need some cash. My stand-up 'career' was not providing any. I made the semi-finals of the 'So You Think You're Funny?' competition after the performance that Kitty had witnessed. But I did not make the final, let alone win it. I continued to do the occasional new-act night, but they were so few and far between that I had little chance of improving. I also suffered terribly with nerves. At the beginning it was new and exciting and I had the excuse of being a novice. But now there was so much at stake, and with every failure my dream of being a stand-up comedian was moving further away and the reality of becoming a supervisor at Dial-a-Mobile was moving closer.

20

My fellow new acts were beginning to make an impact in the industry, something I was simply not threatening to do. Hannah Chambers, who gave me my first gig at the Comedy Café, was moving into management. She saw all the new acts walking through her doors and was picking the best ones. She was, and still is, excellent at talent-spotting. Her initial picks from the open-mike nights were Daniel Kitson and Jimmy Carr. I asked her if she would consider me, but despite being encouraging, she simply wasn't interested.

The truth is, I wasn't very good. I couldn't compete with Jimmy and Daniel. Daniel was honest and open and naturally funny, and Jimmy had wonderfully written material. I was naturally funny, but didn't know how to replicate this onstage, and my material was average. If I were an agent, I wouldn't have represented me. There's a comedy website called Chortle; it's an online bible for British stand-ups and is extraordinarily comprehensive. I knew it was only a matter of time before the site reviewed me and checked every day. When I saw my name on the front page of the website in the 'Latest Reviews' section, I nearly vomited with nerves. I wanted a career in stand-up, and here was the first clue as to whether that was possible. As upsetting and deflating as it was at the time, the review was accurate. It ended with: 'Michael McIntyre is the equivalent of a Marks & Spencer pullover. Dependable and durable, but nothing to get excited about.'

I was devastated. I was so desperate for an endorsement,

for somebody to see that I was talented. But the reality was that comedians were becoming successful around me, and I was being roundly dismissed. I showed it to Kitty, who was typically positive and wise: 'What's wrong with you, Michael? Not only is this just one person's opinion, it's not a bad review. Marks & Spencer is quality. You've seen the adverts, "This is not just any chicken, this is M&S chicken, the finest, most succulent, tender, juicy chicken." That's you, the best.'

'The best chicken?' I said.

'No, comedian. You're not just any comedian.'

'No,' I resisted, 'that's the food. Marks & Spencer's food is the best, the clothes are average. I wouldn't be upset if I had been compared to a Marks & Spencer smoked salmon parcel, but I wasn't. I was compared to a pullover. The food is special, but the clothes are boring.'

'Nonsense, Michael,' Kitty retorted, 'Marks & Spencer stands for quality, whether it be the clothes or the food. Everyone loves M&S and everyone is going to love you. Plus, you're wearing an M&S pullover right now.'

She had a good point, but it was by no means the review of someone who was destined for the top. Kitty believed in me, but nobody else did, until I performed an open spot at a very small club called the Laughing Club in a pub called the Albany in Twickenham. The club was run by comedy enthusiast Adrian Rox. It was a small function room with about fifty people in the audience, and I didn't think it went particularly well.

The following day Kitty's parents, Simon and Alexandra, were visiting our humble abode for dinner. We were sitting in the kitchen/diner/toilet on plastic garden furniture I'd bought from Homebase and eating Tesco value cornflakes. The phone rang, and I excused myself and went to the living room to pick it up. 'Hello, welcome to Dial-a-Mobile. Are you calling about the new Nokia, sorry, hello?'

It was Adrian Rox from the Laughing Club, and he offered me my first paid gig, in Liverpool. I ran into the kitchen but Kitty wasn't there.

'Where's Kitty?' I said to Simon and Alexandra, breathless with excitement.

'She's in the loo,' Alexandra said.

'I'm here, darling,' Kitty said, from the loo, just a few feet from us, 'I can hear you.'

'I just got a paid gig,' I announced, beaming from ear to ear. 'One hundred pounds!'

I couldn't believe I was going to be paid for something that I had been doing for free for so long. The fee didn't include accommodation. We found a B&B in Liverpool for £30, and the petrol there and back cost £80. The £100 is of course taxed at about 20 per cent. So after my first paid gig I ended up owing £30.

The gig was unremarkable, and for only a handful of Liverpudlians; however, Adrian subsequently asked me if I wanted to host his Twickenham club. He thought I was good at talking to the audience and could jovially move the show along. I enjoyed hosting – there was less pressure on me to be funny. I could relax and get useful stage time between acts. I jumped at the chance. This meant that every Saturday night I was the compere.

I had developed about ten minutes of material that was working at the Laughing Club week in, week out. My year-long wait for my open spot at Jongleurs Camden was now nearly over, and I was well prepared. When I had played the Comedy Store the previous year with such mixed fortunes, I was so raw, I had no idea what I was doing. Now I had an act. I had jokes that I had performed every week for months, and they worked. I felt confident this time. I called them to confirm my booking, on my Dial-a-Mobile Nokia 3310 off-peak using my free minutes, and to my horror they told me they had given my spot to someone else.

'Why?' I asked frantically, having waited a year.

'We didn't have your number,' the lady from Jongleurs said.

'That's because I've changed phone. Unfortunately I couldn't keep my old number with my new Nokia 3310, but I did get free weekend calls, 400 free minutes per month and a free in-car charger. I need this open spot – I've been waiting a year for it.'

'We tried for ages to get hold of you,' she said nicely, 'but nobody knows who you are. Nobody has ever heard of you. We presumed you weren't doing stand-up any more. I'll see what I can do.'

She was lovely and squeezed me back on to the bill. The incident made me more determined. I had no standing in the industry whatsoever. Over a year had passed since my first gig, and nobody knew who I was.

It was Saturday night, the best night of the week for comedy. Friday nights can be a bit rowdy, the audience have been working all week and tend to drink too much. But on a Saturday night people are relaxed and in a good mood. I was too. I had been getting laughs with my jokes from an audience of about fifty people in my Twickenham club. Now I had an audience of five times that, so I figured I should get five times the number of laughs. This was simple mathematics, a welcome change from working out how much petrol I had in the car.

I was due on in the second half, so I settled back and watched the acts in the first half. These were well-known circuit comics who made a decent living from stand-up.

233

Watching them gave me more confidence. They were getting a terrific response, but I felt that my jokes were just as good.

'Ladies and gentlemen, please welcome Michael McIntyre.' I strode purposefully on to the stage hell-bent on making sure that in ten minutes' time Jongleurs wouldn't have to phone around to find out who I was.

Good evening, ladies and gentlemen. I don't want any trouble here tonight, I'm not hard, I don't have the accent for it. When I try to sound threatening it sounds more humiliating, I said, hamming up my posh accent. *'Come on then, if you think you're hard enough.' It sounds more like a homosexual invitation. 'You, me, outside now . . . it's a lovely evening, let's take this alfresco on the veranda. Do you want some? Do you want some? . . . Nibbles, they're divine.'*

Comedians have traditionally made jokes about the Irish, saying they're stupid, and I would like to say that I totally disagree with this. I've been to Ireland, I've met a lot of Irish people, I found them charming and wise. Although you can't ignore all the evidence. The fact is they live on an island and called it Island and then spelled it wrong.

I had an amazing gig, much better than at the Comedy Store, by far the best gig I'd had so far. It was exhilarating; the audience erupted when I left the stage. I was walking on air when I returned to the tiny, quite grubby dressing room. Before I could catch my breath, the door burst open and a confident, stocky man with a hint of a Welsh accent cornered me. 'You were good, you were really good, I think you could be the best there is. The very best, that's how good I thought you were. Do you understand what I'm saying? You could be outstanding, unbelievably good.'

He thrust a card in my direction. It read: 'Paul Duddridge, Artist Management'. He was an agent. This was beyond my wildest dreams for that night. I just wanted to get re-booked at Jongleurs.

'Call me!' he said.

I couldn't believe it. This was momentous. I chatted to the other comedians, who all endorsed him as a top comedy agent. He wanted to be my agent. Me! I sold mobiles for a living and hosted a weekly comedy night in Twickenham for fifty people. I'm moving into the big time.

I raced home in my Austin Metro and into Kitty's arms, clutching the now sweaty business card.

'It went so well, it was amazing, the best night ever, and this agent gave me his card. I think I got an agent, he said I could be the best. I don't think I've ever been this happy.'

I showed Kitty the business card. I loved the words 'Artist Management'. I was an artist now. I knew it.

Kitty and I sat on the sofa in the living room (although after thirty seconds, it was a bed), talking late into the night. She told me how she never doubted me and how proud she was. Although it had seemed like a tough year, it had only been one year, that's nothing. Watch out Jimmy Carr and Daniel Kitson, I'm coming! Hannah Chambers made a mistake turning me down, because I'm an artist, an artist with management.

I'm not a Marks & Spencer pullover, I am a Marks & Spencer smoked salmon parcel.

Within days I had a meeting with Duddridge at his offices in Barons Court. He was an amazingly impressive character with strong philosophies on the comedy business. I couldn't really take them all in, but they all sounded wonderful. He said that if I did everything he said, I would be successful.

He was like a comedy guru, a life coach, focusing on the mental side of things. He used a lot of proverbs such as 'You can lead a horse to water, but you can't make him drink', 'Keep your friends close and your enemies closer', 'Act like a king to be treated like a king', 'Lie down with dogs and wake up with fleas'.

I couldn't follow everything, but there was no doubt he was an inspirational orator. I felt uplifted and ready to rule the world.

'Don't make a decision now,' he said ushering me out, 'have a think about it, then call me.'

Driving home, my head was buzzing with his voice. When I got home to Kitty, I tried to remember some of the stuff he had said.

'How did it go, Michael? Tell me everything!' she asked, as I came through the door.

'Well, he said lots of stuff. He's an amazing character; he was like a motivational speaker.'

'But can you remember anything he said?' she pressed.

'Err, something about a king being taken to water . . . and lying down with your enemies' dogs . . . I don't remember exactly.'

'What are you talking about, Michael?'

'He said I need to wake up and drink fleas.'

'What?'

'You had to be there. You're going to love him. He's a successful agent, he really believes in me. I've got to go for it, right?'

Early the next day I called him, and he became my first agent. I waited until 6 p.m., off-peak, and used my free minutes to phone in my resignation to Dial-a-Mobile, and went out for a celebratory dinner. This was the beginning. I knew it. Within days things started to change for the better. The best news of all was that I was being fast-tracked by the mighty Jongleurs empire. A combination of my successful open spot at Camden and the clout of Duddridge meant that I immediately had a whole string of gigs booked at their clubs around the country. Within months I became a jobbing comedian, performing twenty-minute sets at Jongleurs clubs in Oxford, Birmingham, Leeds, Southampton, Portsmouth, Cardiff, Nottingham – in fact, just think of a major city and there was a Jongleurs.

Jongleurs was open on Thursday, Friday and Saturday. So each week I would be in a different city and pulling in around £500 a week. Each bill consisted of three comedians and a compere. The first act would be the most inexperienced, followed by a stronger act and then an interval before the headline act. I was on first. This was to be expected as I was new and inexperienced. I had to work my way up the bill. Being first actually suited me as I liked to drive home when-ever possible, even though it meant covering hundreds of miles a day. I would drive home to be with Kitty.

Since Kitty had told me she loved me in Villa Bianca, we had not spent a night apart. When we first got together, she said to me, 'This is it, you know, I'll be with you for ever, you're the one.' As happy as I was, I couldn't really believe her. But she was true to her word; she loved me like I loved her and after a couple of years of living together, I withdrew the last of my savings and found myself browsing rings in Tiffany. I knew she wanted to get married. You know what girls are like – she would drop occasional hints, like whenever I bought her flowers, she would throw them over her head.

My proposal formed the basis of my first big comedy routine. So before I tell you the story, here's me opening the show at Jongleurs Leeds, Cardiff, Bristol, Oxford, Portsmouth, Southampton, Glasgow, Nottingham, Birmingham or Manchester, week in, week out:

I'm engaged, ladies and gentlemen. I bought her a beautiful diamond ring that cost me a fortune. But you'll like this, I had it engraved . . . with the price.

I got her a Tiffany ring, and I think she was more excited about that than us spending the rest of our lives together. She was like, 'I can't believe it! It's Tiffany! Is it really? Is it really a Tiffany ring?'

'Of course it is,' I said. 'Look, it's a Tiffany box, it's a Tiffany ring,' I replied.

'Yes, but you could have just got a Tiffany box and put a shit ring in it' and I was like . . . 'Why didn't I think of that?'

Girls get hypnotized by diamonds – it's like they turn into Gollum from The Lord of the Rings: *'Precious. Master, give me precious. Precious is mine.' You look outside any jeweller's and you'll see single girls staring in the window saying, 'Soon, precious will be mine.'*

I took her to a lovely Italian restaurant to propose. I was so nervous; this is a major moment. I got the ring out and said, as if in slow motion, 'Will . . . you . . . marry . . . me?'

And she was like, 'Michael, start again.'

'What do you mean, start again?' I said.

'Start again and do it right, you have to get down on one knee,' she said.

'Hang on a minute, you're not directing this scene, I'm proposing, this is how I'm doing it.'

'Michael, stop, I have been waiting my whole life for this moment, it's romantic, it's traditional, you have to get down on one knee.'

'Now listen,' I said, 'I have just spent the equivalent of a small car on this diamond ring, why don't you get down on YOUR knee?'

That was more or less my joke, and it always got a big laugh. It's not what happened of course. I'm not that rude. The only truth was that I did buy her a Tiffany ring. I suppose the shock of the price inspired the routine. I did also take her to an Italian restaurant, Villa Bianca, her favourite, where she finally succumbed to my two-year harassment. I envisaged this to be the perfect romantic setting to pop the question. If Kitty suspected anything, she didn't let on. We were just going out for dinner. I was naturally tense, I wanted to get it right, for it to be perfect. I booked the same table that we sat at before. I thought I would 'pop' the question at the end of dinner. I had a whole speech planned in my mind that I was going to launch into after dessert. But after we ordered, I was struggling to make normal conversation as my mind was preoccupied with the proposal and constantly checking that the most expensive thing I had ever bought was still in my back pocket.

'What's wrong with you?' Kitty said, sternly.

'Nothing,' I said, defensively.

'You're acting really weird, really rude. You're not really listening to me.'

'Sorry, what did you say?' I said, fidgeting with my pocket again.

'You're not even listening to me now are you?' she snapped.

'What?' I said, with a blank expression.

'Why don't we go home, Michael? What's the point in going out to dinner, if you're not going to talk to me or listen to me?'

We were in danger of having a row. This wasn't the plan. I realized I had to change the plan, I had to propose now before we fell out. She seemed really pissed off. We were in danger of splitting up!

'Darling, I've got something to say,' I began, taking her hand.

'What?' she said softly. I was off the hook. She knew what was coming.

'Well, we've been together for nearly two years and I don't know how it's possible, but I love you more every single –'

'MR WILSON!' shouted the maître d'. It was so loud the whole restaurant, including us, turned to see who had just walked in.

Walking into the restaurant was Richard Wilson, the star of *One Foot in the Grave*. Suddenly the whole restaurant was focused on Richard Wilson.

'That's what's-his-name?' said Kitty.

'Richard Wilson. I'm trying to propose here,' I said.

'Sorry, Michael, carry on,' Kitty said. I composed myself and continued.

'Darling, what I was saying was that –'

'I DON'T BELIEVE IT!' shouted an Italian waiter, badly impersonating Richard Wilson's catchphrase, much to the enjoyment of the other waiters, as Richard Wilson and his dinner guest were seated directly next to us.

'MR WILSON, WHAT CAN I GET YOU?' The celebrity diner seemed to be making the normally quite prickly Italian waiters very loud and animated. 'LET ME TELL YOU ABOUT THE SPECIALS . . .'

I had no choice but to pronounce my everlasting love to Kitty and ask for her hand in marriage while an Italian waiter shouted about the specials to Richard Wilson from *One Foot in the Grave* at the next table.

'I have always loved you, I can't imagine the world without you in it . . . WE HAVE A RISOTTO MARINARA, MR WILSON, VERY NIIICE . . . from the moment I met you in the Steeles pub wearing my massive coat . . . WE HAVE A LOBSTER SPAGHETTI TONIGHT, CHEF'S SPECIALITY, MAGNIFICO . . . you became the only girl in the world to me, I loved you more than I knew it was possible to love someone . . . WE ALSO HAVE A VEAL ESCALOPE, MR WILSON, THIS IS MY FAVOURITE . . . I dreamt for so long that we could be together and how it would be if we were together and our love has exceeded . . . AND FINALLY WE HAVE A PENNE ARRABIATTA AL DENTE . . . anything I could have imagined. Kitty, I love, I will love you for ever . . .'

I took out the ring from my back pocket and opened the case.

'Will you marry me?' I said.

'I'll just have the lasagne,' said Richard Wilson.

'I DON'T BELIEVE IT,' said the waiter.

'Yes,' said Kitty.

21

Kitty and I then entered a wonderful magical time of announcements and wedding planning. I was to marry the love of my life, and although I didn't get a chance to express it to her fully in Villa Bianca, the point I wanted to make was that I didn't really know her when I was infatuated by her, but she had surprised me with just how perfect she was, and just how perfect we were together.

Everybody was thrilled for us. Kitty was glowing with happiness, I had never seen her like that, she couldn't stop smiling. The only person who I wished could share in our joy was my grandmother. But it had now been years since we last spoke; she had no interest in me whatsoever. Our relationship was over. I had come to terms with it, but deep down I clung on to the hope that we would see each other again, that she would be at my wedding. It was so brutal for her to love me so wholly and unconditionally and then turn her back on me so completely, so quickly. But it wasn't to be; she died in her sleep a few months after I became engaged. All the memories of our happy times came flooding back and I was devastated, but soon I remembered everything else, all the pain she had caused. The truth was she had gone years before; this just eliminated any chance of reconciliation, but there was probably none anyway.

My engagement routine kept getting laughs at Jongleurs. Kitty not only found it funny, but loved that I was immediately telling an audience containing single girls that I was engaged to someone else. It always made me laugh that she could be jealous, that she could think I might cheat on her. I could never have an affair. Look at my track record with women – it would take me two years of stalking, harassing and hiding in bushes to get another girl to sleep with me.

However, the gloss of earning an income from stand-up was starting to wear thin. Jongleurs was not a traditional comedy club; it was a chain, like McDonald's. The club offered an evening's entertainment for weekend revellers, mainly large single-sex parties on stag nights, hen nights, birthdays or a work night out. The audiences were drunk and rowdy and had short attention spans. Fast, bite-size and usually crude jokes were most effective. The strapline under the Jongleurs logo read: 'Eat, Drink, Laugh, Dance'. 'Laugh' was third on the agenda. I needed to become a better comedian and Jongleurs was not a conducive environment for that.

As an aspiring comedian, you need to play the full variety of gigs up and down the land. Jongleurs should be included in the mix, certainly. The ability to make a few hundred pissed punters laugh is an indication that you've got a bulletproof act, but to develop and improve as a comedian you need more, much more. I played other clubs, but usually only one weekend a month.

Not only was I trapped in Jongleurs, but I was also making no progress within it. I was always going on first, deemed the weakest on the bill, and the other comedians in some cases were astonishingly poor. Many of the comedians who played Jongleurs were old hacks. They never made it, leaving them bitter and cynical. They had lost their ambition and being around them was making me lose mine.

Just remembering the dressing rooms at Jongleurs sends chills down my spine. A typical Jongleurs dressing room had a couple of old smelly sofas, maybe a TV that didn't work, an iron and ironing board, untouched fruit and an A4 print-out of the line-up on the wall. It was depressing enough before you add a few jaded and bitchy comedians. If you met some of these comics, you'd be amazed that they were in the entertainment industry.

That's not to say there weren't some characters. One old-timer from the Midlands always struggled onstage but thought he was God's gift to comedy. I once saw him say to an audience who weren't laughing at him, 'I'm good at this, you know. Google me.' He was convinced that he was brilliant, but the only reason he wasn't successful was that everyone kept stealing all his jokes.

'Peter Kay's at it again,' he announced in the dressing room of Nottingham Jongleurs while ironing his shirt. I looked around the empty room in the hope he was talking to someone else.

'At what?' I asked.

'Stealing my material,' he revealed in his Brummie accent. 'Yep, I was watching him the other night, just ticking off the jokes, mine, mine, mine, mine, it was unbelievable.'

'Unbelievable' was right. I hadn't seen this guy write a joke in years, nobody had.

'He's not the only one, you know,' he carried on, steam pluming from his iron and from his ears.

'Oh really, who else?' I enquired.

He stopped ironing and faced me for added drama.

'Jay Leno,' he revealed.

'Jay Leno? The host of *The Tonight Show* on NBC in America has been stealing your jokes?' I asked, trying not to laugh.

'I know, incredible isn't it?' he said, thinking I was as baffled as him.

'How did he do it? Do you think he comes to Jongleurs and sits at the back with a pad?' I asked, looking forward to his explanation.

'No. Don't be silly. He's a massive star. There's no way Jay Leno would do that . . . He hires people, local people to do it for him. I've seen them, you know, in the audience, at the back, taking notes.'

'I'm shocked!' I said, already itching to share the hilarity of this conversation with Kitty.

'Me too, but there's no other explanation. And he's not the first American talk show host to steal my material, either.'

'This has happened before?'

'A few years ago.' He again put down his iron and dramatically turned to face me.

'David Letterman,' he revealed. 'I sent him a tape of my stand-up set to try and get on his talk show and the next time I watched it, he'd stolen all my ideas.'

'He can't get away with that. What were the jokes?'

'Topical stuff,' he declared.

'He told your jokes, word for word?' I asked, loving his level of fantasy.

'Not exactly, but he took all the subjects. George W. Bush, the Iraq war, Dick Cheney, it was all there. But who's gonna believe me?'

It seemed like this was the best I could hope for by playing Jongleurs. I wasn't going to be famous, but maybe I could be totally deluded. I occasionally played other clubs like the Banana in Balham, Up the Creek in Greenwich, the Glee in Birmingham, the Hyena in Newcastle, and I would come alive and get a sense of how much better I could be. The audience were more focused, allowing me more time to express myself onstage. But I felt any good work that I would do would be undone by returning to Jongleurs for the next few weeks.

Then a genuine opportunity presented itself. Duddridge announced that he was taking me to perform at the Edinburgh Festival. This was what I had been waiting for. This was my chance to make a name for myself. Edinburgh is where stand-up stars are found. There are hundreds of shows in every nook and cranny of the city. Open a cupboard door in Edinburgh during the Festival and there will be a wannabe comedian performing a show to a handful of punters.

The opportunity that Edinburgh provided was the Perrier Award. This is where a panel of about twelve journalists, comedy fans and TV execs see every show, nominate the best five shows and then pick a winner. Just to be nominated will set you on your way to stardom, as demonstrated by the esteemed list of comics the panel have unearthed through the years, including Frank Skinner, Jack Dee, Eddie Izzard, Steve Coogan, Harry Hill, Lee Evans, Dylan Moran, Bill Bailey, Johnny Vegas, Peter Kay, the list runs and runs. Household names who were nobodies before the Perrier panel found them. It seems that if you're going to become a successful stand-up comedian, you will be nominated for the Perrier Award. Very few people slip through the net. The year before I was set to make my debut, 2002, the Perrier panel again proved their worth by nominating the then unknown comedians Jimmy Carr, Omid Djalili and Noel Fielding. The winner was Daniel Kitson.

For all the tough Jongleurs gigs, here was my big chance to break away from the pack. In addition to the main award, there was also the Newcomer Award for which I would be eligible as I was making my debut.

Duddridge managed to book me into the much sought-after Pleasance Courtyard for twenty-five shows in August. The Pleasance Courtyard is a real hub of the Festival. Hundreds of people flock there, drinking and socializing and choosing from a multitude of shows starting hourly in a series of venues ranging from the 350-seat Pleasance One to my venue, the sixty-seat Pleasance Attic. I now had something to aim for, a focus.

Edinburgh, however, is a gamble. For all the success stories aforementioned, there are many more whose dreams were not realized, leaving them in massive debt. The Edinburgh Festival is very expensive, costing between £5,000 and £10,000 to put on a show. It takes a lot of soul-destroying Jongleurs gigs to pay that back. But it was a gamble worth taking, a gamble all aspiring comedians had to take.

I headed to Scotland filled with optimism and adrenaline. The Festival lasts three weeks, and the plan was for Kitty to join me on weekends. I shared a flat with the comedian Paul Tonkinson. Paul is from North Yorkshire and was my only real friend in comedy. We had met at the Glee Comedy Club in Birmingham, and he became my biggest fan. Nobody believed in me like Paul did, he saw something in me that nobody else had, not even me. He lived near me in London, and we had been spending time together, talking about ideas and stand-up. Paul had been a comic for ten years, he had played clubs all over the world, appeared on several TV and radio shows, but he kept telling me he wanted to learn from me. I was flattered, but deep down thought he must be as deluded as the Brummie comedian who was now claiming the sitcom *Seinfeld* was his idea.

Paul was more excited about my Edinburgh show than his own. 'You're gonna win the Perrier Award, mate,' he kept saying over and over again. He even went to the bookies to try and put money on it, but they had as much idea who I was as Jongleurs had when I called up about my open spot.

The night before my first gig, I couldn't sleep with excitement, I was raring to go. I cobbled together all my jokes and just about had an hour's worth. I also had a lot of untried ideas about Edinburgh from my days as a student. My main worry, however, was who I was going to tell these jokes to. My pre-sales for the Festival were one ticket. Just one person had bought a ticket to see me; and it was a 2-for-1 deal. This one person couldn't even convince someone else to come with him for free.

The omens were not good, but when showtime came I got a few last-minute bookings and had an audience of about thirty, thanks mainly to the 2-for-1 deal. The Scots love a bargain. I also benefited from the overspill from sold-out shows like Jimmy Carr and Dara Ó Briain in Pleasance One.

I opened the show commenting on all the Scots who had shown up simply because of the 2-for-1. I impersonated them booking the tickets in my pretty decent Scottish accent, and they lapped it up. I also made jokes about Scottish money, how they had their own money, but not their own currency. I would impersonate the business news on Scottish TV: 'The exchange rate remains stable at one pound to the pound.'

My adrenaline helped me have a successful first few nights, but when the 2-for-1 offer ended and the tickets went to full price, I started to struggle to attract an audience of more than ten, not enough to put on a show and create anything like an atmosphere. I had some awful gigs, getting no laughs at all. I even had people walk out, halving the audience.

My only hope to increase my audience was to receive some positive reviews for my show. With hundreds of comedy shows, the competition to get a journalist to see your show is fierce. I employed a PR girl, but unfortunately she was useless. The first time I spoke to her, I knew things probably weren't going to work out.

'Hi, it's Michael,' I said.

'Michael who?' she replied in her Mancunian accent.

'Michael McIntyre.'

'Michael . . . Macin-tower,' she said, trying to place me.

'McIntyre. You're doing my PR,' I said, wondering how it was possible that the person in charge of publicizing me hadn't managed to publicize me to herself.

'Oh yes, of course. Hiya, love. What are you up to?' she then said like we were old friends.

'I'm performing a show at the Edinburgh Festival,' I said with more than a hint of sarcasm.

'Brilliant, I should come and see that, shouldn't I? I'll check my diary and try to squeeze it in.' This was horrifying. She was supposed to be getting the press to see me, and she could barely book herself to see me.

'What about the newspapers?' I pushed.

'I've got them,' she said, nonchalantly.

Thank God, I thought. She does know what she's doing. She's booked some journalists to my show. I'll find out the dates and make sure those are my best gigs.

'Which ones? When?' I said, my excitement building.

'All of them. This morning. We get the papers every day to see if there's anything in them about the comedians.'

'Oh right,' I said, deflated, realizing she was referring to having bought the newspapers. 'Was there anything in them?'

'Not today, but it's early days yet, don't panic,' she said.

'I think you should try and get the papers to see my show, the *Times*, the *Guardian*, the *Independent*, I'm seeing reviews in them every day. Reviews of new comics like me playing at the Pleasance. Can't we get them to come to my show?' I said, reminding her of her job description.

'What a good idea!' she said. 'I'll see what I can do.'

A few days later she called me back.

'Fantastic news!' she said, 'I've got the *Guardian*.'

'Wonderful, when?' I said.

'The nineteenth, to Gina's show,' she proudly announced, referring to Gina Yashere, another comedian she was doing PR for at the Festival.

'Do you think you could get them to see my show too?' I asked.

'On the nineteenth? I don't think so, they're seeing Gina.'

'No, on another date,' I suggested, losing any remaining hope that she could do her job.

'Great idea, I'll see what I can do.'

The Festival was leaving me behind. All the other shows seemed to have photocopies of reviews pasted on top of their posters that were all around the city. '5 Star, *The Times*. 4 Star, the *Guardian*'. My posters only featured my hopeful smiling face.

I started doing impressions of how bad my PR girl was in my show. I would pretend to call her and she would pick up the phone shouting, 'Four star!'

'Really? I got a review?' I would excitedly respond.

'Oh, no, sorry,' she would say, 'I'm in the petrol station. Who's calling?'

I would pretend to call her another time. 'Three star!' she would say, picking up the phone.

'That's not so bad. At least I got a review,' I would reply.

'What? Sorry, love, I'm just booking a B&B. Who is this?'

And I would end the joke with her picking up the phone saying, 'One star!'

'Hello, it's Michael calling.'

'I know, love, you got a review today in *The Times*.'

This may have been funny, but making jokes about how badly my Festival was going to about ten people in an attic was not ideal. Then things took a turn for the worse. I had a show where I sold the grand total of zero tickets, nil, zilch, none whatsoever. It was as if I wasn't at the Edinburgh Festival at all. Other shows had queues of people snaking all around the Pleasance Courtyard, and not one person wanted to see my show. I headed down to my venue in the hope that somebody might show up, but nobody did. I had never felt like more of a loser. I hung out with the technicians who worked at my tiny venue and tried to make light of the situation, but they seemed genuinely sorry for me. I went back to the flat despondent, deflated and defeated.

Peter Kay's stand-up show was on Channel 4 that night, and I lay on the sofa watching it while my flatmate Paul was performing his show to a packed crowd. Peter Kay was incredible, so funny, his huge loving audience wiping away tears of laughter. Peter Kay had entered 'So You Think You're Funny?' in 1997 and won the whole competition with one of his first gigs. The following year, he had gone to the Edinburgh Festival and been nominated for the Perrier Award. I didn't get anywhere near winning 'So You Think You're Funny?' and here I was in Edinburgh with no audience. Our lives were worlds apart. I thought I was wasting my time, I didn't stand a chance.

I could find comedy in most things, but this wasn't funny. Paul tried to make me feel better but I could tell he hadn't expected me to struggle so much to get an audience. He had been to the Festival several times before and had never heard of anyone not selling a single ticket.

Kitty came up to see me the next day, and I sat with her in Starbucks and burst into tears. I had reached rock bottom. We were sitting by the window facing the pedestrianized Royal Mile that was packed with people handing out fliers for their shows. Not just comedians but magicians, dancers, singers and theatre groups all dressed up in their stage costumes. As I sobbed into my latte, I said, 'It can't get any worse.'

To which Kitty replied, 'There's always someone worse off.'

'Who?' I questioned.

'Him,' she said, pointing out of the window at a man wearing only a nappy, handing out leaflets for his show with his head sticking out of a toilet seat. She was right. It's a jungle in Edinburgh, everybody's trying to make it, to get noticed. I had two weeks left. It was Saturday night, the busiest night of the week, and that night I had sold about forty tickets, enough to put on a show.

I had nothing more to lose. I bought a double Jack Daniels before the show and looked out of the window in the tiny room adjacent to my Attic venue that I used as a dressing room. I could see Arthur's Seat glowing in the last light of the day. I hadn't thought about my history with the city thus far, I had been so consumed with the pressure of my show. But now I thought of my dad, whose ashes I had scattered a few hundred yards away. He was watching over me, he must be. I can do this.

I took a swig from my Jack Daniels and went for it. I ditched most of my mediocre material and just played with the audience. I improvised and enjoyed myself. I wasn't trying to be funny, I was just having fun. Laughter filled my minuscule Attic venue, and for the first time, I was myself onstage, the best of me. I didn't care if there were any press in. That night I learned for myself that I could do it, I wasn't wasting my time.

But luck would have it that there was someone from the press there, Bruce Dessau from the *Evening Standard*. Here are some extracts from his review:

> Michael McIntyre is so sharp, he is in danger of shredding himself. This livewire was so busy bantering brilliantly that I'm not sure he did much scripted material . . . He teased a cabbie, mocked an hirsute schoolboy and snatched a sandwich from a punter . . . His publicity shots make him look like a squeaky clean teenager, but there is a wise head on those shoulders. He has been professional for only two years but worked the room like a man possessed . . . If McIntyre doesn't make the Perrier shortlist, he will have been cruelly overlooked.

I couldn't believe it. I had gone from not selling a single ticket to being talked about in connection with the Perrier, and not just by anybody, by Bruce Dessau, who was on the judging panel. The review had an amazing impact on me, but unfortunately not on ticket sales, as it was printed in a London newspaper, London being the capital city of a country that I wasn't performing in. I could only imagine that Londoners were sitting on the Tube thinking, 'That sounds like a good show. If I was in Edinburgh, I might go to that, but I'm not. This is my stop.'

Bruce went back to his fellow Perrier panellists and reported his discovery. Suddenly I was in the running. The rest of the panel were dispatched to see me, including one night when ten of the twelve judges were the only tickets booked for my show. The remainder of the tickets were handed out for free to make up the numbers. I never quite repeated the heights of that one night but I had done enough. I was nominated for the Perrier Best Newcomer. My show then sold out for the remaining week of the Festival. I didn't win it, but I had arrived. Having plumbed the depths of despair, I found somehow everything had turned around.

Duddridge was thrilled, my mum was so proud, Paul thought I was robbed and should have won the main award, and my PR girl said she didn't like Perrier and preferred Highland Spring.

I was overjoyed with what was a successful Edinburgh, out of the blue. In three weeks' time, Kitty would be marrying a Perrier Best Newcomer Nominee.

Finally, everything seemed like it was coming together.

22

Everybody chipped in to give us a magnificent wedding. My mum and Steve bought Kitty's wedding dress, Kitty's parents provided the flowers and the food, friends purchased our wedding bands, Kitty's parents' friends kindly allowed us to use their wonderful country house in Somerset for the reception, other friends made the cake and hired us an old Rolls-Royce, Lucy paid for the wine and LloydsTSB Bank paid for the honeymoon.

I borrowed £10,000 for the holiday of a lifetime to the Maldives. You only ever have one honeymoon, I was marrying the girl of my dreams, I had just been nominated for a Perrier Best Newcomer Award, I was twenty-seven years old with my whole career ahead of me. I was sure I could pay it back.

The fact that everybody had contributed made for a really special family occasion. People were calling up almost every day offering to help in any way they could. I remember Kitty putting the phone down saying, 'Great news, Michael, my uncle's girlfriend is a professional horse photographer.'

'Sorry? What are you talking about?' I said, confused.

'She's agreed to do the photography at our wedding,' Kitty said.

'There are no horses coming to our wedding,' I commented.

'I know, but I'm sure she can photograph humans as well.'

'I've never even heard of a horse photographer, what does she do?' I asked.

'I don't know, Michael, she goes to horse races and stuff, she's like the official photographer,' Kitty speculated.

'Horse races? I'm not sure about this, darling. Is she going to just take a whole stream of photos at the end of the aisle, like a photo finish? Is our wedding album only going to consist of one photo, you winning by a nose?'

I thought this was funny and could possibly be used as material, then I considered using it in my speech on the big day. I think I was more nervous about my speech than anything else. All my wife's family knew I was a comedian but had never seen me perform, and I picked up an air of genuine concern over the financial security of their daughter. So there was a lot of pressure building on my wedding speech to be funny, especially when I found out her father had suggested the speeches be rescheduled for BEFORE the ceremony. I mean, it's not often a groom has to give an example of his work on his wedding day. If you're a builder getting married, you don't eat lunch, cut the cake, have your first dance and then knock up a gazebo on the lawn.

When the day finally arrived in late September, there wasn't a cloud in the sky. It was beautiful, what the English call an 'Indian summer', and what I presume the Indians call 'summer'. A marquee was set up on the lawn should the weather not hold, and the congregation and I gathered in a small church conveniently and romantically located on the grounds of the house. Kitty's father, Simon, surprised her with a cart pulled by two ponies that took them the short distance from the house to the church.

I waited at the end of the aisle for my bride as the organ began 'Here Comes the Bride'; I turned and there she was, looking stunning. She had her hair up with hair extensions. I was unaware of the existence of hair extensions. She hadn't told me she was going to do this. I didn't know what had happened to her, I had heard of nerves making people's hair fall out, but never double in size. She looked beautiful, my bride. She raced down the aisle at such a speed the organ had only reached 'Here comes' before she was by my side. The vicar went through all the traditional vows; at the bit when he says, 'If there is any reason why these two should not be married, speak now or for ever hold your peace', I couldn't resist doing a little comedy look round to the congregation.

We made our sacred vows to one another and had cued up the Beatles' 'All You Need is Love' on a tape player at the back. We kissed as man and wife and after a bit of fumbling with the tape deck at the back of the church, the music played and we walked out of the church to cheers and applause. It was magical. We climbed into the waiting cart to be pulled by the two ponies up the drive to the house, while the guests walked up to the reception. Some of the locals came out of their houses to catch a glimpse of the bride. Surprisingly few photos had been taken at this point, but as soon as Kitty's uncle's girlfriend saw the ponies, she bolted to life and took a series of shots of them, in some of which Kitty and I can be spotted in the background.

Our budget was so tight that something had to give. It was the main course of lunch. We had a starter of cold salmon and salad and we had the wedding cake for dessert. Nobody mentioned the missing middle course. After lunch it was time for the speeches. This was terrifying for me. There was a lot riding on this, almost as much as the Edinburgh Festival. The one piece of good news is that I was on last, straight after Simon. This was the first time I had headlined.

The pressure ultimately became too much for me, and I

treated the speech too much like a gig and started laying into the front row. Within the first five minutes, I had character-assassinated my new brother-in-law, embarrassed the maid of honour and totally forgot to mention my wife. Simon had to interrupt by raising a toast before Kitty initiated divorce proceedings.

We jumped into our classic Rolls-Royce as confetti filled the air, spent the night at a suite in the Bath Spa Hotel and set off on honeymoon the next day.

It was perfect.

The Maldives were like nothing I had ever seen before. We flew to the capital, Malé, and then took a seaplane to our hotel, the Hilton on Rangali Island, that is literally on a tiny island containing only the hotel. It takes about fifteen minutes to walk around it. We had a room on the blinding white beach, but many of the rooms were on stilts in the turquoise Indian Ocean. The service was immaculate; little Maldivian men would rake the sand you had just walked on. The food was phenomenal, everywhere you looked was breathtakingly beautiful. We were in paradise.

The only downside was I forgot that half-board meant that we only had breakfast and dinner paid for. I had about £150 remaining on my credit card. I couldn't afford to buy lunch at the extortionate restaurants, and there was obviously nowhere else to eat – the closest supermarket was back at Heathrow. So having spent a small fortune of loaned money and travelling halfway round the world, we had to steal food from breakfast every morning to eat for lunch. Kitty would keep watch, and when the waiter turned his back, I would stuff croissants, fruit, yoghurt and mini-cereal packets into our beach bag. One morning we couldn't swipe anything from breakfast and we got so hungry during the day that I tried to spear fish in the ocean. This holiday of a lifetime had shades of the film *Castaway*.

The happy couple, Mr and Mrs McIntyre, returned home looking tanned and hungry. Our lives had revolved around the Edinburgh Festival and the wedding for so long that it felt a bit strange. I was in debt. The loan and credit card had pushed me significantly into the red and Edinburgh had cost about £4,000. It was time for my career to start moving; I needed the money.

My agent's office sent me my gig list and to my horror it was the same as it had always been, Jongleurs gig after Jongleurs gig. I couldn't believe it. I was nominated for the Best Newcomer Award in Edinburgh, but that didn't seem to count for anything. The truth was that being nominated for the Perrier Best Newcomer Award was quite a minor thing compared with being nominated or winning the main award.

The next year of my career was no different from the previous one. I continued to open the show at Jongleurs. I was dedicating my career to Jongleurs and they still only rated me as an opening act. I occasionally played other clubs, as before, and loved it, but I would then not be working on Sunday night, Monday night, Tuesday night and Wednesday night, before heading back to entertain Stags and Hens at Jongleurs. All the while, my debts were mounting. I was borrowing more and more money at extortionate rates, using debt to pay off debt.

I was broke. My mum lent me money, Lucy lent me money, Sam lent me money, I called Paul from a petrol station when my credit card was declined. I sold my grandfather's old cufflinks he had given me and even tried to sell his old enormous cashmere coat. Although, in fairness, Kitty had been asking me to sell that for years. I'm not exaggerating when

I say that our life became quite desperate. I took every gig Duddridge could get me, but it wasn't enough to get me out of the mess I was in. One night Kitty was seriously ill with a sky-high temperature. I needed to be with her, to look after her, but I left her alone to go to Norwich because we so badly needed the £150 from the gig. My financial situation was spiralling out of control.

The only thing that kept me going was the next Edinburgh Festival, all my eggs were in that basket. I would be returning as the Perrier Best Newcomer Nominee. Television producers and comedy bookers would see my show. I could be nominated for the Perrier, I could win it and my career would skyrocket. I obsessed over the Perrier Award. This was my chance of success, my last chance. On top of my mounting debts, the Festival would cost me thousands more pounds. If I didn't get a break at Edinburgh 2004, I didn't know how I could survive in comedy.

My agent, Paul Duddridge, still believed in me. He was bankrolling the Edinburgh Festival, so it was to him that I would be in debt. He continued to try to motivate me. Every time we spoke I would feel uplifted afterwards, but it didn't seem to ever make me funnier. He again booked me into the Pleasance Attic, reflecting how my career had gone nowhere over the past year. The good news was that the Perrier panel was to be chaired by Bruce Dessau, the *Evening Standard* critic who had championed me the previous year. Bruce was my biggest fan, my only fan of influence. He'll make sure the panel come to see my show; he'll support me. It's up to me now.

I was a man on a mission. I was again living with Paul Tonkinson, who had become my comedy corner man. We would talk endlessly about how to get the best out of me. My plan was to play with the audience every night. I would

use my mediocre material as fall-back if my riffing and improvising didn't work. If I could have gigs every night like the
one that Bruce Dessau witnessed the year before, I was
convinced I would be nominated. I had to be.

I hit the ground running. On my first gig there was a man
with long hair and a long beard sitting in the front row.
'You've been waiting long,' I said, and I was off. For the first
week all my shows were different, dictated by who was in the
audience. I was on good form. The problem was that as the
Festival went on, I started to feel the pressure. I began to
worry about whether there were Perrier judges or critics in
the audience. I started to become inhibited. The Festival is
long and gruelling, performing twenty-five shows back-to-
back without a night off. My anxiety heightened on a daily
basis as I knew these were the most important gigs of my
life. I started to worry myself sick.

In addition to the usual stress-related illnesses like headaches and sore throats, my body started to fail me in ways it
never had before. I came out in a rash all over my body, I had
blurred vision and got pins and needles in my face. In my
face? Has that ever happened to anyone before, ever? I woke
up one morning and couldn't hear out of my ear. Christine
Hamilton (from *I'm a Celebrity . . . Get Me Out of Here!*) and her
husband Neil (shamed politician) were doing a daytime chat
show called 'Lunch with the Hamiltons' at the Festival. I was
booked to appear on it to help publicize my show to the audience of about 300. I rushed to the doctor's surgery in Edinburgh
and said, 'You've got to help me, I can't hear out of one ear
and I've got lunch with the Hamiltons in an hour.'

To which the doctor said, 'Would you like me to block the
other ear?'

I, of course, took that story and put it straight into my

261

show. I expected it to get a bigger laugh before remembering my hearing was down 50 per cent. I was falling apart. Halfway through the Festival, Kitty came up to be with me for the remainder. She took control and stuffed me with vitamins and emotional support. It's just such a strange life, every day there was one hour that was vitally important to me. The rest of the day, I was preparing for that one hour. As soon as the show was over, I would go to sleep, wake up and have to do it all over again. It was like *Groundhog Day*.

Despite not coping very well physically with the pressure, my shows weren't suffering too much. I felt I was on track, improvising more than doing material. I got a review in the *Independent* that read:

> Michael McIntyre generates most of his material by chatting to members of the audience. As confident as he is quick-witted, McIntyre is a boyish, likeable chap who improvises as effortlessly as Eddie Izzard and Ross Noble except with an additional knack for characters and accents. No comedian makes his job look easier.

This was exactly the reaction I wanted. Most comedians at the Festival had structured shows, rehearsed shows that were the same every night and usually had a theme. I was focusing only on making people laugh as much as possible, I wanted them to laugh until they had tears in their eyes and their faces hurt. That was my goal. I wasn't interested in props, gimmicks and depth. I'm a comedian; my job is to be funny. I hoped that the Perrier judges wouldn't penalize me for my lack of a 'show' and would reward me for simply being funny.

I was having lunch with Kitty on the last Monday of the Festival. I could now hear out of both ears, but I had an unsightly cold sore. My wife was urging me to relax and enjoy the last few nights: 'Whatever will be, will be. It's out of your hands.' My mobile phone rang; it was Duddridge, telling me that I was down to the final ten and that several judges would be coming to my show for the next two nights before announcing their five nominations on Wednesday. That was the call I was waiting for; it isn't out of my hands, it's in my hands.

I was happy with the way the show went that night, mostly material but flashes of improvisation. On the last night before the nominations I really went for it. Confidence was now flowing through me, I felt like I could make anything funny, anything at all. I felt like Neo from *The Matrix* when he starts to believe, and becomes all-powerful. I was playing with the audience for fun and now the audience contained Perrier judges who had my career in their hands. But to me they were just an audience to play with. I asked, 'What do you do for a living?'

And a rather tall, serious-looking gentleman said, 'I'm a journalist for *The Times* and I'm on the Perrier panel.'

I didn't bat an eyelid and set about trying to make the scenario as funny as possible. I kept referencing my chances of being nominated and certainly overstepped certain boundaries, but it was funny, everyone was having a great time. When the show ended, I felt optimistic about my chances. I told Kitty that night that I had given it everything and I meant it. I knew I had new fans on the panel who enjoyed what I did, which was make people laugh with no gimmicks, no structure, no real content, just laughs. Word got back to me that one of the panellists, the infamously tough critic for the *Scotsman*, Kate Copstick, said she would be fighting to get me nominated. Duddridge received a phone call checking my eligibility for the award. Everything was pointing in the right direction.

Wednesday morning was the most excruciating hours of my life. The result had come through at around midday the year before, 12.12, 12.34, 12.40, 12.47. Still no news. No phone call. Every minute that passed, I felt my chances were dwindling. I kept refreshing the Chortle website – if anything had happened, they would reveal it.

1.05 p.m., the phone rang. It was my mum, I snapped at her, 'There's no news, I'll call you.' Kitty was feeling as sick as I was.

At least another half an hour passed, and I was losing hope. Nica Burns, the founder of the Award, traditionally calls all the nominees personally, so I thought I was only clinging on to the faintest hope when Duddridge called. 'Hello?' I said, as calm as I could.

'It's not good news, you haven't been nominated.'

While I was listening to his words of consolation and support, Kitty ran into the room and I just shook my head in her direction.

I didn't win the Perrier. I wasn't even nominated, and now I was in even more debt.

The following day there was an article in *The Times* by two of the Perrier judges who wrote: 'Only Michael McIntyre stands out from the acts delivering pure stand-up. When his material matches his improvisation – or when he drops it altogether, Ross Noble style – then he might be a major star.'

I hadn't done enough. I was close, but that counted for nothing. My Festival petered out, and I played to about fifteen people on my last night. I returned to London on the Tuesday and on the Thursday to Jongleurs in Nottingham, first on the bill.

23

The 'death rattle' was how I used to describe the sound of the post dropping through the letterbox. Nothing good ever came in the post, just bills, red reminders and threatening letters. Kitty was in the kitchen as I went to see what unopened horrors awaited me. As per usual, there was a pile of brown envelopes with red writing visible through the little window on the front. One of them looked even more threatening than the others. I ripped it open to be met by typical words such as collections, arrears and court. Mostly these were debts I was aware of, but this one was particularly unwelcome. 'Student Loans Company', shit. I had taken out a student loan during my first and only year at university. I had honestly forgotten about it, but they hadn't and I owed them two thousand pounds.

With my wedding loan, credit cards and two Edinburgh Festivals, this made me over £30,000 in debt. Believe it or not, despite my appalling credit record, it was around this time I replaced my 'sofa that turns itself into a bed' with the Montana Ice three-seater from DFS on interest-free credit. The deal was that I paid nothing for a year and then paid about £150 for the rest of my life and the lives of any surviving relatives. Like most DFS customers, I only heard the first part about paying nothing for a year. I always thought it was funny that they give you interest-free credit on sofas. If people don't have the money, they're hardly going to get off their fat arses and make money if all you're doing is making their fat arses more comfortable. Interest-free credit on treadmills, that makes more sense.

I debated telling Kitty about the Student Loan letter. She was worried enough about our mounting money problems. I felt I had to; I had to share it with her. We shared everything. I walked into the kitchen clutching my latest debt.

'Darling, I've got some bad news,' I said.

'Well, I've got some good news,' Kitty said.

'What good news?'

'I think I'm pregnant,' she said, holding up a pregnancy test.

We were both desperate to start a family, but I was terrified about how to pay for a child. I was sinking deeper underwater financially, drowning.

'What was your bad news?' she asked.

'Oh, forget about that,' I said, stuffing the letter in my pocket, out of sight.

I then thrust us into even more debt by buying several pregnancy tests to make sure she was pregnant. There were three different varieties in Boots, all different prices. What's the difference? Don't they all do the same thing? Does the cheapest pregnancy test just say, 'Maybe' and the most expensive one say, 'Yes, you are pregnant, it's a girl and it's not yours, she's a slag'?

They were all positive. She was pregnant; I was going to be a dad. I had nine months to sort my life out. Nine months to take control of the mess that was my life and provide for my family.

I continued to do the same gigs as before. I had no chance of being spotted at these gigs, but what I could do was improve. I had battled with the dilemma over whether I should improvise onstage or do material. *The Times* had even

266

spelled it out for me. I wanted to improvise, that's when I was at my funniest. But the time had come to concentrate on my material. I pulled together all the best bits of improvisation, wrote them up as jokes and learned them. The results were almost instant. I suddenly had an act that was killing everywhere I went. I wrote and wrote and wrote. I was basically improvising and riffing, but this time on my own, in front of my computer. I then fine-tuned and edited my thoughts and then tried them out onstage. I soon had hours of material and started to perform completely different twenty-minute sets every night.

Kitty's pregnancy proved to be a fertile source of material, what with her coping with morning sickness by consuming ginger and Coca-Cola and her bizarre craving for the smell of rubber. One of my best jokes was about Kitty becoming pregnant:

I'm having a baby. It's not easy to make a baby, my wife and I were trying for fifteen months. I say months because it's a cyclical process, you have to wait every month for your opportunity to make a baby because of the way that women function. At the end of every month she would say to me, 'Go to Boots and get the test, get the pregnancy test,' and I would say, 'Why? Why don't we just wait and see if it grows within you, I think that's the best and the cheapest of our options.' 'No, Michael, go to Boots and get the test, I want Clear Blue, because it's the best, I don't want any of the other shit.' It's £13.99! And I had to get it every month . . . I could have got broadband, that's what really pissed me off.

I became so confident in my material that I could also improvise, knowing that if it didn't take off I could fall back on my now bulletproof jokes. Then with my wife heavily pregnant, I reached rock bottom. For four years I had been going on first at Jongleurs, every once in a while I would be on second. Progress. But this weekend I was something called Jongleurs' 'spare'. This is when you are a sort of substitute in case another comedian can't make it to one of the London Jongleurs venues in Camden, Battersea or Bow. I had to go to Camden Jongleurs and wait until they either called me to tell me I was to perform at one of these London venues or, more likely, go home. I couldn't believe it, this was worse than being on first, now I wasn't even on. I was being paid not to work.

I hated Jongleurs dressing rooms when I was working, but sitting there as a substitute was far worse. I couldn't wait for the phone call telling me that I could go home. As the evening went on, however, it appeared that the headliner hadn't shown up. The venue manager gave me a heads-up: 'Get ready, Michael, there's a problem with the headliner, you might have to go on.'

'Finally,' I thought. 'I'll headline this show, blow the roof off and show Jongleurs that I can do it.'

Then Jongleurs called me. 'The headliner isn't going to make it,' the booker said.

'I'll headline, no problem,' I said.

'No, we're sending another act over from Bow. You've never headlined before, we think it'll be too much for you.'

Insult to injury. I had given Jongleurs years of my life, performed hundreds of times for them, and here was the result. They thought it would be 'too much for me' to head-line a show. I left Jongleurs that night feeling dejected and frustrated. It was a stormy night, rain was pouring from the night sky. I felt like such a loser; things couldn't get much worse. Of course they could. I had a flat tyre. Shit! I had to change the tyre of my Austin Metro Princess while getting soaked through.

Cold and drenched, I took the spare tyre out of the boot. What a sight we were, the spare comedian fitting the spare tyre. The tyre looked more like a rubber ring. It turns out that my spare tyre was only a temporary measure designed to get me to the nearest garage. On the side of the tyre it read: 'Maximum speed 40 mph'. The tyre was so flimsy that if I drove over 40 mph, it would burst. After a great deal of blasphemy, I attached the rubber ring tyre to my car and raced home at speeds up to 40 mph.

Kitty was asleep when I opened our front door, passing unopened bills before I climbed the stairs and sat on my interest-free-credit Montana Ice DFS sofa, with my head in my hands, my wet hair dripping on my rented carpet. How was I going to get out of this? I needed a miracle.

On 29 June 2005, I got one. My son Lucas was born.

He was born at UCH hospital in central London in the early hours of the morning. Thirty hours earlier Kitty and I had been lying in bed watching the film *Ray* starring Jamie Foxx when she started to get minor contractions. Our local hospital was the Whittington in Highgate, about ten minutes' drive away, but we had decided to have the baby in central London at UCH, about half an hour away with no traffic. We opted for UCH because my mother's wonderful doctor, who had delivered my three little brothers, worked there. However, a few weeks into Kitty's pregnancy, he retired, and it was too late for us to change hospitals.

'I feel weird, Michael, I don't know what's happening,' Kitty said, clutching at my arm.

'That's because you never concentrate, darling. It's quite simple; it's a biopic about Ray Charles.'

'Ohhhh,' Kitty groaned in pain.

'We can watch something else if you want,' I suggested.

'I think I just had a contraction, Michael.'

'Are you serious?' I leapt out of bed. 'Let's go, let's go to the hospital and have a baby!'

'No, Michael, we have to call them, get me the phone.'

I reached for the DVD controls and paused *Ray*.

'Don't pause *Ray*, fuck *Ray*, get me the fuck phone!'

'The fuck phone?'

'Ohhhh, ohhhhh, just get me the phone, I'm in labour.'

'Sorry, darling.'

Kitty spoke to a midwife, who told her to time her contractions and when they were two minutes apart she should come into the hospital. It could be a long while, they said. What followed was about six hours of increasingly painful contractions in our living room. If you haven't seen a woman in labour, it's pretty intense, animalistic stuff. Two things shocked me. The shocking pain and the shocking language. Every few minutes she was writhing around the floor in screaming agony: 'Ohhhhhhh, ahhhhh, fuuuuuuuck.' Strangely, she was totally fine between contractions and we were able to hold a normal conversation.

'So, I've called my mum and she said, ohhhh, ahhhhhhh, ohhhhhhhh, ahhhhhhh, that she'll wait and hear from you before coming down to the hospital.'

We had a laugh about these moments of normality between agony, but when I suggested we continue watching *Ray* between contractions I was subjected to a stream of insults.

At about five in the morning, the contractions suddenly became far more frequent and severe.

'Do you think it's time?' I asked as she screamed on all fours.

'GET ME OHHHHH, AHHHHHH, OHHHHH-HHH TO THE FUCKING HOSPITAL!!!!'

We grabbed our already packed hospital bag and I helped her down the stairs. Halfway down we had to stop for another contraction. 'WAIT, OHHHHH, AHHHHHHH, OHHHHHH, WHY HAVEN'T YOU PAID THESE FUCKING BILLS?' she screamed seeing all the unopened post I had hidden.

She just about climbed into the back of the car before the onset of the next contraction.

'DRIVE, MICHAEL, DRIVE AS FAST AS YOU CAN!!'

It was at this point I realized I hadn't yet changed the rubber ring tyre. I was waiting to be paid before buying a proper one. It was the dead of the night and the roads were clear, but I was restricted to 40 mph.

'OHHHHH, AHHHHHHH, OHHHHH, HURRY UP, WHY ARE YOU DRIVING SO FUCKING SLOWLY? PUT YOUR FOOT DOWN!'

'I can't drive at more than 40 mph, darling, I'm so sorry.'

'WHAT THE FUCK ARE YOU TALKING ABOUT? I'M IN LABOUR AND YOU'RE TALKING ABOUT THE HIGHWAY CODE!' Kitty venomously yelled on all fours in the back of the car.

'I've got a temporary tyre. Remember, I told you, darling, and if I drive over forty, it might burst.'

'WHY DIDN'T YOU GET IT CHANGED? YOU KNEW WE MIGHT HAVE TO RACE TO THE HOSPITAL AT ANY TIME. YOU FUCKING OHHHHH, AHHHHHHH, OHHHHH!'

I was saved from further abuse by her latest contraction. I could see a green light in the distance and drove towards it at a steady 40 mph, knowing that unless I sped up it would be red before I reached it. I had messed up; this was my first baby. I hadn't considered the rushing to the hospital bit. The lights went red, and I stopped the car as Kitty finished her latest contraction and I waited for the abuse that I was due.

'... STUPID FUCK, I CAN'T BELIEVE YOU. HAVE WE EVEN GOT ENOUGH PETROL?'

A cold chill came over me. The petrol gauge was broken, the milometer was broken, and I couldn't remember the last time I put petrol in the car.

'I ... think so.'

'YOU ARE A TOTAL C— OHHHH, AHHHHH, OHHHHHHH!'

She was screaming in such pain, wiggling her bottom against the window in the back seat. I thought she was going to give birth in the back of our Metro with me driving at 40 mph exactly. I put my foot down; I had to risk it. I reached 50 mph, 60 mph. I could hear the temporary tyre screaming just as loud as Kitty. One of them was about to burst.

They both held on.

The car screeched to a halt outside the hospital, and I helped her inside through the smell of burning rubber. This spared me from further abuse as she had been craving that smell throughout her pregnancy. She lay on a bed with her contractions coming thick and fast. A midwife then came in, lubricated her middle finger, and did something to my wife within two minutes of meeting her that it had taken me two years to achieve.

'I'm sorry, but you're only one centimetre dilated, you've got quite a long time to go yet.'

She was right. Kitty endured another fifteen hours of contractions. She was determined to have a natural childbirth but was exhausted and eventually asked for an epidural. An epidural is an anaesthetic that, when it works, numbs the pain. It worked. The last couple of hours, Kitty was calm and in relative comfort. She pushed and pushed and eased our little messy baby boy out into the world.

Welcome.

I cradled him in my arms in the hospital. I gazed into his little eyes (already bigger than mine) and held his new hand in mine. I looked at him with all the love I have ever felt. He looked back at me in a way that seemed to say:

'Can you afford this?'

In that instant in the hospital, I knew I had to take control of my life. I couldn't take control of my life for myself, but I could do it for him. My son. Everything had to change.

I immediately started to look for an alternative, more conventional style of management. I had stuck with Duddridge for four years, and it just hadn't worked out. He tried hard to make me understand his philosophies on how to find success, but I now had my own philosophy. I wanted to work every night of the week, I wanted to be as good as I could be through hard work, not mantras and proverbs, and I wanted to get out of Jongleurs.

I asked around and researched the biggest agents in the business and one name came up, over and over again, Off The Kerb. What was so attractive about Off The Kerb was that they represented not only comedy legends, like Lee Evans and Jack Dee, but were creating new stars seemingly every year: Sean Lock three years previously, Dara Ó Briain the year before and that year Alan Carr was emerging. It was obvious to me that they were the best in the business, and I set my heart on them representing me. Oh, and if I needed any more convincing, they also represented Jonathan Ross, the then darling of the BBC.

I got their phone number and spent the day trying to pluck up the courage to call them. Off The Kerb have their finger on the pulse of live comedy; not only have they been representing comics of all statures for twenty years, but they also run their own clubs all over the country. So it reflected my low standing that when I called up, although they had heard of me, nobody at the office had seen me perform. I spoke with Danny Julian, who put me at ease within moments. I was a nobody, calling him out of the blue, but he agreed to watch me perform.

It was his job to find the stars of tomorrow, it was his job to take all calls seriously, and he was good at his job. He said he would book me in for a gig and come to see me with his boss, Joe Norris. It was as easy as that. I was elated when I put the phone down. Elated because I had taken that first step and elated because I knew I couldn't fail. I may have spent years in the wilderness, years of making no impact whatsoever, but I had also spent years developing a twenty-minute set that was now near perfect.

I was so confident that Off The Kerb would take me on that I called Duddridge and we separated amicably. I owed him money for the two Edinburgh Festivals. None of the major banks would lend me the money, so I went to the only people who might, DFS. I found out the bank they used and sure enough they gave me the money. (HFC, by the way, in case you need a loan; the rate of interest was about a million per cent.)

Off The Kerb booked me into their toughest gig at Canary

Wharf. I met Danny Julian and chatted with him beforehand. We hit it off immediately. He had just had a baby too, and we compared notes on sleepless nights. What I didn't tell him was that most of my sleepless nights were because I was worrying about my financial situation. I wasn't nervous. I knew my jokes inside out, as long as I told them the right way round, I'd be fine. For about six months, every audience I had encountered had enjoyed them. What could go wrong?

Nothing did. The gig was tough, but I did enough. The next day I was asked to come into the office for a meeting with Danny and Joe. They asked me what I wanted, and I told them I wanted to work every single night, play the Comedy Store and stop doing Jongleurs as soon as it was financially viable.

'That's easy. No problem, we book hundreds of gigs. You can headline them all,' Danny said.

'You'll have too many, Michael, you'll regret asking to work so much,' Joe added.

'I've got a lot of catching up to do,' I said.

Danny explained to me how things worked at the agency. 'I'll look after you on a day-to-day basis. I'd be your agent. But if you get some television work, that's when Addison will step in. He's incredible at all that.'

Addison is the infamous Addison Cresswell, the cigar-smoking, fast-talking, most powerful agent in the business, who brokered Jonathan Ross's mega-deal at the BBC. Everybody has a story about Addison Cresswell, he's one of life's characters and I knew he held the key to my future.

'Is Addison going to come and see me?' I asked.

'Not for a while, mate, let's get you up and running first,' said Danny.

I left the meeting feeling reborn as a comedian. I couldn't

wait to get started. I also had something to aim for: impressing Addison Cresswell. Even though I had never met him, I had a feeling that if Addison got behind me, my debts would be history.

The transformation in my life was instant. Two days later, I had a tryout at the Comedy Store. It was the first time I had been back in six years. I had the gig that I had dreamed of having and was immediately booked in for weekends. Compared to a weekend at Jongleurs, a weekend at the Comedy Store is paradise. You have a gig on Thursday, then two on Friday and Saturday as there is an early show and a late show. Plus you get paid about a grand in cash. The club was such a pleasure to play that even with my debts, I would have done it for nothing.

Danny was true to his word, and I started gigging every night of the week, developing material and chipping away at my debt. It was like a whole new world. Rather than playing to pissed partygoers, I was performing in arts centres and small theatres to people who were there primarily for the comedy. I also started to gig abroad, going to Dubai, Tokyo and Hong Kong. I kept staring at my diary in disbelief. I was booked to appear on the Comedy Store TV series broadcast on the cable channel Paramount. The gig went so well they gave me a *Comedy Store Special*, a half-hour of my own. The turnaround was so satisfying. Gigging so much had exactly the effect I hoped it would; my material, inspired by my life, was getting sharper. I was getting better:

My baby was overdue. People kept telling us the best ways to induce labour. Apparently it's to have sex and eat curry. There are no prizes for guessing who may have come up with that theory. Men are sitting in pubs saying, 'I can't believe we got away with that!

I've had sex and curry all week, last night I had a curry on her back whilst we were having sex.' Of course we tried it, until we were thrown out of the Raj King in Muswell Hill.

My mad drive to succeed took its toll on my young family. Home life was difficult, squashed into our one-bedroom flat. Kitty was totally exhausted as Lucas wasn't sleeping, and I wasn't there to help. It's amazing how you create life, and then immediately hope it goes back to sleep. I had wasted so much time over the last few years that I had to seize this opportunity for our future. Although it was difficult, there were signs almost every day that things were moving in the right direction.

The plan, of course, was to go back to the Edinburgh Festival.

Off The Kerb booked me in for the Edinburgh Festival at an eighty-seater venue at the Pleasance. Kitty and Lucas went to France to stay with my mum, and I went to Edinburgh alone. This would be the longest time I had been away from Kitty, let alone Lucas. It was a massive sacrifice. But as I have explained, there are huge opportunities for stand-up in Edinburgh, and Off The Kerb could get them for me. It was up to me to take them.

Off The Kerb hired an experienced PR girl who got some journalists to see my show in its first week. I got several four-star reviews, and my show subsequently sold out every night. The change was unbelievable.

But the most important gig of the Festival was for Addison Cresswell. I had been with his agency for almost a year and this would be the first time he saw me perform. I spoke to Danny on the day Addison was due to watch me. 'What if Addison doesn't like me?' I asked.

'That's OK, you'll still have me fighting your cause, and

Joe. But put it this way, mate . . . it's better if he does . . . a lot better.'

The pressure of the gig suddenly got to me and I struggled. Sometimes when you chat to the audience as much as I was, you end up going down too many blind alleys, the audience lose confidence and the gig never ignites. It was one of those nights. Addison didn't even stay behind to meet me.

'I blew it,' I said to Danny on the phone the following day.

'Blew what?' said Danny in his usual relentlessly positive way.

'Last night's gig. The Addison gig.'

'Addison wasn't at your gig last night. Change of plan. He's like that, you never quite know where he's going to be. He says he's coming tonight, but I wouldn't hold your breath.'

That night I had the kind of gig I was typically having, lots of banter with the audience, lots of big laughs. Before and after the show, I would hide behind the curtain of the tiny venue as there was no dressing room. When I came out at the end there he was, Addison Cresswell, all on his own, waiting behind. He was puffing on a law-breaking cigar and had a huge grin on his face.

'You are a revelation,' he said in his distinctive deep voice, walking over to shake my hand.

I was thrilled and relieved, but I was also tired. I had been struggling in comedy for years, my family were in another country, I was still in massive debt. Surely this was the moment everything changed for me.

'Are you going to make me famous, Addison?' I said boldly to Lee Evans's agent.

'A couple of years, I'd say,' he replied.

It would be months.

24

My Edinburgh Festival again ended with the disappointment of not receiving a Perrier nomination, but this time it didn't matter. After Addison had seen me, he went into overdrive, practically physically pushing TV execs to see my show. The result was that two days after the Festival ended, I was booked by Channel 4 to appear on the first ever *Charlotte Church Show*.

It was extraordinary. I was picked up from home in a gleaming silver Mercedes and taken to the BBC, where the show was recorded. I was on cloud nine. I kept Kitty updated throughout the day. Here is a selection of my phone calls to her:

'I've got my own dressing room, it's got my name on the door. I've got my own shower and a fridge. There's also a box of Celebrations, I can't stop eating them.'

'A man from Channel 4 just came to my dressing room. I think he's really powerful. He says he loved my Edinburgh show and can't wait to work with me in the future.'

'Shit, darling, I think I left my cufflinks . . . Oh no, false alarm, I found them . . . Love you, bye.'

'I just met Denise Van Outen, she's also on the show. I told her it was my first time on TV and she was so lovely to me.'

'We just had a rehearsal. Charlotte Church is gorgeous . . . No . . . No, I don't . . . I was just saying . . . Why are you being like that? . . . Darling . . . Please . . . I do not fancy Charlotte Church . . . She's in a relationship with a rugby player and

I'm married to you, I was just saying that in the flesh . . . I'm not making things worse . . . I know we've got a baby . . . calm down . . . I'm not obsessed with Charlotte Church's flesh . . . I'll call you after the show.'

'I think it went really well. Everybody said I was really funny. Danny's over the moon. I'm so happy. I'm just going to have a quick drink and then come home . . . I don't know . . . I think she's gone home . . . I don't fancy her.'

1 September 2006 saw my proper television debut. The show got over 2 million viewers. Channel 4 were pleased with my performance and I naively expected to be catapulted into the mainstream, but I soon returned to playing the clubs and Jongleurs. I was hungry for success. Every time my mobile phone rang, I hoped it would be Addison. However, he is an extraordinarily busy man, managing the careers of Jonathan Ross, Lee Evans, Jack Dee, Sean Lock, Dara Ó Briain, Alan Carr, it's a who's who of British comedy. As the weeks passed, my 'Addison calls' were becoming less frequent. I was far from out of the woods.

My next big show was the gala at the Brighton Comedy Festival. Alan Carr was hosting, and I only had to do ten minutes. The gig was my biggest audience to date. The Brighton Dome holds about 1,800 people. The fact that I only had to do ten minutes meant that I could string together all my best jokes. I was looking forward to this night for weeks. I've always felt 'the more the merrier' with comedy audiences. What I didn't know was that Addison was in the audience. He comes from Brighton; he has a second home and family there. So when I had a sensational ten-minute gig in such a big theatre, I showed Addison my true potential. He had only seen me with an audience of eighty. I came alive on the big stage. I love to move around, to express my jokes physically.

I could tell afterwards that I had gone up another notch in Addison's eyes. He was chattier with me, fussing over me and getting me drinks. The next day, I went off for another gig somewhere, continuing to gig almost every night, and Addison had an idea. He had seen me on a big stage, and he thought maybe he could get me on the biggest stage of them all. In a few weeks, the Royal Variety Performance was to be hosted by his client Jonathan Ross. He thought that if I could reproduce my Brighton performance in front of Royalty and on BBC1, I could be fast-tracked to success.

The major problem with Addison's theory was that I wasn't booked for, or wanted on, the show. The comedians had already been selected. Lee Mack, Omid Djalili and Ken Dodd were due to perform, along with Jason Byrne, who was taking the spot of unknown new comic. There was no room for me. Addison sent my *Comedy Store Special* to Peter Fincham, the controller of BBC1, and implored him to give me a chance.

In late November of 2006, I was in the Jongleurs Nottingham dressing room when Addison called me on my mobile. My heart leapt with excitement when I saw his name on the caller display.

'Michael, it's Addison. Are you sitting down?'

I worried for a moment he was telling me I had to do my A-Levels again at Woodhouse College.

'Yes,' I lied.

'Now, I think I've got you a very big gig. I think you're up to it. If it goes well, it's massive. I thought you were fantastic in Brighton. You just need to do that again. Do you think you can do that again?'

'Of course, I do that every night. What is it?' I asked with a bit of trepidation.

'The Royal Variety Performance. They're going to add you to the bill if you want to do it. They'll make an announcement tomorrow. I've stuck my neck out for you, but I've got a good feeling about this. Do you want to do it? I need to know now, 'cos I've got to move fast on this.'

'Yes, yes, of course,' I said feeling faint, clinging to the ironing board for stability.

'Fantastic. You need seven minutes. It's in two weeks. You better start practising what you're going to say,' Addison instructed, before hanging up.

I wanted to share my news and spun around to the other comedians in the dressing room. It was a familiar depressing sight of deadbeat bitter comics ironing, bitching and ignoring the fruit. I felt a rush of joy wash over me. I didn't say anything. They weren't interested in me, or my good news. I'm getting out of this place.

Finally, that was my last night at Jongleurs.

For the next two weeks, I was out every night rehearsing my seven minutes, not that I needed to, I knew my jokes. I was ready. The only unknown was whether I could handle the extra pressure of such a massive occasion. Danny saw me storm the Canary Wharf gig, Addison knew I could do it in Brighton, but could I hold my nerve with the stakes so high? I kept telling myself to treat the Royal Variety like it was just another gig. Let me tell you some of the other names appearing that night: Jonathan Ross was hosting, John Barrowman, Take That, Rod Stewart, Paul O'Grady, Graham Norton, Meatloaf. I was scheduled to perform in the second half, before Barry Manilow. It wasn't just another gig.

Just the year before I was 'spare' at Jongleurs and now I was waking up on the day I was to appear at the Royal Variety Performance. I was determined, focused and, thankfully, healthy. After the peculiar ailments that affected me during my pressure-filled Edinburgh Festivals, I feared I would be struck down with some career-threatening disease, but I was fine. I was picked up from home early in the afternoon. A chauffeur-driven BMW pulled up outside my flat. This is it. I looked out of my living room window and smiled at the driver, who nodded towards me with a look of deep disappointment. He was obviously hoping for Rod Stewart, Manilow or Barlow and ended up with me. I kissed Kitty and my baby Lucas goodbye clutching my newly dry-cleaned borrowed suit.

I wasn't used to such luxury transport. I normally used my amazingly cheap local mini-cab firm. The price was reflected in the condition of their cars. One car I took had no rearview mirror; the driver had his own vanity mirror that he would hold up to see behind him. I sat in the back and waved at Kitty waving Lucas's hand at the window. As we neared central London I got more and more nervous with every passing mile. By the time we arrived at the Coliseum theatre I was dizzy with anxiety. The area was swarming with activity; there were television trucks and police roadblocks and barriers with autograph hunters wedged behind them.

I checked in at the stage door and picked up my 'Artist Pass' and proudly hung it around my neck. Backstage, as you can imagine, is wild. In addition to the comedians, singers and bands were stage shows like *The Sound of Music*, *Wicked* and *Spamalot*. Everyone was rushing around in a frenzy in various states of undress. Proper showbiz, I loved it. The show was being rehearsed throughout the day. I waited in the wings watching Rod Stewart before it was my turn.

'It's a heartache, nothing but a heartache . . .'

I should have been marvelling at watching a legend at such

close proximity, but I was in a trance, I had a job to do, I had to justify having this artist's pass around my neck.

When Rod left the stage, there was on offstage announcement: 'Ladies and gentlemen, please welcome Britain's hottest comedy star . . . Michael McIntyre.'

I walked out as a few of the crew members applauded. If you're thinking my 'Britain's hottest comedy star' introduction was a bit generous given that I had achieved nothing to date other than my few minutes on the *Charlotte Church Show*, allow me to clear that up for you: I wrote it.

There was an enormous orchestra pit directly in front of the stage filled with musicians. I started bantering with them. I said to a man holding a trumpet. 'Hello, sir? What do you do for a living? I'm guessing something in the musical field?' There were chuckles from the crew. I was supposed to go through my set, but there was no way I was going to tell my jokes to an empty room. I wanted to save them. I just messed about and practised my bow to the Royal Box and then exited stage left. I got a feel for the stage and visualized my gig.

'Excuse me?' said an unfamiliar voice from behind me. I turned to see that it was Jason Orange from Take That.

'You were really funny, mate,' said a quarter of Take That.

'But I didn't do any of my jokes,' I confessed.

'Yeah, but you were funny. Good luck.'

This moment from Jason Orange really served to relax me. Addison had tried to calm me down, Danny had a go, I was speaking to Kitty on the phone every ten minutes, but ultimately it was Jason Orange who made me feel good about myself. Who would have thought it?

Before the show, I went outside for some fresh air. I went around the front of the theatre and saw Prince Charles and Camilla arrive in his armour-plated black Jaguar. The Queen and Prince Charles alternate their attendance and it was his turn. I hadn't really thought about the royal aspect of the occasion, I had just focused on this being my big break. A chill came over me. This is huge.

I watched the opening of the show on a monitor backstage with Danny. I had seen Addison earlier, but he now had priorities with Jonathan Ross. I could sense that Addison and Danny were worried. Addison's head was on the chopping block; he had insisted to the BBC that I could handle it and now it was time to find out. Danny had huge belief in me, but who knew what would happen?

As the time approached, I went and paced up and down the corridor outside my dressing room, going through my set over and over again. I was debating whether to start with a physical routine I did about different types of walks. I impersonated the walk you do when you try on shoes, the walk you do when you're crossing the road and the walk you do through the metal detecting arch in the airport. I paced up and down, doing the walk you do when you're incredibly nervous. Danny stood in silence letting me focus. This pacing ritual is common among performers. I don't know what you gain from walking up and down like a caged lion, but I wasn't the only one. Soon I was joined by the three Sugababes. The four of us, three Sugababes and I, pacing up and down the narrow corridor, occasionally bumping into each other. A stagehand came to fetch me. It was time. I took a deep breath and left Danny with his fingers crossed.

A few hours earlier I had stood in the same place watching Rod Stewart, feeling nervous but focused on seizing my moment to make a name for myself. Now I panicked. I caught a glimpse of the Royal Box and the audience. Prince Charles and Camilla were seated overlooking the stage in a box decorated with fresh flowers. My mouth went dry, totally dry, my heart pounded. This was not Brighton, Edinburgh or Jongleurs. I tried to remember the jokes that I had been mentally rehearsing for nearly two weeks, but nothing came to me. Relax. Take a deep breath. Calm down.

'Ladies and gentlemen, please welcome Britain's hottest comedy star, Michael McIntyre.'

This was it. Thirty years after I had got my first laugh, peeing on the doctor when I was born. Seven years since I had taken my first steps on to the stage at the Comedy Café. Seven years of driving around the country trying to work out how to be a comedian. Seven years of failure and frustration and financial stress.

I had been on a journey from having weak material to finding my voice improvising onstage, then harnessing these moments of inspiration and turning them into strong material. Now I was armed with my best seven minutes; seven years had come down to the next seven minutes to change my life, in front of his Highness, his loyal subjects and 10 million people watching at home.

Could I do it?

Could I do it for Addison who had gambled on me? Could I do it for Kitty waiting for me at home, a bundle of nerves, loving and believing in me? Could I do it for my baby son Lucas whose future depended on me? Could I 'go get 'em' for my dad who never lived to see the day? Could I do it for Jason Orange from Take That? Could I do it for me?

I strode on to the stage. The view of the audience was unexpected. They were very well lit so that the television cameras could catch their reaction. In Brighton there were 1,800 people, but with the bright spotlight on me, I couldn't see any of them. I could just hear the lovely sound of their united laughter. Now I could see every member of the audience. They were all dolled-up in dinner jackets, party frocks, their jewels glistening in the over-lit auditorium. They all shared the same expression: 'Who is that?' I glanced up at Prince Charles, who was sporting exactly the same look.

I launched into my walks routine and got no reaction whatsoever. The opening of the joke isn't particularly funny, but you would expect some support from an audience of 2,000. I quickly changed my plan and turned to my best short jokes, including the one about buying Kitty's pregnancy tests. I didn't panic. I inherently knew that my jokes were funny. I just had to perform them well and with a smile on my face and trust that people watching at home would find them as funny as everybody else outside of this stuffy occasion. However, as my act went on, the laughter built, and I started to receive rounds of applause. I ended with the walks routine and the audience were in the palm of my hand.

I was just as good as in Brighton; the audience were tougher, but I had done what I set out to do. I bowed to the Royal Box and the smiling Charles and Camilla and left the stage. I was buzzing with excitement. I passed crew members, other performers and Barry Manilow doing breathing exercises. I half expected them to congratulate me but realized that nobody had seen my gig. Nothing had changed backstage, but everything had changed for me.

I climbed the stairs to return to the pacing corridor I had left not fifteen minutes earlier. I was desperate for someone to confirm it had gone well. The corridor was now empty but for two people, Addison and Danny. As soon as they saw me they ran towards me and into my arms like I had just scored the winning penalty in the World Cup final. We jumped up and down hugging and celebrating.

I did it.

25

That was three years ago. The Royal Variety was my big break. From then on, I did all the things that you may have seen me do. Panel shows like *Mock the Week* and *Have I Got News for You*. Chat shows like *Friday Night with Jonathan Ross*. Stand-up shows like *Live at the Apollo* and the Royal Variety again. My own show, *Michael McIntyre's Comedy Roadshow*. And I released my DVDs, *Live and Laughing* and *Hello Wembley*.

I tried to write the last three years for you in detail, but it was so boring to read. It turns out that writing about success is actually very dull, so I deleted it, for your sakes. It was like a long-winded arrogant CV (the previous paragraph is a clue). I discussed it with Kitty and my mother and Addison and my publishers, and everyone agreed. In fact, only my 27-inch iMac questioned my decision: 'Are you sure you want to delete?' it asked.

I clicked 'Yes', and I made the right decision.

But I still wanted to write a final chapter to fill you in on some of the lovely things that have happened to me and update you on some of the characters in the book. You know at the end of 'films based on a true story' when they have writing on the screen to tell you what happened to the people in the story? I always love that, so I'm going to do the same thing with my book. Now, I don't actually know what happened to everybody, so I will fabricate some. I will indicate the false ones, so that I don't get into any legal strife.

Barry 'Baz' Cryer

A bona-fide comedy legend, Barry has written for the likes of Tommy Cooper, Bob Hope and Frankie Howerd, but maintains that working on *The Kenny Everett Show* with my dad was his favourite. I hadn't seen him since we sat in the studio audience together at my father's ill-fated BBC pilot *The Hecklers*, until fifteen years later he called me at the Lyric Theatre in London, where I was performing. Meeting up with Barry and listening to his stories about working with my father has been so special for me.

Kenny Everett

Kenny died a few years after my father, aged fifty, from an AIDS-related illness. He is greatly missed by his legions of fans and by comedy as a whole. There are photos of him all over my mum's home in France. She misses her friend.

The Tarot card reader

Revealed as a fraud in a Scotland Yard sting days after my mother's reading. The psychic bookshop was actually just a front for money-laundering and drugs-trafficking. The so-called psychics are each serving life sentences. (False)

Sam Geddes

Sam is married and lives in Hong Kong doing a job that nobody understands. He seems to be successful at it. I told him he features quite heavily in my book and he said, 'You haven't mentioned the boxing, have you?'

Sandrine

The girl who popped my cherry found happiness with Panos Triandafilidis, the Greek kid from Merchant Taylors'. He works as a ferry driver and they live in Dover and have a holiday home in Calais. They have three of the hairiest babies the world has ever seen. (False)

Mark Cousins
I was nominated this year for a Royal Television Society Award for my performance on *Michael McIntyre's Comedy Roadshow*. I lost to Harry Hill. Another low point was when Ant and Dec walked towards me and I shouted, 'Ant and Dec!' only to find it was actually Ant and some other guy called Paul. I was just so used to seeing them together that I saw one and assumed the other one would be next to him. The high point of the evening was running into Mark Cousins, who was also nominated for a film he had made. I told him I was writing this book and that he was the first person to believe in me. We shared a hug. It was lovely to see him again, and to meet 'Ant and Paul'.

'It's complicated' guy
I don't give a shit.

Paul Duddridge
Gave up being an agent and answered his true calling. He is now a successful motivational speaker and self-help guru in Los Angeles.

Brummie Jongleurs comedian
After years of legal wrangling, he won substantial damages from Jay Leno, Jerry Seinfeld, Woody Allen, Robin Williams and the estate of Richard Pryor for stealing his material. (False)

Jongleurs

The Jongleurs empire that I used to play went out of business. The original owner is now relaunching a series of clubs still using the Jongleurs name. Good luck to them.

Paul Tonkinson

Paul and I are still very close. He came to one of my shows at the Manchester Arena, where there were 13,000 people in the audience. I thought it was one of my best nights of the tour. 'It was good, but I still think you could be better,' he told me afterwards.

Charlotte Church

Just for the record, I do not fancy her. (False)

Jason Orange

Jason made an incredible comeback with the rest of Take That, who played Wembley Stadium on their last tour. As far as I've been told, they are returning this year to play the Royal Variety Performance alongside the youngest ever host in its history, me.

So what about me?

Well, I cleared my debts and paid off my DFS sofa that my wife re-upholstered and is downstairs as I write. I'm going to be honest; I more than paid off my debts, so thanks to you for buying my DVDs and coming to see my live shows. I also finally got on the property ladder. After much house-hunting, we found our dream family home in Hampstead. When my parents divorced, I thought I would never be able to afford to return to leafy Hampstead. Well, not only have I returned, but in a bizarre twist of fate, I bought a house on the very road where I grew up. Just twenty-two houses up the road from the house we sold to the Osbournes in 1984. Outside Kitty's and my bedroom window is the road I used to walk on with my dad, and the road I walked alone when he died.

It's been a strange circle of life coming back here. Stranger still when my mum and Steve visited, and Steve helped me paint my office walls Brinja No. 222 from Farrow & Ball, although he started having flashbacks and rag-rolled them at first. My mum, Steve and I couldn't resist knocking on the door of our old house, and the present owner, a sweet Jewish gentleman, very kindly showed us around.

It was weird to see my parents' old room again, after all these years, where my dad used to blow his morning breath into my baby face. Surreal to see the once dark jungle-like out-of-bounds living room now light and modernized, and to see Lucy's and my old bedroom with the ceiling that once fell on us. Unfortunately, Steve had another flashback and made a pass at the present owner's wife.

After the Royal Variety, I sold out just about every venue I played. I started in 200- to 300-seat capacity theatres and built my way up to the biggest venues in the UK, selling out fifty-four arenas each of around 10,000 seats in the autumn of 2009. I've had some pretty wild dreams in my life, in fact I've spent most of my life dreaming about success, but what has happened to me was beyond all of them. Things occurred so fast I barely had time to take a breath. It's only now, writing this book, that I have begun to digest everything. I suppose it's part of the reason I don't have many amusing or insightful stories about the past few years. The fact is that I've been working flat out and anything funny that has happened I've turned into stand-up material that you've probably heard.

It's just mind-blowing. One minute I was traipsing around

comedy clubs telling my jokes, and the next minute I'm playing arenas where they're selling merchandise with my jokes written on them. Some of the jokes that couldn't get me to headline Jongleurs were now on T-shirts, key rings and mouse mats.

If there was one moment when I was able to stop and appreciate what was happening to me, it was on my last night at the O_2 in London. The O_2 is the biggest venue I've played: it's the biggest venue in Europe and holds 16,000 people. I played there for four nights. Before my tour started, I saw Madonna there, the first night I did was replacing Michael Jackson, the night before my final night Beyoncé was there. It simply doesn't get any bigger than this.

I arrived for my final O_2 performance at about 4 p.m. feeling at home, having already had three gigs there. I knew it was the last time I would be there for a long while, maybe ever, so I was determined to enjoy it. The gig is surprisingly easy. Despite there being so many people, the spotlights were so bright I couldn't see a single soul from the enormous stage. I could just hear an eruption of laughter. This night was extra special because my mum had come over from France to see the show and my sister Lucy had come over from New York, where she now lives and works.

All through the tour I was looking forward to my mum seeing the astonishing size of these venues. You really have to see it to believe it. She sat in her seat and watched the thousands and thousands of my fans taking their seats, clutching bags of merchandise with my face on them. She was overwhelmed and began to cry as she thought of her visit to the Tarot card reader on Kensington Church Street when she was pregnant with me over thirty years earlier.

'It came true. It all came true,' she thought to herself, smiling through her tears.

I belted out my show with all the passion and exuberance I could muster and savoured every second. I once fantasized about storming the Comedy Store and calling for Kitty at the end like Rocky calling for Adrian. We weren't together then. If I'm brutally honest, I thought that dream was a long shot. I had achieved nothing in comedy and nothing with Kitty and doubted whether I could get close to either. Now the reality of my life was something I wouldn't have dared to dream of. Sixteen thousand people standing and cheering my name, and Kitty among them, rushing backstage and into my arms. My wife, the love of my life and mother of my children, Lucas and our new baby, Oscar.

So many people came to the O_2 that night, and I knew then how special it was. Chilling out after the show in my dressing room with Kitty, Lucy, Danny, my mum, Steve and my brothers, all together, proud of me.

'Where's Addison?' I asked Danny.

Addison has been integral to everything good that has happened in my career. He is an incredible man and agent. From the moment he saw me for the first time in Edinburgh and subsequently squeezed me on to the bill at the Royal Variety, he has been plotting and planning my next move, always one step ahead, masterminding my success. No sooner had I asked about his whereabouts than he burst into the room.

'Michael, congratulations, you were a revelation. Now I need to talk to you about something. I think you're up to it. If it goes well, it's massive. If you want to do it, I need to move fast on this.'

'What is it?' I asked with the now familiar mix of excitement and trepidation.

'How do you feel about writing your life story?'